MW00354982

RACISM
and the
OLYMPICS

To - Frank Del , dentiste
extraordinaire

Bob W.
Kingston, March, 2018

RACISM
and the
OLYMPICS

Robert G. Weisbord

Routledge
Taylor & Francis Group

NEW YORK AND LONDON

First published 2015 by Transaction Publishers

First published in paperback 2018
by Routledge
711 Third Avenue, New York, NY 10017

and by Routledge
2 Park Square, Milton Park, Abingdon, Oxon OX14 4RN

Routledge is an imprint of the Taylor & Francis Group, an informa business

© 2018 Taylor & Francis

The right of Robert G. Weisbord to be identified as author of this work
has been asserted by him in accordance with sections 77 and 78 of the
Copyright, Designs and Patents Act 1988.

All rights reserved. No part of this book may be reprinted or
reproduced or utilised in any form or by any electronic, mechanical,
or other means, now known or hereafter invented, including
photocopying and recording, or in any information storage or retrieval
system, without permission in writing from the publishers.

Trademark notice: Product or corporate names may be trademarks
or registered trademarks, and are used only for identification and
explanation without intent to infringe.

Library of Congress Cataloging-in-Publication Data

Weisbord, Robert G., author.
Racism and the Olympics / Robert G. Weisbord.
pages cm
Includes bibliographical references and index.
1. Olympics—History. 2. Olympics—Social aspects. 3. Racism in
    sports—History. 4. Discrimination in sports—History. I. Title.
GV721.W45 2015
796.48089—dc23

                                                              2014038095
ISBN: 978-1-412-85668-3 (hbk)
ISBN: 978-1-412-86519-7 (pbk)
ISBN: 978-1-315-12798-9 (ebk)

Typeset in Warnock Pro

For Cynthia

Contents

Acknowledgments

Several original sources have been mined by the author. The IOC archives in Lausanne, Switzerland, are a treasure trove for anyone eager to trace the odyssey of the Olympic Movement. Olympic Studies Centre archivist Ruth Beck-Perrenoud was of inestimable help there. Equally informative is the United States Olympic Committee archives in Colorado Springs, Colorado. Archivist Cindy Slater went far beyond the call of duty to be of assistance. Without the Avery Brundage papers housed at the University of Illinois and available on microfilm, no study of the Olympics in the middle decades of the twentieth century would be possible.

The staff of the University of Rhode Island Library was absolutely indispensable to the research for this book, especially Emily Greene of the Interlibrary Loan Department. She ferreted out all manner of materials, some seemingly inaccessible but necessary to tell the story of race and the Olympics.

Librarians Michael Vocino and Mary Ann Sumner also deserve to be singled out as well as Eileen Tierney in audio-visual.

Richard Lapchick and Robert Lipsyte have shared their abundant knowledge.

For his assistance with the chapter on the Berlin Olympics, I would like to thank my colleague, Professor Michael Honhart. Thanks also to Professor Chong Kim for help with the Japanese documents.

A sizeable debt of gratitude is owed to Janine Johnson, Deb Gardiner, Michelle Caraccia, and Sue Myette for their typing skills.

I am also grateful to Bev Swan and Lynn Pasquerella.

Introduction

Karl Marx was wrong. Religion is not the opiate of the people. Sports are in much of the world, particularly in the United States, Europe, and parts of South America. Super Bowl Sunday, a secular extravaganza, dwarfs religious holidays in its popularity. The quadrennial World Cup soccer competition arouses frenzied chauvinism. Globally, billions of fans feverishly focus on the Summer Olympics and the cold-weather Games. In theory, international fraternalism is boosted by these "friendly competitions," but national rivalries often eclipse the theoretical amity.

Of course, the modern Olympics, the subject of this volume, have periodically been convulsed by political and moral conundrums since their revival in 1896. Among the conundrums that engendered strife, often wreaked havoc, led to boycotts, and even threatened the Olympic Movement itself in the twentieth century, race was preeminent. In general, the International Olympic Committee (IOC), the governing body of the Olympics, did not distinguish itself in dealing with racial conflicts. As racial tensions reached their apex under the polarizing presidency of Avery Brundage, the ideal of amateur purity and a favorable reputation for the Olympic Movement, not racial justice, were paramount.

Race in sports cannot be disentangled from societal problems, nor can they be understood separately. Racial conflict must be contextualized. It does not happen in a vacuum. Each chapter in this book, those that deal with specific Olympiads and the ones that concentrate on Rhodesia and the Republic of South Africa, examines the racial landscape against which major disputes evolved.

While hatred and condescension toward blacks is the primary subject of this volume, Nazi anti-Semitism was center stage in the narrative of the 1936 German Games. Adolf Hitler's malevolent Mephistophelian contempt for blacks and Jews was well known and presaged the genocide of the latter. Olympic leaders opted to ignore it.

Brutal Japanese imperialism prevented that nation from hosting the 1940 Olympiads, Summer and Winter, so Nazi Germany offered to replace Japan as host of the Winter Games. The International Olympic Committee showed shocking insensitivity in agreeing to allow Hitler to stage the cold-weather competition (which was ultimately canceled because of the outbreak of World War II). At the time, Hitler's naked domestic tyranny, especially where Jews were concerned, and his unjustified expansionism were undeniable. The world chose not to know.

Before the Olympic cancellation, an acrimonious controversy over amateurism overshadowed the barbarism of Nazism. In that era, elitism, the dominance of the upper classes, was central to the concept of amateurism, a concept that no longer has a role in the Olympics. The time-honored British attitude that sports were the preserve of the moneyed and landed classes had been adopted in large part by Americans in the late nineteenth and early twentieth centuries. For a long time, it was the university-educated "leisure" classes that pervaded the All-American rosters and Olympic teams. A majority of such sportsmen were produced by Harvard, Yale, and other "exclusive" institutions in the period from 1889 to World War I. Very few white athletes were drawn from the working classes. Poor whites were rare at postsecondary schools. For them, financial need was an impediment to high school graduation and a university education. They had to work for a living.

One or two generations after the massive influx of immigrants from southern and eastern Europe (1880s to 1920), the "aristocratic" characteristic of college students underwent change. By the 1930s, the purity of amateurism was being questioned, but Comte Henri de Baillet-Latour, the Belgian nobleman who headed the International Olympic Committee, and his successor, Avery Brundage, were unmovable on the subject. Those who were more sympathetic to "play and pay" and less predisposed to see it as corrupting were stymied.

That black Americans would aspire to a top-tier higher education and to intercollegiate athletic competition was unthinkable to most white Americans. In actuality, a small sliver of the black population, the bourgeoisie, solid middle-class strivers, existed. Some of their sons attended Ivy League schools and distinguished themselves as scholar-athletes. These black pioneers were the nucleus of W. E. B. du Bois's "Talented Tenth," who he hoped and believed would furnish leadership for the oppressed Black masses.[1]

In the 1908 London Olympiad, John "Doc" Taylor of the University of Pennsylvania won a gold medal in the mile relay. Tragically, several months after returning to the United States, he sickened and died. On December 3, 1968, the *New York Times* called him the "world's greatest negro runner," the first ebony track star to be so described.[2]

Another was sprinter Howard Drew of Springfield, Massachusetts. In 1912, Drew, a future lawyer and jurist, was set to compete in the 1912 Stockholm Games, but an injury prevented him from doing so. He had been the favorite to win gold for the United States. It is ironic that Drew was Avery Brundage's Olympic teammate in Stockholm. An intelligent and highly principled person, Drew challenged the Boston Athletic Association when that organization declared that no African American could ever represent it.[3]

Edward "Ned" Gourdin was another remarkable black athlete. He earned a silver medal in the long jump at the 1924 Olympic Games in Paris, setting a new world record. He had been born in Jacksonville, Florida, and attended Harvard. When his athletic career ended, he became a judge.[4]

Southern-inspired racism infected academia, and many universities rejected black applicants. The US Naval Academy at Annapolis and Princeton, to cite just two examples, were egregiously prejudiced. Other universities were more open to the idea of racial integration. However, there was little understanding that utilizing black athletic skills could enhance a school's standing in intercollegiate athletics. That understanding would come slowly. How unfortunate that black, Jewish, and poor youngsters were not warmly welcomed into the sports world the way those of higher social status were. Less inequality in society as a whole would certainly have enlarged the pool of potentially outstanding athletes.

Black achievements are indeed remarkable, given the plight of African Americans in the early twentieth century. Lynchings, abasing Jim Crowism, unprovoked violence against black communities, disfranchisement, job discrimination, shabby and neglected housing, and inferior education were facts of black life. By the time Los Angeles hosted the 1932 Olympics, not much had changed.

Black American protests on the victory stand in Mexico City's Olympics in 1968 is the subject of chapter 4. It dramatized the unhappiness of African Americans with the racial status quo. Progress in race relations had been painfully slow in the 1930s, 1940s, and 1950s. The tumultuous decade of the 1960s was the decade of the civil rights revolution. It was the second Reconstruction. Blacks were determined to succeed where the first Reconstruction had failed by 1877 and was replaced in the South by conditions not far removed from antebellum chattel slavery. After World War II, in the courts, in the Congress, and in the streets, the battle was on to make blacks full citizens. In 1968, black Olympic athletes Tommie Smith and John Carlos were warriors in that battle.

Chapters 5 and 6 deal with discrimination in sports in South Africa and Rhodesia and the international political forces that removed them root and branch from the Olympics. The impetus to impose sanctions came mainly from newly independent African and Asian states.

The last chapter also addresses international politics and the criteria that should be utilized to determine which nations ought to be selected to take part in and serve as venues for Olympic Games. Should undemocratic governments, China, for example, or despotic leaders such as Vladimir Putin be denied the Olympic spotlight? Gays are clearly vilified and victimized in Russia. When the 2014 Games were held in Sochi, there was some talk of boycott, but none occurred.

No crystal ball can foretell the problems of the Olympiads in the twenty-first century. To paraphrase the renowned athlete-philosopher Yogi Berra, predications are difficult, especially about the future.

Notes

1. Robert E. Wells, *Sport and the Talented Tenth: African American Athletes in the Colleges and Universities of the Northeast, 1878–1920* (New York: iUniverse, Inc., 2010).
2. Wen.Wikipedia.org.
3. "Howard P. Drew: The Original "World's Fastest Human," www.howarddrew.com.
4. Wen.Wikipedia.org.

1

A Case of Amnesia: Racism and the 1932 Los Angeles Olympics

In April 2008, with Beijing as their final destination, Olympic torch-bearers in several countries in Asia, Europe, and North America found themselves besieged by demonstrators incensed over China's human rights policies, most notably with respect to Tibet. As had happened periodically in the twentieth century, the choice of Olympic venues was being challenged on political and moral grounds. The campaign to boycott the games in Hitler's Germany in 1936 was bitter and pro-longed, but, in the end, unsuccessful. To show their displeasure with the Soviet invasion of Afghanistan, the United States and dozens of other nations stayed away from the 1980 Moscow Games, and four years later, the Soviets, playing tit for tat, boycotted the Los Angeles Olympiad. But never before had serious questions been raised about the United States as a country morally unsuitable to host the Olympiad.

Ever since the first modern Olympiad in 1896, the United States had been a significant presence at the quadrennial games, and in 1932, Los Angeles played host to the world's athletes. It was not the first time the United States was the venue for the Olympics. In 1904, when St. Louis was staging a world's fair, it also served as the site of the III Olympiad. President Theodore Roosevelt had favored St. Louis, which was cel-ebrating the centennial of the Louisiana Purchase, to host the games over its chief rival, Chicago.[1]

On the contrary, Baron Pierre de Coubertin, the French aristocrat who founded the modern Olympics, frowned upon the choice of St. Louis and, in the end, failed to attend. For him, St. Louis lacked beauty and originality, and he feared that the Games would match the medi-ocrity of the city. Coubertin was further concerned that the athletic festival would simply be an adjunct to the exposition.[2] Racially mixed competition was anathema to him, and two South Africans, members of the Tswana tribe, ran in the grueling marathon. For the first time, a pair of African American sportsmen, Joseph Stadler and George Poage, won medals in track and field.[3] But visitors to St. Louis were strictly segregated throughout.

One 1904 St. Louis innovation was particularly embarrassing for Coubertin: the two so-called anthropological days featuring Turks, Japanese Ainus, Sioux Indians, Filipinos, and Black Africans. Many were aboriginal peoples who, according to Coubertin, had only "barely emerged from primitive barbarism."[4] The "primitives" competed in mud wrestling and in ascending a greasy pole, decidedly non-Olympic events. The euphemistically dubbed "anthropological days" were not officially part of the Olympic program. Rather, they were a circus, a carnival freak show mirroring the raw racism that was reaching its zenith in the United States in 1904.

Among the participants in the anthropological days was Ota Benga, a twenty-three-year-old Pygmy from the ruthless Belgian King Leopold's genocidal Congo Free State, his personal plantation in the heart of Africa. Crowds mocked Ota Benga, tossed brick missiles in his direction, and poked umbrellas at him. Worse humiliation was to come. Two years later, the four foot, eleven inch Pygmy was exhibited in the monkey house of the Bronx Zoo. Tens of thousands turned up to gawk and jeer at the "wild man" from Africa.[5] A sideshow barker was all that was missing. Such was the American mind-set of racism in the first years of the new century.

European cities were the venues for the Olympics after St. Louis. In 1908, it was London and four years later Stockholm. No Olympiad was held in 1916, owing to the fact World War I had broken out two years earlier. Antwerp was the site in 1920 and Paris in 1924. Los Angeles had long been eager to host the 1928 Olympiad, and William May Garland, a prosperous local businessman, made a convincing case in 1920 before the International Olympic Committee (IOC), but to no avail. Amsterdam got the nod.

Still, Garland made a favorable impression on the Lausanne-based IOC, which was predisposed to return the Olympics to the United States for 1932. When Garland made a pitch for the City of the Angels in 1923, the IOC enthusiastically acceded. Baron de Coubertin himself noted that construction for the mammoth Memorial Coliseum gave LA an advantage over its competitors. The Coliseum, which could seat 105,000 spectators, was touted as the most colossal structure of its kind on the planet.[6] Given the extensive participation of the "sporting youth" of the United States in previous Olympiads across the Atlantic, the choice was something of a quid pro quo.[7] Influential Angelinos rejoiced, but the East Coast athletic establishment, which regarded California as an upstart in the world of sports, was clearly displeased.

Business and political interests in LA lost no time in propelling preparations for the Games forward. A bond issue was floated by the city while the state of California appropriated funds to help defray expenses. William Garland became president of the Olympic Committee, and President Herbert Hoover, who personally had no interest in sports in general or in the Olympic Games in particular, nonetheless became honorary president of the X Olympiad.

Because Hoover was deeply involved in his reelection campaign, an eventually unsuccessful one, and because he was profoundly unpopular as the Great Depression ravaged the nation, Vice President Charles Curtis officially opened the Games as the honorary vice president of the Olympiad. Curtis is best remembered, if he is remembered at all, for his Pollyannaish prophecy, made as hunger stalked the land, that prosperity was just around the corner. Hoover remained safely ensconced in Washington, where he partook of a loaf of bread presented to him by a California congressman. It was similar to that served to the world's athletes gathered in Los Angeles. This had been customary since the revival of the Olympics. The bread was meant to symbolize international peace.

Los Angeles's mayor, John C. Porter, relished his moment in the sun and proudly pledged that he would keep the Olympic flag in city hall until the finish of the Games, when it would be transferred to Berlin for the XI Olympiad. The considerable financial risks notwithstanding, the Olympiad thrust Los Angeles into the national and international limelight. Thirteen hundred athletes from thirty-seven nations and in excess of a million visitors descended on sunny Southern California.

Once in Los Angeles, the American athletes were given the royal treatment. They were lionized. Motion picture stars greeted them personally and put on gigantic shows almost every night at the Olympic Village. When the athletes ventured outside the village, they were beleaguered by autograph seekers. Indeed, the Olympic Village itself was a novelty in Los Angeles at the X Olympiad. Prior to 1932, private accommodations were found, and the athletes trained secretly, sometimes individually. All that changed in 1932, at least for the males. Female competitors were accommodated at a local hotel.

In 1932, racial separation de jure and de facto was pervasive in the United States, and sports were no exception. At the same time, there was a realization that black athletes could help win coveted medals in international competition. Perhaps it was inevitable that there would be racial conflicts as the Los Angeles Olympiad approached.

In June 1932, owing to university policy, four African American athletes were barred from Olympic track-and-field qualifying meets at Johns Hopkins University in Baltimore. Both the university and the city were rigidly Jim Crowed then. A dispensation enabling blacks to circumvent the Johns Hopkins trials and compete instead in the sectional trials at Harvard University was proffered by the president of the South Atlantic Association and the chairman of the American Olympic track-and-field committee. A Johns Hopkins official lamely explained, "We often have been called on by Negro organizations for the use of the field and always have declined. Personally, I have no feelings against the boys, but the ruling has remained at the university as long as I can remember and we must be consistent."[8] Only after considerable pressure was exerted by the Baltimore branch of the National Association for the Advancement of Colored People (NAACP) and other organizations did Johns Hopkins relent and permit African Americans to try out for the Olympic berths on their campus.[9]

Black athletes were at a distinct disadvantage in another respect. They were more likely to be shunted aside by the American Olympic Committee, which, at that juncture, was short of money. White athletes were assisted by private clubs, but their black counterparts could not rely on the black community for training and travel expenses because it lacked adequate financial resources.[10]

Nonetheless, Los Angeles catapulted black sprinters on the world stage of Olympic track-and-field competition. Ralph H. Metcalfe and Thomas Edward "Eddie" Tolan captivated the throngs in attendance with their blinding speed. Short, stocky, and bespectacled—the latter ran with his glasses taped to his head—Tolan won gold medals in the 100- and 200-meter events and set two Olympic marks and one world record, but both races were disputed.

In the 100-meter competition, there was a photo finish with both Tolan and Metcalfe clocked at 10:03. It appeared they had broken the tape at precisely the same instant, but, after some deliberation, the judges declared Tolan, the "midnight express," the winner because his torso had supposedly crossed the finish line before Metcalfe's. Tolan thus became the first black American to earn a gold medal in Olympic sprints.[11]

Tolan, a University of Michigan graduate and a one-time schoolboy champion in Michigan, won a second gold medal in the 200-meter event. Again, controversy dogged the race. Metcalfe, the heavy favorite who had dominated the Olympic trials, came in a disappointing third—behind his countryman, George Simpson. It was discovered in short order that Metcalfe's lane had been mismeasured, requiring him to run an additional two or three meters.

Metcalfe declined the offer to have the race rerun lest the American sweep be jeopardized. Was Metcalfe simply motivated by good sportsmanship? His son wondered aloud whether his father was pressured for racial reasons—Simpson, the silver medalist, was white—to not challenge the results after the 200-meter contretemps.[12]

In 1936, the legendary black activist and scholar W. E. B. du Bois wrote in opposition to Americans participating in the XI Olympiad in Berlin, but noted that on the "grounds of poor sportsmanship and discrimination, America, of course, cannot raise a very sincere hand, for she has given the Negro athlete copious doses of both."[13] Among others, du Bois pointed to Tolan, who had been humiliated following the 1928 Amsterdam Olympics. Tolan had been ostracized by his own teammates, who had often left him to dine alone in his hotel room. When his teammates went sightseeing Tolan, was not invited to go along. According to *The Crisis* magazine, the organ of the NAACP, "More than once the group would pack, drive to the station, leave for the next port of call without advising Tolan either when they were leaving or where they were going."[14]

Prior to an Amateur Athletic Union (AAU) meet against Great Britain in 1930, Tolan, along with a couple of black competitors, were denied accommodations by two Chicago athletic clubs where their white teammates were staying. When an angry Tolan announced his intention to leave, AAU officials reportedly informed him that such a rash move would spell finis to his athletic career.[15]

After the 1932 Olympics, Tolan's fortunes took a turn for the worse. Tolan's picture appeared on the front cover of *The Crisis* in September 1932, and the governor of Michigan proclaimed September 6 Eddie Tolan Day. City and county officers raised $300 to enable him to sustain himself. He had considerable difficulty eking out a living. When the mayor of Detroit presented him with a trophy and asked what else the Motor City could do for him, he replied that he needed a job. Tolan did appear briefly on the vaudeville circuit with the African American entertainer Bill "Bojangles" Robinson and taught school for some years. The fruits of his athletic prowess on the international scene were meager indeed. His plans to study medicine came to naught.[16]

Metcalfe's future following Los Angeles was much brighter. The Atlanta-born athlete, whose family had moved to Chicago as part of the "Great Migration" of Blacks seeking greater economic opportunity and racial dignity, competed in the 1936 Berlin Olympiad. A graduate of Marquette University, Metcalfe earned a master's degree at the University of Southern California. In the 1960s, he embarked on a distinguished political career that saw him elected to the United States House of Representatives from Illinois, and he served several terms. In the wake of the 1932 games, Atlanta's white mayor James Lee Key proclaimed September 23, 1932, a day in honor of Ralph Metcalfe but conceded that if "he had remained here, he would probably have been a rose 'born to blush unseen, its fragrance wasted on the desert air.'"

Black American Olympic performances merited front-page treatment in the *Afro-American*, which billed itself as the "Nation's Biggest All-Negro Weekly." A photograph of Tolan appeared prominently on page one, and a banner headline dubbed him the "Fastest Human" and a "dark flashing meteor." Along with much of Black America the *Afro-American* swelled with pride.[17]

On the distaff side, racial prejudice touched two African American runners: Louise Stokes, nicknamed the "Malden meteor" after her Massachusetts hometown, and Tidye Pickett, a Chicagoan who barely weighed 100 pounds. En route to Los Angeles by train, the team had made a stop in Colorado. Racial etiquette there, as in much of the country, did not permit Stokes and Pickett to eat in the dining room of Denver's Brown Palace Hotel, where they were staying. Therefore, the two black female athletes were effectively excluded from the banquet saluting the American contingent. They were further isolated when they were assigned a room in the hotel attic, where their food was served on trays.[18] The luxurious Brown Palace was the second oldest in the "Mile High City," and the first atrium-style hotel ever constructed. It catered to the rich and famous and occasionally hosted presidents of the United States. African Americans were almost never seen there. Nevertheless, it was chosen for the Denver stopover of the Olympic team.

Circumstances surrounding another alleged racial incident after the train left the Mile High City are a bit murky. Tidye Pickett insisted that Babe Didrikson, the track-and-field female supernova, deliberately dumped a pitcher of water on her as she lay in her lower berth. The two then supposedly exchanged sharp-edged words.[19]

Didrikson, twenty-one at the time, was high-spirited, fun loving, self-centered, immodest to a fault, and given to braggadocio and was said to have dashed through the train engaging in rough, boisterous behavior. Pickett opined that Didrikson, who went on to win two gold and one silver medal, had taken a dislike to her. Whether the contretemps was racial in nature cannot be determined with certainty. For her part, Babe Didrikson remained silent on the incident in her autobiography. She simply acknowledged that "most of the girls sat around watching the scenery and playing cards and gabbing. I was busy taking exercise and hurdle bends and stuff. I'd practice in the aisles. Several times a day I'd jog the whole length of the train and back. People in the other cars took to calling out, 'Here she comes again.'"[20] Pickett, who is not mentioned by name, believed Didrikson did not want her on the train: "[I]t was prejudice pure and simple."[21]

Greater disappointment lay ahead. Pickett and Stokes were lionized in the black community, and the African American press took a special paternalistic interest in them. Based on their performances in the Olympic tests, "the two sable sprinters" expected to represent their country in the 4 × 100 relay, where gold medals were a real possibility. However, for reasons still not clear today, Coach George Vreeland replaced them with two white runners. The black women were relegated to the status of alternates. A writer for the popular black newspaper the *Chicago Defender* attributed the eleventh-hour substitution to lily-whiteism. Decades later, Louise Stokes observed that a "pretty fast stunt was pulled." In a 1984 interview, Pickett declared that some people just did not want to admit that the African American women were superior. A columnist for the *Afro-American* had wondered why there were no women to share honors with Metcalfe and Tolan and asserted that "for us to be considered we have to be ten times as good as those of the other race."[22] Before the Games commenced, the NAACP had contacted the United States Olympic Committee to explain its fears that Pickett and Stokes would not be treated equitably. Their fears may have been justified.[23] No black American woman received an Olympic gold medal until Alice Coachman accomplished that feat in the high jump competition in 1948.

Also bypassed at the eleventh hour in Los Angeles was one of the world's fastest runners, James Johnson, an African American from Illinois Central. All but forgotten today, Johnson had defeated three future Olympic champions, including the redoubtable Jesse Owens. There were several tryouts before the 1932 games. In two semifinals, Johnson ran second and third, but his performance in the finals was a disappointing fifth. By tradition, he should have been given a berth on the 4 × 100 relay squad, but he was not selected. A white ran in his place, and the United States won the gold in world-record time. Mystified by Johnson's omission, tennis champion and sports historian Arthur Ashe later wrote, "Maybe the authorities meant to start a new tradition or just continue an old one of dispensing with blacks at will."[24]

In an ironic twist of fate, in 1936, in Berlin, the only two Jewish runners on the American track team, Marty Glickman and Sam Stoller, were replaced in the 4 × 100 by Jesse Owens and Ralph Metcalfe, perhaps at the behest of Avery Brundage, president of the American Olympic Committee, and US track coach Dean Cromwell, both boosters of the isolationist American First committee, which was sympathetic to Nazi Germany and antipathetic to Jews. Until his dying day, Glickman believed that Brundage and Cromwell wanted to spare Hitler further embarrassment by having two Jews stand on the winning podium before 120,000 Germans and the world's news media.[25]

Pervasive apartheid in athletics in this country reflected racial mores in the society at large. With respect to the Olympic Movement, it has been noted by David B. Welky that blacks were completely absent except on the playing fields. African American managers and coaches were nowhere to be seen. Of course, the American Olympic Committee itself was monochromatic in 1932. Ignoring this melancholy reality, the *Los Angeles Times*, on August 3, 1932, crowed about the "first Olympiad unsullied by racial differences."[26] Nonsense.

In general, in the early 1930s, sports and sports facilities were marked by racial separatism. Since 1898, professional baseball had been the national pastime—play-for-pay basketball and football were of secondary importance among sports fans. No "Negro," to use the term then used in popular parlance, could play in the organized major or minor leagues. There was no statute barring them, only a "gentlemen's agreement," an understanding among baseball team owners and league officials. At that juncture, a few prominent sports reporters, white as well as black, took organized baseball to task for maintaining the color bar. Major league officials insisted that no such bar existed. Race was not a criterion in the choice of players, declared John A. Heydler, president of the National League. That was a bold-faced lie echoed by the commissioner of baseball, Kennesaw Mountain Landis.[27]

Such was the situation in 1932 when the Los Angeles Olympics were held. African Americans were restricted to their own leagues. They had their own players, their own umpires, their own sports reporters from the newspapers that served the black communities of Pittsburgh, Kansas City, Baltimore, Chicago, New York, Newark, and Philadelphia, among others. In the Negro leagues, only the ball was white, as Robert Peterson observed. Black teams also played their own world series. It is noteworthy that they sometimes played exhibitions against white major leaguers in which they more than held their own, but the fame, the recognition, and the money available to whites was denied blacks, regardless of ability. Many knowledgeable aficionados of baseball insist that the flamboyant, bigger-than-life Negro leagues' hurler Leroy "Satchel" Paige was the equal of the best major league pitchers and that the legendary Josh Gibson was as powerful a hitter as Babe Ruth.

For their part, the pooh-bahs who ran organized professional football had very little to be proud of where racial issues were concerned. Prior to 1933, there was only a handful of black players on professional team rosters, but that elite group included an all-American out of Rutgers, Paul Robeson, who was eventually recognized as an ebony *Uomo Universale* by virtue of his talents as a singer, actor, lawyer, and athlete. Even the token black presence in football evaporated abruptly in 1933.

For the next fourteen years, until World War II ended and a somewhat more tolerant racial atmosphere prevailed, "Negroes" were missing altogether. Their elimination was surely the result of an unwritten compact among unenlightened team owners and league officials for whom pigskin prejudice was perfectly acceptable. Counted among them was the unashamedly racist owner of the Washington Redskins, George Preston Marshall. Chicago Bear originator, George Halas, angrily denied that skin color was a factor in selecting players. Many of these founding fathers of the National Football League are still venerated today. Several are in the Hall of Fame in Canton, Ohio.

As Andy Piascik has pointed out in his *Gridiron Gauntlet*, there was no Branch Rickey among them.[28] As was the case with organized baseball, in football circles, it was commonly declared, ignorantly or dishonestly, that African American football players possessed talents inferior to those of whites.

In the amateur ranks, the color bar was ubiquitous. In 1932, a team of Cuban stars was kept out of a tournament sponsored by the *Denver Post* after an initial invitation was extended. The sports editor was deluged with objections on racial grounds from Southern baseball executives.[29]

Golf and tennis, both in the professional and amateur ranks, rejected blacks. After all, those were country club sports, and most country clubs shunned blacks. Membership in the Professional Golfers' Association was unavailable to African Americans until 1961. Clifford Roberts, a founder of the Augusta National Golf Club, home of the prestigious Masters Tournament, was quoted as pontificating, "As long as I am alive all the golfers will be white and all the caddies will be black."[30] Blacks were not admitted as members until 1990, almost six decades after the club was founded in 1932.

Future Tennis Hall of Famer Arthur Ashe discovered as a young man in his native Richmond, Virginia, that the taxpayer-supported municipal courts were also off-limits to him. Talent, determination, and grit enabled Ashe to become the first and only African American male to win the US Open championship, and today a statue of Ashe stands outside the stadium where that prestigious tournament is held annually.

Competitive swimming was not an option either. Swimming pools were few and far between in the ghettos and in the rural South, where blacks were typically denied entry. Instruction in swimming was a rarity, leading to a dearth of black swimming champions and, more significantly, a much higher rate of drowning among African Americans. Between the world wars, northern municipalities, fearful of racial contamination, typically segregated swimming facilities, many publically funded. Whites' health could be jeopardized by sharing the waters with blacks, whose hygiene was thought to be questionable. African Americans who had the temerity to cross the racial divide were often intimidated and sometimes physically assaulted. To cite one instance, in Pittsburgh, in 1931, blacks attempting to bathe in the new Highland Park pool were beaten by white toughs. Gender integration among whites, which occurred simultaneously with the influx of blacks from the South, accentuated racial distinctions. White womanhood was allegedly threatened by lascivious black males.[31]

Southern universities fielded all white basketball and football teams. Northern schools usually deferred to southern prejudices by not using their own black athletes when they competed against those Caucasian-only squads in Dixie and even in the North. New York University located in "cosmopolitan" Gotham was no exception. Its surrender to racism in intercollegiate football has been movingly and accurately chronicled by Donald Spivey. In 1929, NYU removed halfback David Meyers from the lineup in a home game against the University of Georgia in deference to Southern racial sensibilities. Apparently, black sensibilities did not count. Eleven years later, a major brouhaha developed when running back Len Bates was not allowed to play against the University of Missouri in that state, where racial segregation was the norm. Ignoring a vocal "Bates Must Play" protest campaign organized by NYU students, the university administration honored its Jim Crow "gentleman's agreement" with Missouri. The white press, including the liberal *New York Times*, downplayed this shameful event.[32]

In sharp contrast to the pusillanimous NYU administration in the Bates case, the University of Pittsburgh, in 1955, refused to play in the Sugar Bowl against Georgia Tech without Bobby Grier, a black, who broke the racial barrier in the face of the racist comments by Georgia's Governor Marvin Griffin, a staunch segregationist. Griffin wanted the Sugar Bowl to remain lily-white. Fourteen years earlier, a black football player for Boston College was kept out of the Sugar Bowl and not allowed to practice with his team.[33]

A flagrant example of some selection committees' unwillingness to "sully" the New Year's Day games by allowing black players on the gridiron came in 1951. In that year, San Francisco University, clearly one of the top football teams in the nation, perhaps the best, received no bid at all. The fact that the Dons fielded "Negro" players, including the legendary Ollie Matson, a future Hall of Famer, explains why San Francisco was passed over in favor of Southern teams. Had the San Francisco squad been amenable to playing without the redoubtable Matson and a second African American standout, Burt Toler, they almost certainly would have received a bid to the coveted Orange Bowl in Miami.[34]

Bowing to sectional prejudice, Southern state universities were long unwilling to integrate their football teams. Kentucky relented in 1966. Alabama, coached by the near-mythical "Bear" Bryant, buckled in 1970, and then only after the University of Southern California, led by Sam Cunningham, a punishing African American running back, demolished the Crimson Tide. A 1970 lawsuit challenging Bryant's white-only recruiting policies also contributed to his change of mind.[35] Interracial football games between black college teams and predominantly white universities were taboo in the South until 1969, when Florida A&M took on and defeated the University of Tampa. A truly dark era had ended.

What was true of football was also true of basketball. For years, historically black college quintets were ignored when postseason tournaments were begun in the late 1930s. There is good reason to believe that they were as good as those of the white colleges, perhaps better.

Conventional wisdom, really self-delusion in the white sports world, held that black basketball players were not up to white standards. It was said in some quarters that "Negroes" could jump but not shoot, a notion that is patently absurd in retrospect. That attitude changed most dramatically after a 1966 NCAA championship game, when Texas Western, now the University of Texas–El Paso, started five black players and beat the perennial all-white basketball power, the University of Kentucky. The triumph has been called "one of the most meaningful victories in the history of sports. The Schmeling-Louis fight of college basketball."[36]

African American track-and-field athletes encountered formidable barriers throughout the first half of the twentieth century. For example, take Ted Corbitt, a Hall of Fame pioneer in long distance running, especially marathoning and ultramarathoning. Corbitt was born in South Carolina but attended high school and college in Cincinnati. Many interstate competitions, including AAU meets, were closed to him. Segregation was common in northern states such as Indiana, Michigan, and Ohio. Where Corbitt could run, he sometimes did not because he never knew whether Jim Crowism would prevent him from finding a hotel or restaurant to accommodate him.[37] Major athletic clubs usually drew the color line. Corbitt and many fellow black athletes were often persona non grata in their own country. Following the 1932 Olympics, Corbitt met and was inspired by Ralph Metcalfe. He was determined to excel, especially at the longest distances, despite the common prejudice of that era, before Ethiopians and Kenyans entered the national sports consciousness, that blacks lacked the requisite endurance.[38]

A virulent racial bacillus also infected professional boxing. In 1908, Jack Johnson won the heavyweight championship of the world, beating Tommy Burns in Australia. Johnson's victory was a catastrophe for many whites who thought the heavyweight championship was symbolic of masculinity and strength. In 1910, Johnson defeated the former champion Jim Jeffries, who came out of retirement to regain the crown for the white race.

Johnson was supremely confident, even cocky, not at all like the cowering, shuffling stereotype of black Americans. He was a "bad nigger."[39] His unconventional lifestyle made him repugnant to white Americans. He wore fancy clothes and drove expensive cars. Worst of all, he married three white women in succession and had numerous white girlfriends. Such behavior, in contravention of America's racial tradition, outraged whites, who conspired to bring him down. They succeeded by trumping up charges against him of violating the Mann Act, which prohibited transporting women across state boundaries for immoral purposes. Johnson felt compelled to flee the country to avoid prison. For all practical purposes, his pugilistic career was over. There was not to be another black champion in the heavyweight division until Joe Louis burst onto the scene in the thirties.

Sports hold up a mirror to society as a whole. Racism in sports reflected the racism that was crucial to the warp and woof of America's culture until midcentury. Bias in employment limited most blacks to menial work—hewers of wood, drawers of water—regardless of their educational attainments and qualifications. There were black college graduates (all addressed as "George") working as Pullman porters to keep body and soul together.

In 1932, at the Boulder Dam construction site, which provided employment for several thousand desperate men, Blacks were barely in evidence. Only with the advent of the New Deal were some black workers hired, owing to the efforts of Harold Ickes, Franklin Roosevelt's secretary of the interior. But conveniently located and affordable accommodations in Boulder City were not available to African American workers. Segregated housing required them to live farther from their work.

Professionals had the same experiences as manual laborers. Los Angeles was typical. Blacks understood that the teaching field was closed to them, as was medicine. In the majority of hospitals, physicians and nurses of color were unwelcome. Discrimination in the admission of patients was common in the 1930s and for years afterward.[40]

Jim Crowism in housing was widespread. Los Angeles in the 1930s was well on its way to becoming an apartheid community. Real estate interests aided by the Ku Klux Klan fostered segregated housing patterns in the city, some of which persist to this day.[41] What was true of Los Angeles was true of most American cities, including the nation's capital, where ghettoization was achieved through voluntary restrictive covenants that perpetuated all-white neighborhoods. In the 1920s, blacks in Washington DC lived in a "secret city," a city of which whites were completely unaware.[42] A mammoth parade by the Ku Klux Klan through the district's streets in 1926 was symbolic of racial sentiment in the city, and indeed the country as a whole. Poverty there was deeply entrenched. Because of the Great Depression and discrimination by businessmen, the government, and unions, job opportunities in both private and public sectors were meager. Even before FDR's 1933 inauguration, only 1 percent of the district's police force was African American. His New Deal, which depended on racist Southern support, was not a very good deal for blacks.[43]

In much of the nation, education was separate and unequal despite the separate but equal *Plessy vs. Ferguson* dictum (1896). Generation after generation of blacks attended underfunded and ill-equipped neighborhood schools. Especially south of the Mason-Dixon Line, per student spending for blacks was disgracefully lower than that for whites, and in Washington DC, the situation was no better. Second-class citizens, which is what African Americans were, received a second-class education.

Many states prohibited interracial marriage between whites and people of African or Asian descent. At the time of the Los Angeles Olympics, California was one such state and remained so until 1948, when the Supreme Court of the Golden State struck down the eugenics-based statute.[44] Such prohibitions of miscegenation designed to achieve racial purity were similar to the infamous Nuremberg Laws that outlawed sex and marriage between Jews and so-called Aryans in Nazi Germany.

In American race relations, the vigilante justice perpetrated against blacks, usually by bloodthirsty, racist mobs, was shockingly scandalous. This practice went on year after year, decade after decade. Neither the churches nor the press challenged such lawlessness. Between 1889 and 1918, more than 3,200 lynchings were authenticated; 2,522 of the victims were black. There were 13 lynchings in 1931 (all but two involving blacks) and 21 in 1930. America's record of antiblack mayhem in the 1920s had been even worse. Sometimes the hapless victims were mutilated before, during, or after the fiendish deed was done. And not all lynchings were carried out furtively. Some were public entertainment watched by large crowds of whites—men, women, and children—who left carrying relics, that is, body parts. "To hell with the Constitution" if it interfered with lynching rapists, roared South Carolina's "Pitchfork" Ben Tillman, who as a US senator had sworn to uphold the Constitution.

Most of the victims, incidentally, were not even accused of rape. These were the "Strange Fruit," the black bodies swinging in the Southern breeze of which Billie Holiday and other African American performers sang poignantly beginning in 1939. Efforts to enact a federal antilynching law were stymied by Congress, which continually turned a blind eye to racially motivated mob rule.[45]

Murderous onslaughts on black communities were common in the early twentieth century. In the last seven months of 1919, there were twenty-five *pogroms*, to use the Russian word employed to describe czarist-age assaults against Jews. Summer bloodshed that year led to the term "Red Summer" being coined. June 1921 witnessed a particularly sanguinary riot in Tulsa, Oklahoma, which may have claimed as many as three hundred African American lives. An estimated ten thousand may have been left without homes, but that figure cannot be verified. White Tulsans reduced Greenwood, the black section of Tulsa, including the prosperous "Black Wall Street," to rubble. Martial law was declared, but the riot ran its course. None of the malefactors were punished. As was often the case, the racial convulsion was touched off by a rumor that a black man had sexually assaulted a white woman. The saga of the Tulsa paroxysm was suppressed until recently. Even today, the complete story has not been revealed.[46]

Racial cleansing was a feature of the American landscape. The eviction of black folks from towns and even whole counties was achieved by threats, intimidation, and, of course, force. It is still one of the country's dirty little secrets about race relations. "Leave now or die" was the all too common warning.

Forsyth County, Georgia, in 1912 is a case in point. Under severe duress, blacks frantically fled for their lives. Their land was stolen. Most towns in the county were left with no African Americans in much the same way that many jurisdictions in Germany were made to be *Judenfrei* (free of Jews) by the Nazis. Expulsion had been the fate of African American residents of Pierce County, Missouri, in 1901. Their only crime was being black. The same type of depredation had occurred in Harrison, Arkansas, twice in the first decade of the century, in 1905 and 1909.[47]

In the aftermath of a Ku Klux Klan rally on New Year's Day in 1923, the very year in which the International Olympic Committee accepted Los Angeles's bid to host the 1932 Olympiad, there was a brutal racial attack on the blacks in Rosewood, Florida. Once again, the catalyst was an unverified allegation that a black man had assaulted a white woman. Rampaging whites put to death at least eight people, slaughtered livestock, and destroyed homes. Surviving blacks departed the town, never to return.

Popular racist images of black Americans were reinforced by the media in the 1920s. Films especially stereotyped them. D. W. Griffith's 1925 silent blockbuster *Birth of a Nation*, which offered a racist portrayal of the Civil War and Reconstruction, is illustrative. Just as the Nazis characterized Jews as a sexual menace in the 1930s, Griffith showed blacks as sexually predatory. In one scene that miseducated millions of moviegoers, a young white woman jumps off a cliff to her death rather than be ravished by a black in the Reconstruction period. Another white woman is coerced into an interracial marriage. Griffith romanticized the recently revived Ku Klux Klan, which used the film as a successful recruiting instrument. President Wilson, a former college history professor and a friend of Griffith's, declared the film's version of history to be accurate.[48]

Miscarriages of racial justice were commonplace, but few stunned international opinion on the scale of the notorious Scottsboro case. It began in March 1931, when nine black adolescent males were accused of raping two white women on a freight train passing through Alabama. In little more than two weeks, eight of those indicted were found guilty and sentenced by all-white juries to die in the electric chair. Appeal followed appeal as protest rallies were held around the globe. There were no fewer than seven retrials. Twice the Supreme Court felt compelled to intervene, but almost certainly it was worldwide and domestic agitation that saved the lives of the "Scottsboro boys," who served prison sentences of varying length.[49]

Evidence that black Americans in the 1930s were consigned to subhuman status is abundant and incontrovertible. Look at the so-called Tuskegee study, a US Public Health Service research undertaking designed to monitor the effects of untreated syphilis on black men, mostly poor sharecroppers in rural Alabama. The project began in the autumn of 1932, just after the LA Olympiad. None of the human subjects were told why they were recruited nor were they given medical attention, although antibiotics were available. The racial element was key. Not a single white afflicted with venereal disease was chosen to be a human guinea pig for the project. Like the uncivilized Nazi medical experiments on concentration camp prisoners, the syphilis investigation was technically legal albeit highly unethical. Progress reports were periodically published in medical and public health journals, a fact that makes the entire episode all the more disturbing.[50] Almost forty years elapsed before the startling revelation to the general public of the Tuskegee project.

Congressman Ralph Metcalfe, the former "Black Panther of Marquette," spearheaded the inquiry that gave a new meaning to Tuskegee, which until then was only associated with the educational institute founded by Booker T. Washington.

Throughout the late nineteenth and early twentieth centuries, medical care for blacks was typically abominable. North and south, some white physicians turned away black patients. Julie M. Fenster claimed, "In all of Baltimore in 1910, there were only eight beds available for black children." No one will ever know how many African-American lives were needlessly lost.

There long existed what Harriet A. Washington aptly called "medical apartheid." For all practical purposes, "Black, need not apply" signs hung outside America's medical schools. Consequently, most black physicians were educated at black medical schools: Meharry in Nashville, Tennessee, and Howard in Washington DC. Racism created additional barriers for African American doctors who wished to pursue their medical training. Internships, residencies, fellowships, and hospital privileges were difficult to come by. One black physician-reformer observed in 1938 that the American Medical Association, which was closed to blacks, had shown "as much interest in the health of the Negro as Hitler had in the health of the Jew." Black doctors had formed their own National Medical Association in 1895. The AMA did not apologize for its history of racial exclusiveness until 2008.[51]

No less insidious was the unconscionable abuse of black labor in the South, which continued for almost six decades after the adoption of the Thirteenth Amendment that officially ended chattel slavery in 1865. Peonage and the convict lease systems enforced by a corrupt judiciary enriched white factories, mines, and plantations, helped build corporations such as U.S. Steel, and facilitated the rapid growth of cities such as Atlanta. Untold thousands of blacks living in the states of the old Confederacy worked brutally long hours under appalling and often life-threatening conditions. Some had been imprisoned without cause other than white greed and racism. They were politically powerless, penniless, and frequently illiterate. Douglas A. Blackmon tells this still little-known, shameful story of "neo-slavery" in shocking detail in his Pulitzer Prize–winning opus *Slavery by Another Name*. He draws an analogy between America's exploitation of post–Civil War black slave laborers and Nazi Germany's exploitation of Jewish slave laborers during the Holocaust.[52] At least the latter received some compensation from the postwar German government and from corporations such as Daimler-Benz, Volkswagen, and I.G. Farben, to mention just a few. It was, to use Blackmon's apt title, "slavery by another name." The practice was very much in effect as the world's athletes converged on Los Angeles in 1932.

Given this gloomy cavalcade of racial exploitation both within and beyond the realm of sports, did the United States deserve the honor of hosting the 1932 Olympics? In 1936, a vocal, if ultimately futile, boycott campaign was waged in the United States. The boycotters urged the American Olympic Committee, headed by Avery Brundage, to keep the American team away from Berlin and Garmisch-Partenkirchen, the site of the Winter Games. No serious talk of a Los Angeles boycott was heard in the years before the X Olympiad.

There was small-scale agitation. "Los Angeles offers greetings to the world and guarantees a royal welcome to everyone attending the Olympic Games," read the flashing Coliseum scoreboard. However, not all Californians shared the enthusiasm of Olympic boosters such as Garland and movie studio mogul Louis B. Mayer. With the nation reeling from the Great Depression, with perhaps 350,000 unemployed in Los Angeles and its environs and double that number statewide and soup kitchens and Hoovervilles, wretched, ramshackle dwellings for the homeless, dotting the Southern California landscape, it is not surprising that there were demonstrations, occasionally violent ones, in several cities, including Los Angeles. Protesters denounced the "trivial" nature of the Olympiad and the extravagant expenditures for Olympic facilities when hunger stalked the land. "Groceries not Games" was the message on signs carried by indignant workers, but their efforts were futile. Local pride in housing the Games trumped humanitarian concerns.[53]

In addition to the foregoing, it should be recalled that a counter-Olympics was sponsored and organized by American Communists and kindred spirits. It took place at the end of July 1932 at Stagg Field in Chicago and attracted an estimated four hundred athletes. Although Communists were deeply involved in racial questions, it was not the so-called Negro problem that motivated them to stage a rival workers Olympics. Rather, they saw athletics as an impediment to getting workers active in politics. Sports, in their Marxist view, was an opiate. "Bosses" avoided costly wage disputes by providing games and circuses instead of more bread for the proletariat. In other words, the capitalist class understood the importance of sports in preventing labor restiveness. Moreover, the Communist *Daily Worker* was appalled by the astronomical costs of the Los Angeles Olympics.[54]

Some five thousand spectators were drawn to the track-and-field competitions. Marxist ideology pervaded the gathering, and revolutionary songs were sung. A 1,500-meter relay was named in honor of Tom Mooney, a militant labor leader who had been convicted of a bombing that claimed the lives of ten persons. Radicals had hoped to disrupt the 1916 San Francisco War Preparedness Day parade. In 1932, then in the sixteenth year of his imprisonment for the crime, Mooney applauded the workers' athletic meet for "boycotting the California Olympics held in the state which keeps me a prisoner in spite of the absolute proofs of my innocence." In return, the athletic festival sent a telegram to Mooney and to the "Scottsboro boys" promising continuing efforts on their behalf.[55]

Given the deplorable state of American race relations, the raw racism that permeated the nation, should there have not been protests and more calls for the world to boycott? Between 1933 and 1939, the plight of blacks in the United States was on a par with the lamentable Jewish dilemma in Germany.

There are those who reject an equation of America's persecution of blacks and Germany's oppression of Jews in the 1930s. Historian Joshua Stein has argued that there was "never . . . a federal attempt or a state attempt to justify or promote lynchings."[56] But in truth, there were US senators from Mississippi and elsewhere who defended this vigilante justice that claimed so many black lives, and for decades, the government in the nation's capital and state capitals refused to take meaningful action to curtail lynchings. Professor Stein wrote that "Blacks in America were citizens; Jews in Germany were stripped of their citizenship."[57] The historical fact is that in much of this country, a country that proclaimed itself the land of the free and the home of the brave, a country that supposedly provided liberty and justice for all, dark-skinned Americans were second-class citizens discriminated against and humiliated on a daily basis.

Professor Stein had averred that blacks could approach the police for help. Jews could not. Little help was actually available to blacks with legitimate grievances in many cities and towns. Police were often part and parcel of the racial structure. Was life really better for black Americans than for Jews in the Third Reich? Probably not. Prior to Kristallnacht in November 1938, when the Nazis coordinated pogroms throughout Germany, few Jews were murdered. During the Kristallnacht rioting, an estimated one hundred were killed, and their position deteriorated quickly thereafter. The noose would soon tighten.

Of course, Hitler's blitzkrieg against Poland on September 1, 1939, touching off World War II and paving the way for the Holocaust, dramatically changed the equation. Discrimination and persecution gave way to annihilation. Ghettoization and death camps marked a new phase in Hitler's Jewish policy, his "Final Solution," but it should be recalled that when the 1936 Olympiad took place, more than two years before Crystal Night, Jews were not yet a majority in the concentration camps.

This is not to minimize the shocking treatment of German and Austrian Jews in the six years preceding the invasion of Poland. Rather, the purpose is to show that selective historical amnesia has led Americans to lose sight of the fact that subjugation of blacks was still rife in the 1930s, seventy years after emancipation.

In 1936, the world had a golden opportunity to say no to Hitler's dictatorship. Alas, it did not. Instead, it tacitly put its stamp of approval on his regime. Would a rebuff have deterred the Führer and changed the course of history? The "if" questions are history's most intriguing, but, of course, they are unanswerable. Still, asking those questions may serve as a guide for future decision makers.

Back in 1932, the International Olympic Committee had turned a blind eye to America's horrendous racial practices. Had it not, the glacial pace of racial progress might have been somewhat accelerated. It took a new climate of opinion after World War II to bring on the civil rights movement of the 1950s and 1960s. In the interim, a generation of black Americans had their dignity insulted, their lives circumscribed, their hopes deferred, and their dreams crushed.

Much of the white world ignored the racial criminality of both the United States and Germany. Imperial nations—England, France, Belgium, the Netherlands, Germany until 1918, and Italy—by virtue of their military superiority and industrial strength denied darker-skinned peoples in Africa and or Asia their most fundamental rights.

Japan, in occupying Korea after 1910, was no better. It can be argued from an ethical standpoint that these countries were unworthy of hosting Olympic Games, but they were the heart and soul of the Olympic Movement. They dominated the executive board of the IOC. However desirable, eliminating them from the quadrennial games would have been totally impractical. The ethical dilemma, which was not recognized as such, did not disappear. If anything, it worsened.

Notes

1.   International Olympic Committee, *One Hundred Years—The Idea—The Presidents—The Achievements*, vol. 1 (Lausanne: International Olympic Committee, 1994) Vol. 1, 90, 123–125, 170; George R. Matthews, *America's First Olympics: The St. Louis Games of 1904* (Columbia: University of Missouri Press, 2005), 205; Gaston Meyer, "St. Louis 1904," in Lord Killanin and John Rodda, *The Olympic Games* (London: Macdonald and Janes, 1979),

50; Pierre de Coubertin, *Une Campagne de Vingt—et—un Ans 1887–1908* (Paris: Librairie de L'education physique, 1909), 161.

2. Pierre de Coubertin, *Olympic Memoirs* (Lausanne: International Olympic Committee, 1997), 43; Matthews, *America's First Olympics*, 43.

3. James A. Page, *Black Olympian Medalists* (Englewood, CO: Libraries Unlimited, Inc., 1991), 94–95; Bill Mallon, *The 1904 Olympic Games: Results for All Competitors in All Events, with Commentary* (London: McFarland and Co., 1999), 12.

4. International Olympic Committee, *One Hundred Years*, 170; de Coubertin, *Olympic Memoirs*, 43.

5. Geoffrey C. Ward, "The Man in the Zoo," *American Heritage* (October 1992): 12, 14; Robert Moor, "Pygmy Caged in Monkey House," *New York* (April 9, 2012): 38.

6. *Olympic News*, vol. 6, nos. 1 and 2 (January/February 1932): 7.

7. International Olympic Committee, *One Hundred Years*, 249–250.

8. *New York Times*, June 2, 1932

9. W. E. B. DuBois, "Negroes Allowed," *The Crisis*, vol. 9, no. 8 (August 1932): 263.

10. Ibid., 252–253.

11. Page, *Black Olympian Medalists*, 81; David Guiney, *The Friendly Olympics* (Dublin: PR Books, 1982), 61–62. Also see "Eddie Tolan, a Victim of Race Prejudice," Eddie Tolan Vertical File, Bentley Historical Library, University of Michigan.

12. *Congressman Ralph H. Metcalfe: The Man, the Legacy*, USOC archives (Colorado Springs, CO), DVD; *Afro-American*, August 13, 1932, and August 20, 1932; Ralph Metcalfe Jr., personal interview, August 14, 2009, in Chicago. He is the curator of the Metcalfe Collection.

13. *The Crisis* 42 (September 1935): 273.

14. *The Crisis* 39, no. 9 (September 1932): 295.

15. Arthur Ashe, *A Hard Road to Glory: A History of the African-American Athlete*, vol. 2 (New York: Warner Brooks, Inc., 1988), 81.

16. *The Crisis* 39 (October 1932): 327.

17. Ibid., 39 (November 1932), 295; *Afro-American*, August 6 and 13, 1932.

18. Doris H. Pieroth, *Their Day in the Sun: Women of the 1932 Olympics* (Seattle: University of Washington Press, 1996), 47; *Northern Illinois University Alumni News* (Summer 1984). Henry Brown, who enriched himself in the aftermath of the 1849 gold rush, founded the hotel in 1892. See Chris Warren, "If These Walls Could Talk," *American Way*, May 1, 2011.

19. Michael B. Davis, *Black American Women in Olympic Track and Field* (Jefferson, NC: McFarland and Co., 1992), 131.

20. Babe Didrikson Zaharias (as told to Harry Paxton), *The Life I've Led: My Autobiography* (New York: A.S. Barnes and Co., 1995). Also see Susan E. Cayleff, *Babe: The Life and Legend of Babe Didrikson Zaharias* (Urbana, IL: University of Chicago Press, 1996).

21. *Northern Illinois University Alumni News* (Summer 1984).

22. Pieroth, *Their Day in the Sun*, 111; *Northern Illinois University Alumni News*: *Afro-American*, August 27, 1932.

23. *Jean Shiley Newhouse*, interview, September 1987, by George A. Hodak. Shiley, a gold medalist in the high jump in 1932, turned the telegram over to Vreeland. The Hodak transcript was provided courtesy of Doris Pieroth.

24. Ashe, *A Hard Road to Glory*, 82.
25. Marty Glickman and Stan Isaacs, *The Fastest Kid on the Block: The Marty Glickman Story* (Syracuse: Syracuse University Press, 1996), 26–29. Marty Glickman, "For Glickman, Berlin Memories Still Tinged with Regret," *New York Times*, August 7, 1994; Peter Levine, *Ellis Island to Ebbets Field: Sport and the American Jewish Experience* (New York: Oxford University Press, 1992), 227. Interview with Marty Glickman, June 29, 1989, Kingston, Rhode Island.
26. David B. Welky, "Viking Girls, Mermaids, and Little Brown Men: U.S. Journalism and the 1932 Olympics," *Journal of Sport History* 24, no. 1 (Spring 1997): 36. Also see Patricia Vertinsky and Gwendolyn Captain, "More Myth Than History: American Culture and Representation of the Black Female's Athletic Ability," *Journal of Sport History* 25, no. 3 (Fall 1998): 543.
27. Robert Peterson, *Only the Ball Was White: A History of Legendary Black Players and All Black Professional Teams* (New York: Oxford University Press, 1970), 175. In 1942, Commissioner Landis asserted, "There is no rule, formal or informal, or any understanding—unwritten, subterranean, or sub-anything—against the hiring of Negro players by the teams of organized ball." Quoted in Jules Tygiel, *Baseball's Great Experiment: Jackie Robinson and His Legacy* (New York: Vintage Books, 1984). 30.
28. See the introduction to Andy Piascik, *Gridiron Gauntlet: The Story of the Men Who Integrated Pro Football* (Toronto: Taylor Trade Publishing, 2009); Charles K. Ross, *Outside the Lines: African Americans and the Integration of the National Football League* (New York: New York University Press, 1999), 45. Actuated by both humanitarian and pecuniary considerations, Branch Rickey, the pioneering Brooklyn Dodger executive, brought up Jackie Robinson to break the racial barrier of the major leagues. Cleveland Indian owner Bill Veeck (rhymes with *wreck*), an effervescent, high-spirited showman, integrated the American League by signing Larry Doby.
29. *The Crisis*, vol. 9, no. 8 (August 1932).
30. Karen Crouse, "From Striking Symbol of Segregation to Victim of Golf's Success," *New York Times*, April 3, 2012.
31. Jeff Wiltse, *Contested Waters: A Social History of Swimming Pools in America* (Chapel Hill: The University of North Carolina Press, 2007), 121–131; Martha Southgate, "Water Damage," *New York Times*, August 11, 2012.
32. Donald Spivey, "'End Jim Crow in Sports': The Leonard Bates Controversy and Protest at New York University, 1940–1941," in *Sport and the Color Line: Black Athletes and Race Relations in Twentieth Century America*, edited by Patrick B. Miller and David K. Wiggins (New York: Routledge, 2004). In 2001, NYU tried to atone by honoring student protestors who had been suspended six decades earlier. Better late than never. *New York Times*, May 4, 2001.
33. Peter Thamel, "Taking on the Governor and Winning," *New York Times*, January 1, 2006. Also see Michael Oriard, *King Football: Sport and Spectacle in the Golden Age of Radio and Newsreels, Movies, and Magazines, the Weekly and the Daily Press* (Chapel Hill: The University of North Carolina Press, 2001), 308–313.
34. Kristine Setting Clark, *Undefeated, United, and Uninvited: A Documentary of the 1951 University of San Francisco Dons Football Team* (Irvine, CA: Griffin Publishing Group, 2002). See the Introduction and page 96.

35. Samuel G. Freedman, "Southern White Teams Just Didn't Play Black Ones, but One Game Ended All That," *New York Times*, October 26, 2009; Jay Reeves, "FBI Had Monitored Lawsuit by Blacks versus Tide's Bryant," *Providence Journal Sports*, August 22, 2010.

36. The statement made by Rick Majerus, a veteran college basketball coach, was quoted in obituaries for Bobby Joe Hill, one of the Texas Western starters. *New York Times*, September 9, 2009. Also see the film *Glory Road*, directed by James Gartner, 2006.

37. Obituary of Ted Corbitt, *New York Times*, December 13, 2007.

38. John Chodes, *Corbitt: The Story of Ted Corbitt, Long Distance Runner* (Los Altos, CA: TAF News, Book Division of Track and Field News, 1974), chapter 5.

39. Al-Tony Gilmore, *Bad Nigger!: The National Impact of Jack Johnson* (Port Washington, NY: Kennikat Press, 1975); Jack Johnson, *Jack Johnson Is a Dandy: An Autobiography* (New York: Chelsea House Publishers, 1969). Also see Geoffrey C. Ward, *Unforgivable Blackness: The Rise and Fall of Jack Johnson* (New York: Alfred A Knopf, 2004).

40. Charlotte A. Bass, *Forty Years: Memoirs from the Pages of a Newspaper* (Los Angeles: Charlotte Bass, 1960), 52.

41. Cynthia Hamilton, *Apartheid in an American City: The Case of the Black Community in Los Angeles* (Los Angeles: Labor/Community Strategy Center, nd), 11.

42. Constance McLaughlin Green, *The Secret City: A History of Race Relations in the Nation's Capital* (Princeton, NJ: Princeton University Press, 1967), 202.

43. Ibid., 223.

44. Peter Wallenstein, "Interracial Marriage on Trial," in Annette Gordon-Reed, ed., *Race on Trial: Law and Justice in American History* (New York: Oxford University Press, 2002), 178.

45. *New York Times*, January 1932. These statistics were provided by Robert R. Moton, who succeeded Booker T. Washington as the principal of Tuskegee Institute. David Margolick, *Strange Fruit: The Biography of a Song* (New York: The Ecco Press, 2002). Also see NAACP, *Thirty Years of Lynching in the United States, 1889–1918* (New York: The Lawbook Exchange, Ltd., 1919).

46. Tim Madigan, *The Burning: Massacre, Destruction and the Tulsa Race Riot of 1921* (New York: St. Martin's Griffin, 2001); Alfred Brophy, public lecture on the Tulsa Race Riot, Brown University, November 30, 2004.

47. *Banished*, directed by Marco Williams (Two Tone Productions and the Center for Investigative Reporting, 2007), film. See Elliot Jaspin, *Buried in the Bitter Waters: The Hidden History of Racial Cleansing in America* (New York: Basic Books, 2007).

48. See Donald Bogle, *Toms, Coons, Mulattoes, Mammies and Bucks* (New York: Bantam Books, 1974); Thomas Cripps, *Slow Fade to Black: The Negro in American Film 1900–1942* (London: Oxford University Press, 1974).

49. Dan T. Carter, *Scottsboro: A Tragedy of the American South* (Oxford: Oxford University Press, 1971).

50. Eunice Rivers, Stanley H. Shuman, Lloyd Simpson, and Sidney Olansky, "Twenty Years of Follow-up Experience in a Long-range Medical Study," *Public Health Reports* 68, no. 4 (April 1953): 391–392.

51. Harriet A. Washington, *Medical Apartheid: The Dark History of Medical Experimentation on Black Americans from Colonial Times to the Present* (New York: Doubleday, 2007); "Apology Shines Light on Racial Schism in Medicine," *New York Times*, July 29, 2008, Science section, D5; Julie M. Fenster, "A Deadly Inheritance," *American Legacy* (Winter 2001): 54.

52. Douglas A. Blackmon, *Slavery by Another Name: The Re-enslavement of Black Americans from Civil War to World War II* (New York: Doubleday, 2008).

53. A. J. Stump, "The Olympics That Almost Wasn't," *American Heritage* 33 (1982): 64–71; Robert K. Barney, "Resistance, Persistence, Prudence: The 1932 Olympics Games in Perspective," *Research Quarterly for Exercise and Sport* 67 (June 1966): 154.

54. *Daily Worker*, July 27, 1932.

55. Ibid., August 1–2, 1932.

56. Joshua Stein, "'Olympic Games' Comparison Doesn't Measure Up," *Jewish Voice and Herald*, September 10, 2004, 5.

57. Ibid.

2

Jews, Blacks, and the 1936 Nazi Olympics

Gallons of ink and reams of paper have been expended by historians and journalists alike to tell the story of the 1936 Olympics, or "Hitler's Games," as they have been called. None of the quadrennial Olympic competitions can match 1936 for no-holds-barred controversy. In the rich tapestry of the modern Olympics, nothing, except for the tragic murder of the Israeli athletes in Munich in 1972, has equaled 1936 for sheer drama. More than six decades later, the United States Holocaust Memorial Museum in Washington DC mounted an exhibit on the 1936 Games, and the exhibit has traveled around the country, reviving memories among the dwindling few who can recall them and the many who have read about them or seen grainy images of Berlin and Garmisch-Partenkirchen, where the Games were played.

Germany had been chosen to host both the Summer Games of the XI Olympiad and the Winter Games of the IV Olympiad in 1931, when the country was still governed by the democratic Weimar constitution, but the republic's days were already numbered. Plagued by the devastating effects of the Great Depression, Weimar, which since its inception had been burdened by the punitive terms of the Versailles Treaty ending World War I, was supplanted by the Third Reich. Adolf Hitler became chancellor on January 31, 1933, and the National Socialist German Workers' Party, or Nazi Party, quickly tightened their grip on the fatherland.

In less than a year, Hitler transformed the economically ravaged Weimar into a police state. Persecution of Jews, Gypsies, Jehovah Witnesses, gays, and political dissidents proceeded apace. Dachau, the first concentration camp, was opened on the outskirts of Munich in March 1933. Thousands of mentally and physically impaired "Aryans" were sterilized as were hundreds of Black German mixed-race children as part of Hitler's quest to purify the "master race."

The Nazis reserved their most venomous wrath for the almost 600,000 German Jews. A boycott of Jewish businesses was launched at the very beginning of the new regime. A torrent of laws and decrees, perhaps 2,000, most notably the Nuremberg Laws of 1935, deprived Jews of their German citizenship and made them pariahs in a land they had inhabited for almost two millennia. Jews were now forbidden to marry or have sexual relations with Aryans, lest they pollute the German blood. They were virtually eliminated from the nation's economy, academia, and culture to which they had made monumental contributions over the centuries.

Jewish communal and individual life became increasingly unendurable. Signs declaring, *"Juden werden hier nicht bedient"* ("Jews are not served here") proliferated in shop windows, and Jewish-owned businesses were often vandalized. Humiliation became a daily experience for Jews, who were told in countless ways that they did not belong in the land of their birth. Even choral societies and chess clubs excluded them. Jewish children were ridiculed in schools by other children and by teachers. Information about the perils posed by Jews for German society was inculcated in mandatory classes about race and heredity.

In the sports world, there was comprehensive discrimination against Jews too. Gymnastic associations were declared off limits, as were ski clubs. Many communities barred Jews from swimming clubs and pools. In Breslau, Jews were even prohibited from working as lifeguards. Jews had been ubiquitous in German boxing in many capacities—as trainers, managers, promoters, and fighters throughout the Weimar years. No more. They were purged. Tennis clubs were made *Judenfrei* (free of Jews). Because he was a Jew, Daniel Prenn, a standout in German tennis, was summarily dismissed from the Davis Cup Team, an action that drew a courageous protest from the anti-Hitler Baron Gottfried von Cramm, perhaps the country's preeminent tennis player.[1]

In August 1933, the German Jewish Maccabiah team, one hundred strong, was denied the right to go to the World Maccabiah Games, the Jewish Olympics, in Prague. In October 1933, a prominent Jewish sports association, Hagibor, was declared illegal and its property expropriated. In February 1934, Bavarian police authorities padlocked those Maccabi sports clubs still functioning. Almost all practice facilities were closed to Jewish athletes, and Jewish teams were no longer allowed to compete with Aryan teams. Clearly, there was nothing subtle or clandestine about the Nazi policy on Jews in sports. It was a policy that accurately mirrored that toward Jews in German society in general. In a nutshell, the policy was that there was no place for Jews in Hitler's Germany. They would be removed, one way or another.

Brownshirt (SA) sport leader Bruno Malitz bemoaned the fact that "Frenchmen, Belgians, Polaks and Jew-Niggers run on German tracks and swim in German pools."[2] He added, "There is no room in our German land for Jewish sports leaders and their friends, infested with the Talmud, for pacifists, political Catholics, pan-Europeans and the rest. They are worse than cholera and syphilis, much worse than famine, drought, and poison gas."[3]

Within months of the Nazi takeover, questions were being asked in the United States and elsewhere about the appropriateness of Berlin and Garmisch-Partenkirchen as the locales of the 1936 Games. In short order, there developed a full-fledged movement in the United States whose goal was to transfer the competition out of Germany to another country. The American Jewish Congress (AJC) and the Jewish Labor Committee were especially vocal on this matter. The former praised the American Olympic Committee (AOC) in October 1933 for having extracted a promise from Germany that Jewish athletes would not be excluded from the 1936 Games but voiced skepticism nonetheless. The Nazi promise seemed to them a "subterfuge intended to mollify an aroused public opinion." Germany, the AJC charged, had no intention of permitting Jews to participate.[4]

Emanuel Celler of New York was one of the few Jews in Congress who was outspoken on the Olympic controversy. Fair sportsmanship was uppermost in his mind, and there was indisputable proof of "racial proscriptions of athletes."[5] In his judgment, pledges by Germany's sports mandarins were meaningless. At that juncture in American history, Jewish political influence had little impact on national issues such as the Olympics nor, for that matter, the admission of German Jewish refugees.

The boycott campaign was not limited to Jews. There was, for example, the Non-Sectarian Anti-Nazi League to Champion Human Rights, founded and headed by Louis Untermyer, a distinguished trial attorney. The league wrote to the American Olympic Committee on September 26, 1934, that the "Olympic ideal of fair play and good sportsmanship irrespective of creed, color, race and social condition, constitute a criminal utterance in Germany today for which large numbers of innocent citizens have been exiled, expropriated, tortured and slain."[6]

Proclaiming that the boycott was a moral substitute for war, the League argued in May 1935 that there was incontrovertible evidence that mistreatment of Jewish athletes had not diminished one jot and that Catholic sports organizations were persecuted as well. Despite guarantees by Hans von Tschammer und Osten, the Reich's sport leader, there was not a "single stadium in Germany today that admits Jews for sports purposes. Even the swimming pools and other sports places in various German cities and towns have since been closed to Jews and life has been made so wretched and humiliating for them that training has been rendered impossible."

In pleading for a cutoff of funds for the Olympics, Untermyer wrote that despite Nazi propaganda, the "major sports among the Nazis continued to be street brawling hooligan mob assaults, the goose step of the barracks and the lock-step of the concentration camp."[7] Untermyer and Rabbi Stephen Wise, a highly respected spokesman on Jewish affairs, fomented the ire of Avery Brundage, the president of the American Olympic Committee, who called them "radical individuals [who] have done much to alienate sympathy from the Jewish cause by their unwarranted attack on the American Olympic Committee and the Amateur Athletic Union."[8]

More than forty presidents of American universities and colleges urged the United States to stay away from the Olympiad. Several political luminaries, such as US Senator Robert Wagner, a German by birth, and the colorful, diminutive mayor of New York City, Fiorello LaGuardia, who was half-Jewish himself, also wanted the United States to give the Games a wide berth. As early as 1934, the prescient "Little Flower," whose sister Gemma was to be interned in Ravensbruck, the notorious women's concentration camp, during the war, prophesied that the Führer planned to annihilate the Jews of Germany.[9] In December 1935, LaGuardia was joined by several governors and US senators and Eric Seelig, an amateur boxing champion from Germany, who was forced to relinquish his title because he was Jewish. They told a crowd of 25,000, in no uncertain terms, that America should withdraw from the Games.[10]

The Christian Century, a respected Protestant periodical, asserted that Christians as well as Jews had been targets of "malevolent forces" in Germany. "Why should America and the rest of the nations," it asked pointedly, "continue to condone even tacitly what is taking place in Germany by acting as though Berlin were today a seat of fair sportsmanship?"[11] Two days later, *Commonweal*, an influential Catholic magazine, reached the same conclusion. America should stay away. It highlighted the Nazi mistreatment of German Catholics and opined that "participation in the approaching games means endorsement of willful and violent persecution."[12] Catholic War Veterans took a strong anti-Nazi position also, but *The Tablet*, a conservative Catholic weekly published in Brooklyn, asked why the campaign against Hitler did not also object to the persecution of Christians in Mexico and Russia.[13] Of course, Mexico had not been selected to host the Olympiad, and the Soviet Union would not even put in an appearance in Germany in 1936.

Avery Brundage, the president of the American Olympic Committee since 1929, who became president of the International Olympic Committee (IOC) in 1952, led the ultimately successful antiboycott movement. Brundage had competed in the pentathlon at the Stockholm Olympics in 1912 and subsequently enjoyed a highly successful career in the construction field in Chicago. As a sports administrator, his long career was marked by pugnacity and dogged by embittered conflict. The 1936 Games were his first major battle, but by no means his last.[14]

Brundage's position was that he would not meddle in German domestic or international affairs that did not concern sports. In accepting the invitation to participate in the 1936 Olympiad, he explained that the American Olympic Committee was not endorsing Hitler's policies. *Fair Play for American Athletes*, a 1935 AOC publication, baldly asserted that, "The committee considered nothing but sport and its requirements. Germany's political policy within or without its borders has no bearing on the subject."[15] A forty-year-old practice of paying no heed to religious, racial, or political issues was being followed, stated the pamphlet, whose author was surely Brundage himself.

General Charles H. Sherrill, an American member of the International Olympic Committee and a one-time champion sprinter at Yale University, shared this thinking. A prolific writer, Sherrill had served as the American ambassador to Argentina and, in the early 1930s, briefly as ambassador to Turkey. Described as suave and gregarious by contemporaries, Sherrill was an admirer of the Italian *Duce* Benito Mussolini. His lack of sensitivity to oppressed minorities was evident by his 1935 observation that "it does not concern me one bit the way Jews in Germany are being treated, any more than lynchings in the South of our own country."[16] Still, he pleaded with German sport authorities and even the Führer himself to allow some Jewish presence on the German Olympic squad to forestall boycotters.

Stories of anti-Jewish practices in German sports were circulating widely in the United States, prompting the German Reichssportführer to assert unequivocally in November 1933 that no order had been issued excluding Jews from athletic clubs, that no order had been issued barring Jews from public training facilities, nor had any order been issued prohibiting Jews from any competitions.[17]

Theodore Lewald, president of the Olympic Organizing Committee for Germany, conceded that a number of "athletic clubs and federations spontaneously voted the exclusion of Jewish members and that consequently the Jewish athletes concerned had discontinued their training unless they were willing to join a Jewish club."[18] Lewald emphasized incredibly that these measures had not been taken under any government decrees. He further asserted that Jewish clubs in Berlin were not subject to limitations in training or competitions. This was clearly dissembling on Lewald's part.[19]

There was an Everest of proof of discrimination that could not be ignored. At the meeting of the American Olympic Committee, held in Washington DC on November 22, 1933, the treatment of Jews in Germany took center stage. Gustavus Kirby, the AOC treasurer, alluded to the prominent Jewish population in the United States. It had a "bitterness of feeling which sometimes runs beyond the facts of the case and sometimes produces proposed remedies which would be ineffectual."[20] There was strong sentiment at the gathering against voicing threats not to participate. Kirby said it was not their desire to shake their fists under the nose of any nation or under the nose of any Olympic committee and say, "We will not, we shall not, we are through." However, it was noted that Lewald, who had been temporarily removed from his position as chairman of the organizing committee because he had a Jewish grandmother, was subsequently restored to his post because of AOC pressure.

Charles Ornstein, a Jewish member of the AOC, was distressed in light of the fact that Jewish jockeys had only recently been excluded from all horse races. Aryanism, it was said, was a criterion for candidates for sharp shoulder events. Ornstein recited an additional forty to fifty cases of discrimination. Nevertheless, at that point, he still wanted to go to Berlin if conditions improved.[21]

Throughout the debate, the AOC took great pains to demonstrate that politics would only be minimally important in the upcoming Olympic festivals in Berlin and Garmisch-Partenkirchen. But on November 26, 1935, the New York Times reported that the Winter Games had received official recognition as a "Nazi propaganda undertaking." A representative of Josef Goebbels was assigned to a position with the German organizing committee. His task was to act as liaison with Goebbels, whose ministry of propaganda would henceforth be even more involved in planning the Berlin Games. Propaganda dividends for the Nazi regime would surely be yielded. The wife of Arthur Hays Sulzberger, the *Times* publisher, could not resist the temptation to send the *Times* article to Kirby.[22]

White racial exclusiveness in the United States made it considerably easier for Olympic authorities to deflect complaints about Aryan exclusiveness in the Third Reich. "It is absurd," Count Henri Baillet-Latour, the president of the International Olympic Committee, wrote the members of the AOC in October 1935, "to pretend that the IOC ought to have taken the Games away because Jews are not admitted in the clubs. Could we claim the same for negros [sic] in american [sic] clubs, although in other countries black men are on the same footing as white men."[23] It was surely Los Angeles in 1932 that he had in mind.

German sport officials frequently reminded their American counterparts that discrimination against "Blacks" was rife in their own country, inside and outside the realm of athletics. Frederick Rubien, then the secretary of the AOC, confessed that the charge of unfair treatment could be leveled at the Amateur Athletic Union (AAU), which often banned African Americans from competition. In cities such as Baltimore, "They do not accept colored entries and we bar them entirely in swimming."[24]

American Jim Crowism was apparent even in the run-up to the Olympics. On May 30, 1935, four black athletes were denied permission to enter the AAU track trials at College Park, Maryland, virtually on the doorstep of the nation's capital. This elicited a letter to Jeremiah T. Mahoney, an AAU luminary, pleading with him to have his organization "clean its own house." Otherwise, people in other countries would respond with utter contempt to Americans who raised the fair play issue in connection with Berlin. Mahoney concurred, but he had already resigned his AAU post.[25]

AAU support was deemed necessary to repulse the boycotters. "The opposition," wrote Brundage, had been visiting "every AAU district attempting to pledge delegates to a program to keep the United States out of the Games."[26] In his estimation, their tactics were more severe than those they complained of in Germany: "intimidation, bullying and threats and maybe worse."[27] Brundage found it ironic that the Southern Association voted for keeping the teams at home because of Nazi "race discrimination." Apparently, continued Brundage, who was the embodiment of racial prejudice for almost his entire career, "the Southerners do not realize how ridiculous they have made themselves."[28] Introducing

31

religion, race, and politics will only wreck the AAU, which, according to Brundage, did not have the right to prevent amateur athletes from competing in a sanctioned world championship. For Brundage, Jews were the real enemy. In a postscript, he added, "When we told the Germans to keep hands off two years ago there was nothing but applause from the Jews. Now we must force the Jews who wish to use the Games as a weapon to strike the Nazis to mind their own business and let sport alone."[29] Brundage finally vanquished the AAU and his nemesis, Judge Mahoney, in December 1935, when that organization voted very narrowly to approve US participation.[30] Brundage succeeded Mahoney as president of the AAU, adding insult to injury.

Though he had been anointed the world's fastest human, the soon to be Olympic legend Jesse Owens was still not immune from the lacerating insults that punctuated the lives of black America. In the summer of 1935, competing for Ohio State University, Owens won four events in a dual meet against the University of Southern California but was humiliated when a hotel turned him away because of the color of his skin. It was the Los Angeles Olympic hotel located near the Coliseum, which had a strict segregation policy. Arrangements were made to accommodate the entire team at a USC fraternity house. At the time, it was alleged that the same Olympic hotel had shunned Eddie Tolan and Ralph Metcalfe back in 1932.[31]

Owens commented that he had tolerated hundreds of racial incidents, maybe even a thousand. Traveling in Indiana, in February 1936, Owens and fellow blacks waited in a car while their white teammates and coach ate in a restaurant that refused service to nonwhites. Owens's white teammates brought some plates of food to the car, but the owner of the restaurant even objected to that, ungrammatically exclaiming, "I don't want no money to feed no niggers." He attempted to retrieve the plates and spilled much of the food in the process. Violence was narrowly averted.[32] Owens, no militant, observed that black athletes could not take showers with white athletes and drove to meets in separate automobiles. At Ohio State, they lived and ate separately, which was typical.

Such racial hypocrisy surely undermined efforts to prevent the United States from sending a team to Germany. Still, the boycotters persevered. Restrictions on Jewish athletes could not be ignored by Brundage and his allies. He recognized that fact as early as November 1933 and said he wanted the restrictions removed. In late 1934, he made a short "fact-finding" visit to the Third Reich. He was escorted by an old friend, Karl Ritter von Halt, a member of the IOC and of the German organizing committee. A former Olympian, von Halt was also a Nazi. He gave reassurances that Jewish sportsmen would not be subject to restrictions. Sportführer Hans von Tschammer und Osten had given a similar pledge, although in May 1933, he had unambiguously stated that sports were for Aryans only.[33] It was he who, to his discredit, gave the Nazis complete control over German sports. Brundage concluded that the Games could proceed as scheduled with American participation. Of course, in the end, German guarantees proved meaningless, their promises empty.

In November 1935, Count Baillet-Latour was still uneasy and went to speak to the chancellor. As a result of their conversation, a few Jews were to be added to the German team, the president crowed to the secretary of the IOC, André G. Berdez. Moreover, the Führer had, in response to Baillet-Latour's request, "promised that all the posters, which may be offensive to foreign visitors will disappear from Berlin, Munich, and Garmisch."[34] The posters in question were undoubtedly blatantly anti-Semitic ones, which indicated that Jews were unwanted. Such a sign greeted visitors in Garmisch: "Juden zutritt verboten," ("Jewish entry forbidden"). Baillet-Latour saw this as a "fine gesture" on Hitler's part.[35] "Charade" would be a more apt description.

A fig leaf to conceal the virtual total exclusion of German Jewish athletes was provided by Helene Mayer, a half-Jewish fencer with "blonde Aryan looks" who had been awarded gold at the Amsterdam Games in 1928. After the 1932 Los Angeles competition, in which she had fared poorly, she emigrated to the United States. Lacking proper Aryan credentials she had been ejected from the Offenbach Fencing Club. This rendered her ineligible for the German national team. Because a "Jew" was needed in 1936, Mayer was invited back to the fatherland and qualified to fence under the swastika. She eventually earned a silver medal, and the crowd cheered lustily as she smartly heiled on the victors' podium.[36] Ironically, the gold medal was awarded to a Hungarian Jew. Back in October 1935, Brundage wrote to Arthur Hays Sulzberger that he was confident that any Jew of Olympic caliber would be a candidate for a place on the German squad and cited Helene Mayer. If Jews were not more conspicuous, Brundage said, it was because "they are not athletically good enough to make the teams."[37]

Rudi Ball, an ice hockey star, was a second "alibi Jew," to use Arnd Kruger's felicitous phrases. Ball, the son of a Jewish father and Christian mother, had gone abroad to play. But he was summoned to skate for

Germany in Garmisch in 1936. Hoodwinking the authorities at the IOC and AOC was accomplished by the use of these token *mischlinge*. The inference is obvious. Baillet-Latour, Brundage, and the rest wanted to be deceived to take the wind out of the sails of the boycott movement.

Eager to thwart boycotters, the Nazis also arranged a special training camp for the thirty best German Jewish sportsmen. Margaret Lambert (also known as Gretel Bergmann) was the most promising in this elite group. An outstanding high jumper, she had emigrated to England in 1933 to escape the oppressive atmosphere of her native land. She was ordered back to Germany, and fearful of possible repercussions for her family and Jewish athletes in general, she returned and was placed on an Olympic nucleus team from which the German competitors would be picked. Despite being denied access to some training grounds and being excluded from some track meets, in June 1936, she equaled the German high jump record, leaping high enough to have won a medal in Berlin. That was not to be.

Reich sport officials notified her in writing that she had failed to qualify for the German squad. Her recent performances, it was ludicrously claimed, had been mediocre. By that time, the American contingent was crossing the Atlantic, effectively dooming the boycott. In retrospect, Lambert observed that "Snow White and the Seven Dwarfs" had as much chance to make the Olympic team as any of the thirty or so athletes assembled.[38]

In her autobiography, published in 2005, Bergmann wrote bitterly of the cat-and-mouse game that Hitler had played and won. "The Nazis needed a crackerjack Jewish athlete to show the world that discrimination, as far as the Olympics were concerned, did not exist.[39]

The whole ordeal left lasting scars on Bergmann's psyche. A recurring, ugly nightmare haunted her for many decades. In it she saw herself

in the Berlin Olympics stadium, waiting for the most momentous competition of my life to begin. I stand alone. The 100,000 seats in the huge arena are filled. When I dare to look around it seems as if each spectator is dressed in a Nazi uniform, either the black of the SS elite or the brown of the storm troopers. There are swastikas everywhere. I feel as if 100,000 pairs of eyes are burning holes into my body. My consuming desire to compete against all odds battles with an overwhelming impulse to hide or run away. The call to report to the high jump comes over the loudspeaker. I take a deep breath; this is it. But I am paralyzed, rooted to the spot, my feet encased in cement. I wake up trembling, drenched in perspiration, angry with myself. Why can I not let go? Why must I keep dreaming of something so painful, something I desperately want to erase from my mind?[40]

Daniel Prenn's tennis records, Eric Seelig's boxing prowess, and Bergmann's feats stood as a rebuke to the attitudes of Baillet-Latour and Sigfrid Edstrom, a Swedish Olympic official and close ally of Brundage. From their bigoted perspective, the German Jewish community produced few world-class athletes. They believed that the "New York Jews" were "constructing a lot of incidents that are based on minor, unimportant details." They informed Kirby when they were at the IOC meeting in Athens in May 1934 that there were no Jews on the German team in Los Angeles nor at Amsterdam four years earlier. "The Jews are no [sic] athletes." Therefore, Baillet-Latour and Edstrom continued, it "would not be fair that the Jews in New York should compel the Germans to put on bad athletes simply because they are Jews."[41]

Boxer Max Schmeling, the German athlete best known in the United States, had been assigned the task of contacting key people to subvert the boycott. He agreed to serve as a courier for the worried German Olympic Committee and delivered a letter to Brundage guaranteeing that all participants would be treated fairly and cordially, regardless of race or religion. Schmeling personally told Brundage that the German sportsmen would not permit discrimination of any kind. Writing in 1977, he admitted that such matters were beyond his influence. Hitler could do whatever he wished. In his autobiography, Schmeling further acknowledged that Jewish and black medal winners were not given their due at the Olympiad. He concluded that his plea may have averted the boycott. The Nazis apparently thought so. They awarded Schmeling a medal for his efforts.[42]

Theodore Lewald, the veteran German sports functionary, was one who benefited from the controversy. Lewald was ousted as president of the German Olympic Committee when the race-obsessed Nazis discovered that his paternal grandmother was Jewish, but he was reinstated because his removal would have bolstered the case of the boycott movement and made things difficult for the IOC.[43] Sometime later, Lewald was removed again and replaced by a loyal "pure race" National Socialist stalwart.

The AOC was deeply disturbed by the adverse publicity generated by the boycott movement. Some AOC officials, such as Brundage, reacted with fury. Others, Gustavus Kirby, for one, responded with concern, even as they argued that nonparticipation was misguided. Kirby, who did not relish being despised by Jews, wrote to Brundage at the end of May 1936, "You live in Chicago where the Jewish issue may be dead or gone; I live in New York where, notwithstanding your thought to the contrary, Jewish opposition and Jewish action is still very much alive."[44]

Brundage had sailed to the Winter Games in Garmisch-Parten-kirchen on January 24, 1936. His rage over the boycotters' activities had already reached a boiling point. Two weeks earlier, he had written to Edward James Smythe, a prominent Republican editor, about what he saw as an appalling increase in Communist influence under the Democratic administration of FDR. The Bolshevik presence in educational circles was especially worrisome to him. As far as the anti-Olympic campaign in New York was concerned, he assured Smythe, "We are not depending on any Jews or Communists." Not one to brook dissent, Brundage told the members of the AOC to "re-affirm their loyalty. We intend to clean house. If the traitors, the lukewarm and the indifferent do not resign, they will be thrown out."[45] Among Brundage's fears was that some first-rate competitors would not compete.

The American hope of collecting coveted Olympic gold, silver, and bronze in track and field largely rested on the shoulders of black athletes. But given the racist nature of the Third Reich, there was some question about whether they would go to Berlin. New York's *Amsterdam News* begged black American Olympic athletes "to display that spirit of self-sacrifice which is the true mark of greatness." In a front-page open letter to the athletes, it called upon them to stay home rather than be used by Hitlerism through their appearances in the Berlin Games. The *Amsterdam News* warned that "the use of your magic names to attract thousands of tourists and sports fans in that country would undoubtedly furnish... moral support" to a racist regime. Taking the measure of the German chancellor and the threat he posed, the Harlem-based newspaper said it spoke for "Black America and exploited colonial peoples and in the name of humanity, of civilization, of all forces of enlightenment which are threatened by the rise of Adolf Hitler and his barbarous National Socialist philosophy."[46] To drive home its point about the Nazi menace, the letter pointed to the notorious Jew-baiter Julius Streicher, who published the revoltingly racist weekly *Der Stürmer*. In a speech to a throng of 12,000 ardent Nazis, he openly defended lynchings in the United States: "Here in Germany we say that when a Negro is lynched for assaulting a Whiteman he gets what is coming to him."[47] Perhaps it was Streicher, whose association with Hitler stretched back to the early 1920s, who more than anyone provided the inspiration and rationale for Nazi genocide. After the war, he was convicted at Nuremberg and executed.

W. E. B. Du Bois, a titanic figure in twentieth-century Afro-American history and the Pan-African movement, editorialized in the pages of *The Crisis*, the organ of the National Association for the Advancement of Colored People (NAACP), which he edited, that the United States should steer clear of the Nazi Olympics. His reason was that the "games are being held in a country whose government is founded officially upon suppression of religious political and social liberty, and upon terror and brutality."[48] Neither prestige nor money should be contributed to a government of that sort, said Du Bois, who had studied in Berlin, knew Germany well, and admired German culture.

Walter White, the executive director of the NAACP, the oldest and largest civil rights organization in the United States, expressed basically the same sentiments. In December 1935, White sent a telegram to the Amateur Athletic Union (AAU), which was about to open its convention. White requested that the AAU vote decisively against US participation in the German Olympiad. Why? Because "Germany has violated her pledges against racial discrimination and for American athletes to participate would be to negate every principle upon which the Olympic Games are based." A refusal to take part "potentially could do incalculable good in helping Germany and the world to realize that racial bigotry must be opposed in its every manifestation. To participate would be to place approval upon the German government's deplorable persecution of racial and religious groups."[49] The venerable White took note of the fact that his own country discriminated, particularly against black athletes in the South. Racism was still a fact of American life. In an address he gave on December 3 at a mass meeting of the Committee on Fair Play in American sports, he pointed out that there was plenty of work to be done in the United States.

Discrimination against Black America notwithstanding, *The Crisis* of September 1935 contended that the American Olympic Committee should withdraw from the Berlin competition: "No colored American can read the news which comes out of Hitler's Germany without profound and poignant sympathy for the Jews and Catholics under the heel of Europe's mad man. The tales of humiliation . . . have a familiar ring to us."[50]

Black Americans were keenly aware that the Nazi hierarchy held them in contempt. In his execrable tome *Mein Kampf*, Hitler spoke disparagingly of Africans, calling them "primitive and inferior."[51] They may not have known that the *Völkischer Beobachter*, the Nazi Party newspaper since 1921, declared after the Los Angeles Games in 1932 that black people had no business in the Olympics. Competition between the races debased the Olympic ideal. Therefore, blacks had to be expelled: "We demand it." Nazis were stunned and repelled by the talents of black Americans and fearful that Aryan competitors would be embarrassed in Berlin.[52] Their fears were well founded of course. For the time being, Nazi racist rhetoric had to be muted somewhat in light of the boycott campaign. But would African American athletes absent themselves of their own volition?

In the midst of the Great Depression, which adversely affected the black American population disproportionately—they were usually the last hired and the first fired and not very many had been able to save for a rainy day—black athletes understood that fame, if not fortune, beckoned in Berlin in 1936. They dominated the US track contingent. There was not only the redoubtable Jesse Owens, but Mack Robinson, Jackie Robinson's older brother; John Woodruff; Archie Williams; Cornelius Johnson; and Ralph Metcalfe—all medal contenders. Whatever their misgivings, this coterie believed that the Olympics would afford them a golden opportunity to showcase their talents and garner medals for the United States, whose government was unwilling to help them and their people achieve true equality but was delighted with their contributions to the American medal count.

Ralph Metcalfe, one of the American stars of the 1932 Olympiad, went on record in opposition to the boycott because of an "internal political situation" overseas. He had no reason to believe that he would be mistreated if he were to compete in Berlin. Ben Johnson, a black sprinter at Columbia University, told the AAU that it should clean its own house before it started to clean Germany's. The South in particular needed cleaning up because "Negroes are barred from membership in the AAU." He went on to cite cases of discrimination in AAU and Olympic competition.[53]

While some Jewish American athletes and Jewish sportsmen from several other nations journeyed to Berlin to compete, others bypassed the Games to dramatize their policies and practices. Short-distance runner Herman Neugass, a star on Tulane University's strong track team, wrote to the American Jewish Congress in December 1935, "I feel it to be my duty to express my unequivocal opinion that this country should not participate in the Olympic contests if they are held in Germany."[54] Milt Green, the Jewish captain of Harvard's track team, who won the regional 110-meter high hurdles qualifying trials, was among the boycotters. His Jewish teammate Norman Cahners followed suit. Long Island University's nationally renowned basketball squad, with a majority of Jewish players, was also counted among the protesting stay-at-homes. In Canada, Sammy Luftspring, his nation's highest-ranked lightweight pugilist, declined to box in the Olympic tryouts. His countryman, Toronto-born Henry Cieman, a world-class walker, took the same position. In France, Philippe de Rothschild, an outstanding bobsledder, and coreligionist Jean Rheims chose not to go to Garmisch.

Three Jewish female swimmers from Vienna's Hakoah sports club were selected to represent Austria but elected not to compete because of Nazi villainy. One, Judith Deutsch, stood an excellent chance of winning a medal, perhaps a gold medal, in Berlin in 1936, but her conscience prevented her participation. Because she opted to rebuff the Führer by not swimming in the Games, she became a pariah in her own country. Although she had previously been chosen the preeminent Austrian athlete of the year, she was barred for life by the Austrian Swimming Federation. It was alleged that Deutsch had tarnished the image of Austrian sports. In 1938, following the merger of Austria and Germany, her records were expunged. *Sixty years* later they were restored.[55] American swimmer Charlotte Epstein boycotted the Berlin competition along with Lillian Copeland, a discus thrower who had won gold in that event in Los Angeles in 1932, setting new world and Olympic marks. A third superstar, broad and high jumper Syd Koff, also decided to join the boycotters.

Jewish no-shows had virtually no impact on the boycott movement or the Games themselves. Jewish American athletes, most famously Marty Glickman and Sam Stoller, traveled to Berlin, as did many Jewish athletes from other countries, several of whom won medals. One Polish Jewish boxer, Shepsel Rotholz, the flyweight champion of his country, competed under duress. A member of the Polish armed forces, he protested in vain about boxing in Berlin.

There is no gainsaying the fact that the Nazis attached tremendous importance to the Olympiad. Eric Phipps, Britain's ambassador in Berlin, reported so in November 1935. Hitler, who never evinced any interest in sports, save boxing, realized the public relations value of the Games.[56] Crowds from overseas descending on Berlin and Garmisch would be impressed with the solidity of the Nazi regime, which determined early on that the boycott would have to be undermined. Olympic international idealism was skillfully blended with German nationalism and Nazism. A brand-new Olympic calendar was distributed throughout the Reich by the German Olympic Committee. It contained a large photograph of the Führer next to one of von Tschammer und Osten wearing the uniform of a storm trooper. Adjacent to the Olympic bell was the Olympic slogan: "I summon the youth of the world." Few foresaw that in less than a decade millions of young people would forfeit their lives in the charnel house that the Führer would create.

Masters of public relations, the Nazis were determined to extract the maximum positive, even worshipful, publicity from the Games. Special Olympic postage stamps and picture postcards often featured swastikas, the Olympic rings, and Olympic medals. There were lovely photos of the new Olympic stadium in Berlin, the Garmisch facilities, and the Olympic Village. An especially popular postcard pictured the German chancellor arriving at the Olympic stadium in the company of Baillet-Latour. Hundreds of commemorative black-and-white photos, 3 × 4 1/2 inches, were printed. There was Brundage; von Tschammer und Osten; Lewald; Werner March, the architect who designed the Olympic stadium; Herman Goering at an ice hockey rink; and Helene Mayer giving the Nazi salute on the victory dais.

During the competition, medal-winning German athletes invariably heiled as *"Deutschland Uber Alles"* was played. It was common for their uniforms to be emblazoned with swastikas; that twisted cross was to be found in profusion inside the Olympic stadium as well as throughout the German capital. Brown and black uniforms were ubiquitous, commented Bella Fromm in her Berlin diary.[57]

Hiding the true face of Nazism was imperative. In keeping with their grand deception, the Nazis transported the Gypsies, who had been stereotyped as antisocial and petty criminals, out of Berlin to Marzahn, a nearby internment camp, and postponed enforcement of the flagrantly racist Nuremberg Laws. In January 1936, William E. Dodd, the United States' envoy to Berlin, notified the secretary of state that some manifestations of the Nazi anti-Semitic campaign were being suppressed. Julius Streicher's venomous *Der Stürmer* was no longer prominently displayed. "The Nazis are putting great store by the Olympic Games to rehabilitate the reputation of the 'New Germany' and if all goes smoothly, their hopes are likely to be fully justified," Dodd predicted.[58] Because the Führer yearned for a great propaganda triumph, Jew-baiting was officially off for the duration of the Olympiad, wrote the venerable journalist and historian William L. Shirer.[59] Berlin's Jewish-owned department stores, so often the target of Hitler's animosity, were ordered to fly the Nazi flag, a practice that had been expressly forbidden them. But outside of Berlin, out of the international spotlight, the persecution and humiliation of Jews continued unabated.

Some gay bars previously padlocked by the Nazis were reopened, presumably to make a favorable impression on homosexual overseas tourists. They would not be subject to the infamous paragraph 175 provision of the criminal code that would cause thousands of German and Austrian homosexuals to be incarcerated.

Even after the boycott had been derailed, the Nazis worked assiduously at burnishing their image. American athletes were feted on their arrival. Their royal reception included all manner of social functions. On the first day of the Berlin Games, at a luncheon held at a former imperial palace with members of the IOC in attendance, the Führer stated that his government would resume excavations that had been discontinued sixty years earlier on the site of the ancient Olympics. With a flair for the dramatic, Hitler received an olive branch—the symbol of peace—which supposedly came from Olympia, from the winner of the marathon in the first modern Games in 1896, Spiridon Louis. One gullible writer remarked that Hitler, a man later responsible for the needless, senseless deaths of millions, was "visibly touched."[60]

Visitors to Berlin were easily fooled. They commented on the extraordinary courtesy with which they were treated. Train conductors were particularly polite, they noted. The German capital was spruced up for the occasion. One of its main thoroughfares, the elegant Unter den Linden Boulevard, which Nazis often favored for demonstrations and marches, was cleared of all eyesores, such as scaffolding. Streets were clean, peaceful, and free of turmoil and labor strife. Built for the Games, the new Olympic stadium was imposing and immaculate. Clockwork efficiency characterized the organization and operations of the Olympiad.

Archie Williams, the gold medalist in the 400 meters, recalled that it "was like a movie set. Everything was so clean. The streets were freshly paved. The stadium was new. . . . [T]he hotel where we (athletes) were staying had just been built. We had everything we wanted—a rec room, bowling alley, barber shop. I even got a tooth filled while I was there." When asked how those "dirty Nazis" had treated him, Williams replied, "I didn't have to ride in the back of the bus over there," a sentiment expressed by several black Americans, including Owens.[61]

There was a "glittering swirl of Olympic receptions," Bella Fromm, the Berlin-based Jewish gossip writer, observed in her diary on August

16, 1936. "The foreigners are spoiled, pampered, flattered and beguiled. Using the pretext of the Olympics; the propaganda machine has gone to work on the visitors to create a good impression of the Third Reich. The entertainment varies. Warmhearted, friendly gatherings of the international set, showy and spectacular parties at German official houses."[62] Guests such as William Shirer were served the most delectable food and wine. Members of the Berlin Philharmonic and the State Opera sang and danced. No expense was spared.

At the opening ceremonies, Reich Minister Rudolf Hess, Hitler's deputy, declared that the Olympic spirit could pave the way to the "type of true and honorable peace so necessary for our troubled world of today."[63] Another speaker, State Commissioner Julius Lippert, spoke of Deutschland's wish to live in the "spirit of mutual understanding, thus establishing a bulwark of international peace."[64] Throughout the Games, there was great deference paid to Hitler, who was the official patron and protector (against whom?) of the XI Olympiad. Hitler engaged in a nationalistic frenzy when German athletes were victorious. "This is his show," Fromm wrote. "His Germans are superior. That the whole world must admit."[65]

Before departing Berlin at the conclusion of the Games, Baillet-Latour expressed his gratitude to Hitler. In turn, Hitler thanked the IOC for their "generous co-operation and willing self-sacrifice, which were responsible for the success of the Games." In addition, he voiced his hope that the Games had "served to strengthen the Olympic ideals and thereby create new ties between the nations."[66] His sentiments, contained in a letter to the president of the IOC, have the hollowest of rings in light of his bloody violations.

Hitler had clearly demonstrated his clout with the international community by retaining the Games. George Messersmith, formerly the chief American consul in Berlin, had understood the nature, scope, and even the potential of Hitler's war on the Jews in its early stages. He informed Secretary of State Cordell Hull that the Olympic dispute seriously threatened the Führer's prestige and specifically his prestige among the youth of the fatherland. Conversely, Messersmith believed that US participation constituted the nation's dereliction of moral duty where American youngsters were concerned.[67]

Ambassador Dodd in Berlin observed in September 1936 that the Olympiad had been an unqualified success for Germany. The perception of Germany had been distorted to the advantage of the Third Reich.[68] William Shirer concurred and pronounced them a dazzling success.

That the Nazis had won a great propaganda victory is abundantly plain. Signals had been sent by the global community to Hitler that Germany, despite its crimes, was still a member in good standing. The world would acquiesce to his repressive policies. If anything, that acquiescence emboldened the chancellor. He could literally get away with murder and did. Would Hitler have changed course if the tempest over the Games had had a different outcome? Clio, the muse of history, never discloses alternatives.

Those who think the United States made the correct decision in 1936 invariably point to the remarkable track-and-field exploits of the redoubtable Jesse Owens, whose four gold medals won in Berlin have become Olympic lore. Owens, who dominated the sprints and dramatically bested his opponents, especially Lutz Long, a German, in the long jump, is said to have exploded the myths of Aryan racial supremacy. There is not a scintilla of evidence that the hateful Nazi racial ideology was altered in the least by the triumphs of Owens and the other black medalists. In the overall Olympic competition, Germany had a higher medal count than the United States, a fact that is often conveniently forgotten. Germany garnered more golds, thirty-three to twenty-four; more silver medals; and more bronze. Hitler had the dubious distinction of being the embodiment of racism. Baldur von Schirach, head of the Hitler Youth, remembered the Führer shrieking that he would not allow himself to be photographed shaking a Negro's hand. Hitler had said he found it shameful that Americans permitted blacks to win medals for them.[69] These sentiments were hardly in keeping with the Olympic spirit.

Nevertheless, the frequently told story that the chancellor snubbed Owens in the Olympic stadium is apocryphal. The Führer had been told by the IOC president that he could not congratulate some winners and not others. Indeed, Owens himself felt that President Roosevelt was the one who had snubbed him by completely ignoring his monumental achievements in the German capital. Nazi contempt for people of African origin remained pervasive throughout the entire history of the Third Reich. Half-African children fathered by French African troops in the 1920s, pejoratively called "Rhineland bastards," were sterilized, some before the Olympics, some after. "Pure Aryan" bloodlines had to be protected against contamination by darker breeds. During the war, the German military made sharp distinctions between captured white French troops and French African soldiers. The latter were sometimes massacred.[70]

Owens returned to a rigidly segregated society that continued to subject him to humiliation on account of his pigment. After Berlin, he was arguably one of the most famous Americans in the world, but in New York City, he and his wife had much difficulty obtaining lodging for a night. When they finally found a hotel willing to accommodate them, there was a degrading condition: the pair could only use the hotel service entrance.[71] Furthermore, Owens had trouble earning a living and, on one occasion, had to resort to racing against a horse in Cuba and, on other occasions, against a dog and a motor vehicle. Of course, Owens found these experiences demeaning.[72]

Brundage had stripped Owens of his amateur status when Jesse, living hand to mouth, refused to accompany the Olympic squad to Sweden. Unlike many Olympians who harvested gold, particularly in subsequent Olympiads, the star of the Berlin Games did not command lucrative commercial endorsements, hefty appearance fees, or significant prize money. Far from it.[73] Owens was invited to become a member of the USOC only after the 1968 Olympiad.[74]

Racial and ethnic ramifications are also evident when one looks closely at those who captured the silver and bronze medals at the 200-meter event in 1936. Their post-Berlin lives were deeply disappointing, even tragic, but in very divergent ways.[75]

Mack Robinson, four and a half years Jackie's senior, came in second to Owens. After migrating from Georgia, the Robinson family had settled in Pasadena, where blacks were viewed as unwelcome interlopers. Racial epithets, especially "nigger," were frequently hurled at them. The city was thoroughly Jim Crowed. In the cinemas, blacks were relegated to the balconies. Whites sat downstairs, a system designed to remind blacks, if they needed reminding, who was in charge. Blacks were allowed in the municipal swimming pool only one day a week. Interracial swimming, it was contended by some, could lead to sexual familiarity, even, God forbid, marriage. Archie Williams told an interviewer that a sign indicating that blacks could not enter the water was posted outside a pool in Oakland where he grew up. In Pasadena, the Boy Scouts were segregated, and the YMCA excluded blacks altogether.[76]

Even after winning his Olympic silver medal in Berlin, Mack Robinson was not hailed as a hero in his hometown. Straitened financial circumstances forced him to earn a living as a street cleaner on the night shift. Employment opportunities were meager, and more so for African Americans. Arnold Rampersad, Jackie Robinson's biographer, wrote that "Mack irritated a number of white people by sweeping the streets decked out in his leather U.S.A. Olympic jacket. Some saw this act as provocative." When a court order integrated the local swimming pool, the whites were furious. Mack Robinson and other black employees were given pink slips.[77] As an old French maxim says, we never forgive those whom we have wronged.

Martinus Bernardus Osendarp is not exactly a household name in international sports, not even in his native Holland. In 1936, at the age of twenty, he was a Dutch athletic icon, perhaps the preeminent Caucasian sprinter in the world, as a contemporary Dutch newspaper claimed. At the Berlin Olympic Games, "Tinus," as he was popularly known, won bronze medals in the 100- and 200-meter races. Two years later, Osendarp came in first in both sprints at the European Championships.[78] Goebbels's newspaper, *Der Angriff* contended that had the United States not employed the services of its "Black Auxiliaries" in Berlin, Tinus would have won both races.[79] Historian Paul Gallico wrote at that time that the huge crowds in the Olympic stadium cheered more lustily for Osendarp, a third-place finisher but a fellow Aryan, than for Owens.[80]

After the Nazis brutally conquered and occupied Holland in 1940, Tinus showed his dark side. His behavior was such that he went from national hero to national pariah. Osendarp, a policeman, joined the NSP, the fascist Dutch National Socialist Party, and the SS. He collaborated with the Germans in hunting down members of the underground and in rounding up Jews who were then deported to the Westerbork and Vught transit camps, which were stations to the gas chambers of the east. About three-quarters of the roughly 105,000 Jews residing in Holland perished in the Holocaust, proportionally speaking the highest percentage in any occupied Western European country.[81] Although it produced a very substantial number of resisters, including "righteous Gentiles" who risked their lives to save Jews, there were the turncoats such as Osendarp who abetted the killers. Some of the collaborators were executed after the Netherlands were liberated. Osendarp, who later repented, was tried, convicted, and sentenced to prison. He was released after four years but was shunned by many of his countrymen. Tinus died in 2002. Ignominy has been his legacy.

It has already been noted that some Jews from the United States, Canada, and elsewhere had been unwilling to compete in Germany, but sixteen Jews won medals in 1936. The Nazis regarded them as *Untermenschen* (subhumans) before 1936, and the Nazis regarded them as

Untermenschen after 1936. Their triumph on the playing field did not prevent the calamity that would shortly engulf their people. In fact, a number of Jewish athletes were killed in the Holocaust.

One can imagine a radically different Olympic scenario. With the Berlin Olympic boycott moribund in the United States, France, and elsewhere, alternative games were organized by Socialists, Communists, labor unions, and leftist sporting groups. They were slated to get under-way in Barcelona just before the starting date for the Berlin Olympiad. Barcelona had been the runner-up to host the 1936 Olympiad.

The so-called Committee on Fair Play in Sports, Judge Mahoney's anti-Berlin enterprise, which chose the American athletic contingent in July, stated its objective bluntly: to make a final gesture against the "Hitler Nazi Games."[82] Among the athletes selected to compete for the United States was Charley Burley, a talented left-handed boxer from Pittsburgh's hard-scrabble Black "Hill" district who had refused to try to qualify for the squad going to Germany. Why? Because, he explained simply, he wanted to challenge Nazi terrorism.[83]

The team sheet listing the members of the American contingent said of Burley that he refused to compete in Berlin "on grounds of racial and religious discrimination in Nazi Germany."[84] Burley's English biographer, Harry Otty, believes there may have been more to his decision. Burley, one of three African Americans on the squad, was petulant at times; in fact, he was a prima donna who may have felt that the American Olympic Committee had disrespected him.

Burley was no run-of-the-mill amateur. Rather, he was a superlative fighter who, had he gone to Berlin, would have been a good bet to bring home an Olympic medal. Shortly after Barcelona, he turned professional and became perhaps the greatest boxer who never won a world title. Archie Moore, the legendary light heavyweight champion, nicknamed the "Mongoose," ranked Burley as one of the two best fighters he ever fought. But Burley should also be remembered because, back in 1936, not yet nineteen years of age, he held fast to his principles in preference to career advancement.

The organizers claimed, somewhat hyperbolically, that ten thousand sportsmen would gather in Catalonia. Not only sporting events were contemplated. Competitive cultural events in music and chess were to be featured as well. Unlike the Nazis who barred Jews, leftists of many shapes, and producers of *Entartete Kunst* (Degenerate Art) from the arts festival, which traditionally accompanied Olympiads, the Barcelona planners forbade such discrimination. Indeed, a Jewish victim of Nazi persecution was asked to compose a special hymn, and *Esperanto*, the artificial language devised by a Polish Jewish eye doctor, Ludwig Zamenhof, was one of the languages to be used in Barcelona. Esperanto had been condemned by Hitler in *Mein Kampf* as an element in the international Jewish conspiracy, and two of Zamenhof's children were later counted among the fatalities in Nazi-occupied Poland.[85]

Alas, the rival sports festival never materialized as fighting broke out in Barcelona between the Republican forces and the right-wing nationalist insurgents loyal to the future Fascist dictator of Spain, *El Caudillo*, Generalissimo Francisco Franco. The Spanish Civil War, a dress rehearsal for World War II, had begun and would drag on for three long, sanguinary years. Instead of returning immediately to their home countries, some athletes joined the pro-Republican side. While the athletes were in Barcelona, they helped construct barricades, collected food, and addressed crowds on the solidarity of the working class. Upon arrival in New York City on the transatlantic steamship, the *Normandie*, the American teams received a heroes' welcome arranged by the Young Communist League.[86]

With the Barcelona Games aborted by civil strife, anti-Berlin hopes were focused on New York's Randalls Island Municipal Stadium, east of Manhattan. In July, the US Olympic track-and-field trials had taken place there. Now, the World Labor Athletic Carnival was to be run on Saturday, August 15, 1936, and Sunday, August 16, 1936. That happening was reminiscent of the 1932 Stagg Field Games in Chicago and was aimed at figuratively sticking a finger in Hitler's eye. Sanctioned by the Metropolitan AAU, the carnival was supported by powerful labor unions and the Jewish Labor Committee. New York's governor, Herbert Lehman, and Mayor Fiorello La Guardia heartily endorsed the sports festival. Charles Ornstein, who had been pushed out of the AAU, and Jeremiah Mahoney were also boosters of the Randalls Island weekend. Jewish newspapers throughout the nation helped with publicity.[87]

There were some twenty-three track-and-field events in which AAU-eligible athletes could participate. Other competitions were reserved for trade union members. Black athletes were particularly conspicuous. Their number included Eulace Peacock, who had defeated Jesse Owens three times; Eddie Gordon, who had earned a gold medal in Los Angeles in 1932 in the broad jump; and the previously mentioned Ben Johnson of Columbia University, an Olympic-caliber sprinter. Some of the competitors were there for ideological reasons, that is, principled opposition to Nazism. Others were there to display their athletic skills.

Also listed among the stellar performances competing at Randalls Island was George Varoff, nicknamed the "Jumping Janitor," a working-class pole-vaulter, perhaps the preeminent pole-vaulter on the planet. His winning vault was superior to that of the gold medal winner in Berlin.[88]

Present at the labor games was Robert Rosenkirchen, a New Jersey–based schoolboy track star who had been born in Germany and emigrated with his family to the United States when he was nine. At age nineteen, shortly before the 1936 Olympics commenced, he had broken Eddie Tolan's 1932 200-meter world mark in the American Olympic trials. But it turned out that Rosenkirchen was ineligible to run for his adopted homeland because he had not completed his American citizenship requirements.[89]

At the eleventh hour, Rosenkirchen was courted by the Nazis. According to his daughter, Rosenkirchen was approached by the German ambassador, who delivered a written request from the Führer himself that Rosenkirchen compete for the land of his birth. Although he still had close relatives living in Germany who would be vulnerable to the wrath of the Nazis, Rosenkirchen courageously refused. He stood on his anti-Fascist principles and, in effect, told the Führer to go to hell.[90]

Described by one sympathetic periodical as a "mighty demonstration of opposition to the Nazi controlled Olympics," the labor carnival hardly lived up to its billing. Attendance was poor for a variety of reasons, including infighting among leftist groups. Few athletes from outside North America came to what the Communist *Worker* unrealistically called, "America's greatest demonstration against Hitlerism in sports."[91]

It was the boycotters' last gasp. In the final analysis, Berlin had succeeded in holding the spotlight. Hitler had won. It was business as usual for the Olympic Movement. Humanity had been vanquished. The world would soon face the prospect of an inconceivably bloody war that would entail the slaughter of millions. No Olympiad would be held for twelve years. Although there had been an eight-year hiatus from 1912 to 1920 because of World War I, few could have foreseen that.

Notes

1.   Richard Mandel, *The Nazi Olympics: Sport, Politics and Appeasement in the 1930's*, (Urbana, IL: University of Illinois Press, 1971), 58–59. A listing of the abuses of German Jewish athletes can be found in a letter from Samuel Untermyer to Avery Brundage published in *Nazis against the World* (1934). Nazi anti-Semitism in sports was not uncommon in the last years of the Weimar Republic. See Jacob Borut, "Jews in German Sports during

the Weimar Republic," in *Emancipated through Muscles: Jews and Sports in Europe*, edited by Michael Brenner and Gideon Reuveni (Lincoln: University of Nebraska Press, 2006), 87. A very popular German athlete, von Cramm lost a celebrated tennis match to America's Don Budge in July 1937 and quickly fell out of favor with the Nazi authorities. Contributing to his downfall was the fact that he was gay and had a lover who was Jewish in an increasingly homophobic, anti-Semitic atmosphere. Von Cramm was sent to prison on a "morals" charge and was deployed to the Russian front during the war but survived. See Marshall Jon Fisher, *A Terrible Splendor: Three Extraordinary Men, A World Poised for War, and the Greatest Tennis Match Ever Played* (New York: Crown Publishers, 2009). Some Nazis had tried to rationalize Prenn's exclusion by claiming that he was not German born and that there were questions about his amateur status. Letter, H. de Pauer to Gustavus Kirby, June 27, 1934, Gustavus Kirby Papers, box 6, folder 112, USOC archives, Colorado Springs, Colorado.

2. Duff Hart-Davis, *Hitler's Games: The 1936 Olympics* (New York: Harper and Row Publishers, 1986), 63.

3. Ibid., 64.

4. Letter, Bernard S. Deutsch to American Olympic Committee, October 8, 1933. Quoted in AOC Executive Committee meeting, November 22, 1933, Washington DC, USOC archives.

5. Telegram, Emanuel Celler to Gustavus Kirby, September 25, 1935, Kirby Papers, box 6, folder 102, USOC archives.

6. Letter, Untermyer to Brundage, September 26, 1934, in *Nazis against the World* (New York: Non-Sectarian Anti-Nazi League to Champion Human Rights, 1934), 115–116. Among the prominent non-Jews were Colonel Theodore Roosevelt, eldest son of the late president; Reverend John Haynes Holmes; and Oswald Garrison Villard.

7. Letter, Untermyer to the President, Intercollegiate AAAA, May 31, 1935, Kirby Papers, box 6, folder 115, USOC archives.

8. Letter, Brundage to John Grover, June 10, 1935, Kirby Papers, box 6, folder 103, USOC archives.

9. Gemma La Guardia Gluck, *Fiorello's Sister: Gemma La Guardia Gluck's Story*, edited by Rochelle G. Saidell (Syracuse: Syracuse University Press, 2007).

10. *New York Times*, December 4, 1935, 10, 26. Johann Rukeli Trollmann, a recently crowned boxing champion, had his title taken away because he was a Sinti. He was murdered during the Holocaust.

11. "Move the Olympics," *The Christian Century*, August 7, 1935.

12. "The Olympic Games," *Commonweal*, August 9, 1935. Christians could not maintain their own sports clubs unless they were Nazi-affiliated. *New York Times*, November 7, 1935, 1007.

13. See Letter, Patrick Scanlon to Kirby, March 5, 1934, Kirby Papers, box 6, folder 115. Scanlon, the managing editor of the *Tablet*, wrote that "Catholics in Mexico are undergoing a far worse persecution than the Jews in Germany."

14. A comprehensive treatment of Brundage's career is Allen Guttmann. *The Games Must Go On: Avery Brundage and the Olympic Movement* (New York: Columbia University Press, 1984).

15. American Olympic Committee, ed., "Fair Play for American Athletes" (Chicago 1935). Also see Arnd Kruger, "Fair Play for American Athletes: A Study in Anti-Semitism," *Canadian Journal of History of Sport and Physical Education* (May 1978), 43–47.
16. See "Fair Play for American Athletes."
17. Letter, von Tschammer to Lewald, November 21, 1933, Kirby Papers, box 6, folder 113.
18. Letter, Lewald to Kirby, December 14, 1933, Kirby Papers, box 6, folder 113. Lewald reminded Kirby that there were limits to the number of Jews admitted to Ivy League schools and referred to a woman, an American of Jewish background, who told him that the gulf between Christian and Jewish society in the United States was "unbridgeable."
19. Ibid.; Carl Diem wrote that "the government has not imposed any restrictions" on Jews. Letter, Diem to Kirby, undated, Kirby Papers, box 6, folder 109. Frederick Rubien declared that because he had "Jewish blood," Lewald would certainly see to it that German Jewish athletes were given fair treatment. Letter, Rubien to Kirby, October 31, 1933, Kirby Papers, box 6, folder 116.
20. American Olympic Committee Meeting, November 22, 1933. Minutes of meetings for the X Olympiad, vol. 10, no. 2, USOC archives.
21. Frederick Rubien, American Olympic Committee secretary, back from a trip to Germany in September 1935, asserted categorically that there was "absolutely no discrimination" against Jews. *New York Times*, September 10, 1935. According to "Fair Play for American Athletes," Harold (Dutch) Smith, the 1932 Los Angeles Olympics diving champion, could find "no trace of open discrimination against Jewish sportsmen." Smith was living in Germany and traveling there but saw no hint that the authorities were differentiating between non-Aryans and Aryans.
22. Mrs. Arthur Hays Sulzberger to Brundage, December 2, 1935, Kirby Papers, box 6, folder 117.
23. Letter, Baillet-Latour to William May Garland, Charles Sherrill, and Ernest Lee Jahncke, October 5, 1935, Baillet-Latour Correspondence, IOC archives, Lausanne.
24. Letter, Rubien to Kirby, October 31, 1933, Kirby Papers, box 6, folder 116.
25. Letter, G. T. Lattimore to Mahoney (nd) quoted in the *Afro-American* (Baltimore), June 18, 1936. Lattimore was described as a theatrical magnate.
26. Letter, Brundage to Major P. J. Walsh, October 5, 1935, Avery Brundage Collection, (hereinafter ABC), box 10, reel 6.
27. Ibid.
28. Ibid. The Southern Association of Colleges and Schools is the accreditation agency for eleven Southern states.
29. Ibid.
30. David Clay Large, *Nazi Games: The Olympics of 1936* (New York: W. W. Norton and Company, 2007), 99.
31. "Tried to Bar Jesse Owens," *New York Amsterdam News*, June 22, 1935, 14, 16.
32. Jesse Owens with Paul G. Neimark, *Blackthink: My Life as Black Man and White Man* (New York: William Morrow and Company, Inc., 1970), 15–18.
33. *New York Times*, May 29, 1933.

34. Letter Baillet-Latour to A. Berdez, November 15, 1935, in Baillet-Latour Correspondence, IOC archives.

35. Letter, Baillet-Latour to Charles Sherrill, William May Garland and Ernest Lee Jahncke, November 17, 1935, Baillet-Latour Correspondence, IOC archives. "Absolutely absurd" were the words used by Rubien to describe reports that strongly anti-Jewish posters were to be found around Garmisch-Partenkirchen. *New York Times*, September 10, 1935, 10. Though heavily censored, the Munich press reported in November 1935 that in Garmisch, in the recreation hall and elsewhere, signs read that Jews were prohibited from entering. *New York Times*, November 7, 1935.

36. George Constable, *The Olympic Century: The XI, XII, & XIII Olympiads* (Los Angeles: World Sport Research and Publication, 1996), 83. Confronted by a proposed African American boycott of the 1968 Mexico City Olympics, Brundage remembered how *he* had pressured the Führer to accept two Jews on the German team. See *Jewish Post* (Chicago), December 29, 1976. The so-called Aryan rule of the German Fencing Association had to be waived in Mayer's case. See Joshua Cohen, "Fencing for Hitler: Helene Mayer (1910–1953)," in *Jewish Jocks: An Unorthodox Hall of Fame* (New York: Twelve, 2012).

37. Letter, Brundage to Arthur Hays Sulzberger, October 29, 1935, ABC, box 29. Also see letter, Brundage to Untermyer, July 8, 1935, ABC, box 29. Brundage was not concerned about the presence of Jewish sportsmen on the American team. He was sure there would be some Jews, and there were.

38. Margaret Lambert, "A Jewish Athlete and the Nazi Olympics of '36," *New York Times*, February 3, 1980. Also see the documentary, *Hitler's Pawn*, HBO Sports, 2004, Director George Roy. Henry Laskau, né Helmut Laskau in Berlin, was one of the best in his native land in two walking events, 5,000 meters and 1,500 meters. He was overlooked when Germany fielded teams for international competition. Because of his Jewishness, he wound up in a Nazi labor camp but fortunately was able to escape to the United States, where he distinguished himself as a race walker for years. See the obituary for Laskau in *New York Times*, May 9, 2000.

39. Margaret Bergmann Lambert, *By Leaps and Bounds* (Washington DC: The United States Holocaust Memorial Museum and the Holocaust Survivors Memoirs Project, 2005), 86.

40. Ibid., 2.

41. Letter, Baillet-Latour and Edstrom to Kirby, May 17, 1934, Kirby Papers, box 6, folder 109.

42. Max Schmeling, *Max Schmeling: An Autobiography*, translated and edited by George B. von der Lippe (Chicago: Bonus Books, 1998), 109–110.

43. Sigfrid Edstrom called him "half a Jew." Letter, Edstrom to Brundage, ABC, box 42.

44. Letter, Kirby to Brundage, May 27, 1936.

45. Brundage to Edward James Smythe, June 1, 1936, Kirby Papers, box 6, folder 103.

46. *New York Amsterdam News*, August 24, 1935. *The Philadelphia Tribune*, another Black newspaper, opined as follows: "The AAU shouts against the cruelties of other nations and the brutalities in foreign climates, but conveniently forgets the things that sit on its own doorstep." December 19, 1935.

47. See Randall L. Bytwerk, *Julius Streicher* (New York: Dorset Press, 1983).
48. "Stay Out of Nazi Olympics," *The Crisis* (September 1935).
49. *Pittsburgh Courier*, December 14, 1935.
50. "Nazis, Negroes, Jews and Catholics," *The Crisis* (September 1935).
51. Adolf Hitler, *Mein Kampf*, trans. Ralph Manheim (Boston: Houghton Mifflin Company, 1971), 403. Also see Alfred E. Senn, *Power, Politics and the Olympic Games: A History of the Power Brokers, Events and Controversies That Shaped the Games* (Champaign, IL: Human Kinetics, 1999), 50.
52. *Der Angriff* (The Assault). The argumentative Nazi newspaper created by Goebbels referred derisively to America's "Black Auxiliaries." The daughter of the US ambassador in Berlin, Martha Dodd, heard an aide to Foreign Minister Joachim von Ribbentrop express his opinion that as animals, as nonhumans, blacks should not have been allowed to compete against Aryans. It was bad sportsmanship. Martha Dodd, *Through Embassy Eyes* (New York: Harcourt, Brace and Co., 1939), 212.
53. The Metcalfe and Johnson quotes may be found in "Fair Play for American Athletes."
54. "Stories from the Berlin Olympics: Herman Neugass," *United States Holocaust Memorial Museum Update* (Spring 1997).
55. *Watermarks*, 2004 film, directed by Yaron Zilberman, distributed by Cinephil.
56. Historian Alfred E. Senn has written that Germany had withdrawn from the League of Nations. The Olympiad "could turn the world's attention from international practical conflicts and was seen by Berlin as an opportunity to offset foreign criticism of its domestic policies." Senn, *Power and the Olympic Games*, 52.
57. Bella Fromm, *Blood and Banquets: A Berlin Diary 1930–1938* (New York: Simon and Schuster, 1992), 225.
58. Dodd to Cordell Hull, January 30, 1936, in the United States Department of State/Foreign Relations of the United States, Diplomatic Papers 1936, vol. 4, Europe/Washington DC, 1954, 198–199. Dodd, a history professor and sometime farmer, served from 1933 to 1938. He was appalled by Hitler's brutality to the German Jews. Many in the highest echelons of the Third Reich viewed him as pro-Jewish and hostile to the Nazis, whose carefully staged rallies he refused to attend. Dodd's philo-Semitism stood in sharp contracts to the anti-Semitism of many in the State Department. Erik Larson, *In the Garden of Beasts: Love, Terror and an American Family in Hitler's Berlin* (New York: Crown, 2011).
59. William L. Shirer, *20th Century Journey: A Memoir of the Life and the Times*, vol. 2, *The Nightmare Years 1930–1940* (Boston: Little, Brown and Company, 1984), 230.
60. James P. Barry, *The Berlin Olympics: 1936 Black American Athletes Counter Nazi Propaganda* (New York: Franklin Watts, Inc., 1975), 20.
61. A. Glenn Dicky, "Hitler's Games: A High Time for Gold Medalist," *San Francisco Chronicle*, June 12, 1984.
62. Fromm, *Blood and Banquets*, 226.
63. *Official Bulletin of the International Olympic Committee* (1937), 2.
64. Ibid., 3.
65. Fromm, *Blood and Banquets*, 225.

66. Letter, Hitler to Baillet-Latour, August 16, 1936, in *Official Bulletin of the International Olympic Committee* (1937), 4.

67. George Eisen, "The Voices of Sanity: American Diplomatic Reports from the 1936 Berlin Olympiad," *Journal of Sport History*, vol. 11, no. 3 (Winter 1984), 69–70. Also see Large, *Nazi Games*, 96; Stephen R. Wenn, "A Tale of Two Diplomats: George S. Messersmith and Charles H. Sherrill on Proposed American Participation in the 1936 Olympics," *Journal of Sport History*, vol. 16, no. 1 (Spring 1989), 27–43.

68. Eisen, "The Voice of Sanity," 74–75, from Dodd's Report to the Secretary of State, September 2, 1936.

69. Baldur von Schirach, *Ich Glaubte an Hitler* (Hamburg: Mosaic Verlag, 1967), 217–218. In 2013, Siegfried Michner, a German sports writer, belatedly "revealed" that he had seen Owens and Hitler shake hands behind the stands at the Olympic stadium. See *Daily Mail* (UK) online, August 12, 2013.

70. Clarence Lusane, *Hitler's Black Victims: The Historical Experiences of Afro-Germans, European Blacks, Africans and African-Americans in the Nazi Era* (New York: Routledge, 2003), 138–141; Rafael Scheck, "The Killing of Black Soldiers from the French Army by the Wehrmacht in 1940: The Question of Authorization," *German Studies Review* 28 (3) (2005): 595–605. Also see David McBride, "Medical Experimentation, Racial Hygiene and Black Bodies: Afro-German and African-American Experiences in the 1930's, *Debatte*, vol. 7, no. 1 (1999): 63–80. Hitler blamed the Jews for introducing blacks into the Rhineland to ruin the "hated white race" by bastardization. Hitler, *Mein Kampf*, 325.

71. Jeremy Schaap, *Triumph: The Untold Story of Jesse Owens and Hitler's Olympics* (Boston: Houghton Mifflin Mariner Book, 2007), 234.

72. Donald McRae, *Heroes without a Country: America's Betrayal of Joe Louis and Jesse Owens* (New York: Harper Collins Publishers, 2002), 159–161.

73. Schaap, *Triumph*, 232.

74. Owens remained a genuine American sports hero among whites, but many blacks saw him as an "Uncle Tom" after Mexico City. See chapter 4.

75. Robert Weintraub, "Two Lives after Losing to Jesse Owens," *New York Times*, July 21, 2012.

76. A good source of information about Mack Robinson is Arnold Rampersad, *Jackie Robinson: A Biography* (New York: Alfred A. Knopf, 1997). Also see Archie F. Williams, "The Joy of Flying: Olympic Gold, Air Force Colonel, and Teacher," interviews conducted by Gabrielle Morris, 1992. See page 14.

77. Rampersad, *Jackie Robinson*, 31, 35, and 64. Also see Jules Tygiel, *Baseball's Great Experiment: Jackie Robinson and His Legacy* (New York: Vintage Books, 1984), 61.

78. See "Tinus Osendarp," *Wikipedia*, http://en.wikipedia.org/wiki/Tinus_Osendarp.

79. Schaap, *Triumph*, 208.

80. Ibid., 192.

81. Manfred Gerstenfeld, "Wartime and Postwar Dutch Attitudes toward the Jews: Myth and Truth," *Jerusalem Letter/Viewpoints*, August 15, 1999.

82. Ibid.; *Sunday Worker*, August 1, 1936. Also see Large, *Nazi Games*, 286–287.

83. US Team Sheet, "American Team for Olimpiada Popular: Barcelona, Spain," July 19–26, 1936. Copy provided by Harry Otty.

84. Harry Otty, *Charley Burley and the Black Murders' Row* (United Kingdom: Tora, 2006). E-mail from Harry Otty to author, October 20, 2009. Burley's widow, Julia Burley, told Otty that her husband was not eager to go to Berlin because of all the "trouble and fighting that was going on." E-mail from Harry Otty to author, November 8, 2009. Rob Ruck, an authority on black sports in Pittsburgh, has noted that Burley's family and that of August Wilson, the eminent African American playwright, were neighbors and that one of Wilson's stage characters was inspired by Burley. Ruck was referring to Troy in *Fences*, a one-time athlete who, like Burley, was forced to haul garbage to make a living. See Rob Ruck, "Sport and Black Pittsburgh 1900–1930's," in *Sport and the Color Line: Black Athletes and Race Relations in Twentieth-century America*, edited by Patrick B. Miller and David K. Wiggins (New York: Routledge, 2004), 23, fn. 30.

85. Hitler, *Mein Kampf*, 307.

86. *New York Times*, July 28, 1936.

87. Edward S. Shapiro, "The World Athletic Carnival of 1936: An American Anti-Nazi Protest," *American Jewish History*, vol. 74: 265–266.

88. Ibid., 276; Arieh Lebowitz, "Labor's 1936 Counter-Olympics, *Unionist*, December 8, 1996.

89. Ira Berkow, "The Man Who Told Hitler 'No,'" *New York Times*, August 28, 1990; Laurie Kohanik, telephone interviews with author, December 18, 2008, and January 5, 2009.

90. Berkow, "The Man," and Kohanik interviews.

91. Shapiro, "The World Labor Athletic Carnival of 1936," 269; *Daily Worker*, August 15, 1936.

3

The 1940 Winter Olympics: The Games That Never Happened—Politics, Morality, and Sports

From the IOC's perspective, it was imperative that plans be made for the next Olympiad. On June 9, 1937, at the 34th executive meeting of the IOC, held in Warsaw, Japan's bid to host the Winter Games of the V Olympiad in 1940 in Sapporo, on the northernmost island of Hokkaido, was approved unanimously. A year earlier, Tokyo had been selected as the site of the Summer competition. The IOC was eager to expand the Olympic Movement to Asia and was most probably influenced in its choices by the fact that the upcoming games would coincide with the 2,600th anniversary of the founding of the Japanese imperial dynasty.

Henri Baillet-Latour observed that the Land of the Rising Sun possessed the "same qualities of order and organization as the Germans, like them respecting law and authority, imbued with Olympic principles."[1] He confidently prophesied that the Japanese would carry out their task as Olympic organizers efficiently.

Baillet-Latour and the leaders of the IOC had chosen to ignore the egregious misbehavior of the Japanese in international affairs since the beginning of the decade. Japanese military expansion had escalated in the 1930s. Chauvinism, the quest for raw materials and markets, and the perceived need for an outlet for surplus population all motivated Japan's avaricious aggression against its neighbors.

In 1931, a trivial incident was used by jingoists to justify the attack on Chinese Manchuria and the ensuing creation of the puppet state of Manchukuo. Because of the assault on Manchuria, the League of Nations condemned Japan, which promptly withdrew from that impotent Geneva-based body. The IOC was unfazed by these developments.

55

Again in 1937, Japanese troops, brutalized by their own officers, brutally occupied key cities in the heart of China, a country whose people were viewed as vastly inferior to themselves. Appalling atrocities committed in Nanking, a nationalist stronghold, in December have been vividly chronicled by many, perhaps most vividly by journalist Iris Chang: widespread rape, unspeakable torture, and the grisly butchery of innocent noncombatants, possibly as many as 300,000 of them. Barbarism seemed to have no bounds. This was total war.

At the same time, the Japanese Olympic Organizing Committee pushed ahead with preparations for the 1940 Games. Its members included Isoroku Yamamoto, who later masterminded the stealthy air attack on Pearl Harbor, and Hideki Tojo, then the vice-minister of war and subsequently the wartime prime minister. Elitist racial considerations aside, Germany, an Axis ally, backed Japan, and so did Iran and the Philippines when questions were raised about Japan's suitability.[2]

The almost mystical belief that sports competition could erase international belligerency can be found in a letter written to Baillet-Latour by a South African member of the IOC. He was still optimistic that the war between Japan and a "certain portion of China" would end shortly. In any event, he opined, the Chinese were almost 50 percent of the global population, and "even if a small portion of her population, say a couple of millions, are at war, I do not think it would prevent the Chinese from sending a team to take part in the 1940 games."[3] Indeed, it was the IOC's duty to convince the Chinese to compete. This, he predicted, "would hope to bring about again a friendly feeling between these two very important nations."[4]

On the other hand, rumbles of discontent and anxiety were heard in several nations, both inside and outside sports circles. A decision to boycott was taken by the British Amateur Athletic Association. It resolved that no British sports ambassadors should be dispatched to Tokyo.

In the United States, the Move the Olympics Committee claimed that it had collected a million signatures in support of its stance. The US State Department had serious reservations about bellicose Japan as well. Two members of the American Olympic Committee, G. R. Manning and William J. Bingham, resigned in protest over American participation in the Japanese games. Judge Jeremiah Mahoney of the AAU, Brundage's old nemesis, took the position that if the world went to Tokyo and Sapporo to compete, it would be authorizing Japanese aggression.

An editorial in the *New York Times* seemed to concur. It noted that, "Hundreds of thousands, perhaps millions of Chinese are marked for death because of what the Tokyo Government had done."[5] Japan's actions were the very antithesis of the Olympic ideal, and American involvement in the Games would appear to bestow "approval on a Government which has lost the right to command it."[6]

Avery Brundage begged to differ. He adamantly repeated that sports transcended all political or racial considerations and reiterated the notion that he had advanced a few years earlier in connection with the debate over Berlin: if the IOC had to find a nation where history was without war and free of aggression in which to hold the games, there would be no Olympics. This elicited a rejoinder from Chengting T. Wang of the Chinese embassy in Washington DC in June 1938: "In the face of what Japan is actually doing in China at this moment, bombing open cities, killing and maiming civilians—men, women and children by the thousands." Wang thought the United States would wish to show its disapproval of such atrocities.[7] Wang, who was also a member of IOC, cabled Baillet-Latour to move the Games elsewhere. His efforts were to no avail.

But shortly thereafter, in July 1938, Japan abruptly relinquished its right to host the 1940 Games because precedence had to be given to the ongoing war effort. In the same month, Count Michimasa Soyeshima, a highly regarded Japanese member of the IOC, resigned. Soyeshima had been crucial to winning the 1940 Games for his nation, but he reluctantly concluded that the continuing fight against China posed insuperable obstacles to a successful Olympics. Canceling in 1938 was preferable to putting on a second-rate Olympics or withdrawing at the eleventh hour. National honor was at stake.[8] Japanese athletes were also barred by their government from competing in the upcoming Games, wherever their location.

It was clear that steel and sundry natural resources could not be spared to erect a sports stadium and other Olympic facilities. Moreover, a world's fair scheduled in conjunction with the games and the imperial celebration also had to be scrapped. What the Japanese euphemistically called the "China incident" meant that the games in Sapporo and the capital city would have to be forsaken.[9]

In March 1938, in light of continuing hostilities, the IOC warned Japanese sports authorities that if they gave up the Games at a late date, there might not be any Olympics at all in 1940. An unsuccessful Olympiad would harm the Asian Olympic Movement and cause a great loss of prestige for Japan.

The secretary of the IOC was also concerned that Chinese athletes might not be given a fair chance to participate. He was worried that Tokyo's geographical remoteness would impose great financial burdens on some nations, but the IOC had no moral compunctions about belligerent Japan hosting Games designed to foster international goodwill.

For his part, Avery Brundage remained stalwart in his backing of Japan. Tokyo's Mayor Kobashi wired Brundage expressing his regret over the Japanese cancellation and thanked him most sincerely for his "continued friendship."[10] On the very day Japan dropped out, a Japanese sports official also thanked Brundage for his "wholehearted support."[11] Brundage had ignored Japan's uncivilized aggression against her Chinese neighbor and insisted that the Olympics be held in Japan or not held at all.

Throughout 1937 and into 1938, Brundage was preoccupied with the dates for the Summer Games that, he feared, could conflict with American university calendars and preclude many athletes, especially in track and field, from competing under the Stars and Stripes. He and other Olympic mandarins fretted about the misappropriation of the term "Olympics," for example, by the Workers' Olympics, the World Bridge Olympics, and even by a horseshoe pitching organization. Doping of athletes and the admission of new sports (e.g., *vol à voile* (gliding)) were given much higher priority than genocide.

Japan's abandonment of the games had been the subject of international rumors for some time. In September 1937, several countries— Finland, Norway, and Britain among them—had approached Baillet-Latour to sound out the president about their chances of replacing Japan. The count was of the opinion that the vocal antagonism of the Japanese militants toward the Olympics fueled the rumors.[12]

The IOC had been kept abreast of the woefully sluggish Japanese preparations for the 1940 Games by Werner Klingeberg, a protégé of Carl Diem's, who served as a technical adviser to the Japanese Olympic Organizing Committee. Progress had been impeded by bureaucratic snafus and tepid political and financial backing.[13] There was also a failure to appreciate that presenting an Olympiad was a truly monumental task. Preoccupied with waging war, the somewhat paranoid Japanese also feared that Olympic visitors might engage in espionage.

Organizing Olympic Games is a formidable challenge indeed. For that reason, host countries are usually given several years to make the necessary preparations. Japan's late withdrawal, while not wholly unexpected, put the IOC in a quandary.

Helsinki, which had the know-how and the facilities, was eager to stage the Summer Olympiad, much to the relief of the IOC. Thomas Fearnley of Norway, an IOC member, declared Oslo ready to take on the task of organizing the Winter Games, despite the limited time available.[14] But St. Moritz, the popular Swiss ski resort, which had been the venue for the successful 1928 Olympiad, won out.

It was not surprising that the question of amateurism emerged as an impediment, for it had long bedeviled the IOC and, in 1935 and 1936, put that body and the Federation Internationale de Ski (FIS) on a collision course. In 1932, the latter had decided that paid ski coaches retained their Olympic eligibility. After all, ski instructors had competed in the Lake Placid Games and four years earlier in St. Moritz. As Arnold Lunn of the FIS explained to a British member of the IOC, the majority of the ski associations represented by the FIS maintained the view that a "ski teacher may be a professional teacher but is not a professional racer, a view for which there is a great deal to be said. You yourself would not regard as a professional cricketer a schoolmaster who had been engaged to teach small boys history (and cricket) because he played for England in the Test matches."[15]

The IOC saw things differently. It was unwilling to budge and, at a meeting in Oslo in 1935, restated its position. The FIS was no less recalcitrant. Switzerland and Austria, two skiing powerhouses, stubbornly refused to participate in the ski competition in Garmisch in 1936. Owing to the centrality of the ski events, total cancellation of the 1940 "snow games" was a real possibility.

Viewed from the vantage point of the early twenty-first century, when professional athletes such as National Basketball Association superstar multimillionaires represent the United States at the Olympics, it is difficult to fathom the veritable obsession with amateurism that characterized the Olympic movement for at least the first half of the previous century. IOC deliberations were replete with affirmations of the necessity of preserving amateurism in its purest form. In 1894, two years before the modern games were revived in Athens, the founding father, Baron de Coubertin, a passionate advocate of things Hellenic, contrasted the lofty Olympic ideal with the base practice of transforming athletes into circus gladiators. "Amateurism fosters sport, professionalism kills it," wrote Dr. Carl Diem, a trailblazer in German Olympism who had been the secretary general of the organizing committee for the Berlin Games.[16]

Avery Brundage, a very prosperous businessman who came from modest origins, also deplored money-chasing professional sportsmen, whom he later likened to trained seals. Civilization itself, not just Olympism, according to the Olympic leaders, depended on the exclusion of anything that smacked of professionalism. Without a doubt, the aristocratic backgrounds of many of them—counts and barons abounded, including Baillet-Latour, a Belgian nobleman whose childhood playmates included a future king of the Belgians—colored their jaundiced view that play for pay was corrupting. Most of the Olympic officials were very wealthy. Bedecked in top hats and swallow coats, they were members of an exclusive club of gentlemen who ate in the finest restaurants and stayed at the most luxurious hotels. They lived in baronial splendor. Class prejudice toward hoi polloi, working-class athletes who lacked the leisure time and financial resources necessary to achieve athletic excellence, was widespread in their set.[17] "The afterglow of the old Victorian distinctions in sport" was the way the Olympic attitude was described. Athletes, wrote Arnold Lunn, "were divided into those who wore evening dress and competed against each other as amateurs and those who did not wear evening dress and whose duty it was to coach amateurs for the events that were both athletic and social."[18]

How to define *amateurism* was at the heart of the dispute that was to deny St. Moritz the opportunity to host the V Winter Olympiad. According to IOC regulations, any reimbursement or compensation for loss of income was a basis for disqualifying an athlete. Playing for money in one's chosen sport or any other sport was as well. Because he had briefly played professional baseball, the legendary Jim Thorpe forfeited his medals, won at the 1912 Stockholm Olympics, where, incidentally, Avery Brundage had competed against him in the pentathlon. Not just competitors, but compensated trainers, coaches, and instructors were disqualified by Olympic rules.

Exchanges between the IOC and the FIS became more acerbic throughout 1937 and 1938. Writing in the official *Olympische Rundschau*, Diem opined that the skiing federation was "lacking in foresight" and predicted that its attitude would "soon be a thing of the past."[19] Brundage, who had become a member of the International Olympic Committee in 1936, said that two FIS officials had "poisoned the minds of a large section of the ski world."[20]

Both the FIS and the IOC remained inflexible on the sensitive matter of professionalism. No compromise, it seemed, could be reached.

A proposal to present slalom and ski jumping as demonstration sports rather than competitive sports proved unworkable. A suggestion that non-Olympic ski races be held simultaneously with the Games was deemed impractical. On February 8, 1938, N. R. Ostgaard, the president of the FIS, informed Baillet-Latour that his organization might be left only with the option of renouncing all participation in the upcoming Winter Games. Later in the year, Baillet-Latour told the IOC that, because of the impasse, he regretted that the "IOC had been obliged to deprive the Olympic programme of this splendid sport."[21]

Given that the Swiss Olympic Committee sided with the FIS, the IOC decided to cut the Gordian knot. On June 6, 1939, the executive committee convened in London and voted unanimously to take an unprecedented step: to remove the games from St. Moritz. Everything possible, it stated, would be done to celebrate the games elsewhere.[22] At that juncture, the IOC asked Germany to undertake the Olympiad at Garmisch-Partenkirchen for a second time.

Since the 1936 Olympics, the Nazis had continued their twin policies of international expansion and domestic repression. With the concurrence of Hitler's Italian Fascist partner, *Il Duce*, Benito Mussolini, Germany reoccupied the demilitarized Rhineland in 1936. Thereafter, his hunger for *Lebensraum* (living space) could not be satiated. In his 1924 magnum opus, *Mein Kampf*, Hitler had written of his yearning for the union of Germany and Austria by every means. Austria had to return to the German mother country, wrote the future Führer, because "one blood necessitated one Reich."[23]

Fifteen years later, in March 1938, his dream came true when the *Anschluss*, which had been prohibited by the Versailles Treaty, became a reality. German soldiers goose-stepped across the border and were greeted with cheers by many Austrians. Austria's Jews were not cheering. In the wake of the *Anschluss*, they were in the crosshairs. Austrian Nazis joined their German counterparts in humiliating Jews, rich and poor alike. In the capital city, Jews of both sexes were compelled to scrub the streets and to clean latrines under the menacing eyes of the SA and the SS. Viennese Jews were forced to eat grass for the amusement of the Nazis. Physical assaults were a daily occurrence.

Jewish schoolchildren were shunned by their classmates, some of whom had been their closest friends. Among them was eight-year-old Eric R. Kandel, who, accompanied by his older brother, fled to the United States after their apartment was rifled and they were evicted. Kandel was "roughed up" in the yard because of his Jewishness.

Kandel went on to become an internationally acclaimed neurobiologist and won the Nobel Prize in Physiology and Medicine in 2000. When the press in his native land boasted about having another Austrian Nobel laureate, Kandel corrected them, saying emphatically, "You've got this wrong. This is an American, American Jewish Nobel Prize."[24]

Kandel had been fortunate indeed, as many thousands were imprisoned for the crime of being Jewish. Their properties were looted and, in many cases, confiscated. Those who could, relinquished their remaining possessions as the price exacted for the privilege of emigrating. In August 1938, the enormous Mauthausen concentration camp was established on the Danube River. Tens of thousands were put to death.

Naively hoping to avoid war, Britain and France abandoned Czechoslovakia and allowed Hitler to annex the Sudetenland with its large German-speaking population. Dismemberment soon gave way to disappearance. Czech independence vanished completely in March 1939 when the Nazis occupied Prague and the provinces of Moravia and Bohemia.

Meanwhile, the Jewish predicament worsened markedly. As the IOC and the FIS grappled with the thorny issue of amateurism versus professionalism in 1938, the persecution in Germany reached a climax in the Kristallnacht pogroms.[25] In November 1938, the very existence of the Jewish community was imperiled. On November 7, a seventeen-year-old Polish-born Jew, Herschel Grynszpan, assassinated the third secretary at the German embassy in Paris. His target had been the German ambassador, who was inaccessible. The event served as the excuse for the Nazis to unleash their fury on the Jews of Germany, who were collectively held responsible for the assassination. Throughout Germany and Austria, countless cities and towns witnessed coordinated attacks in what has passed into history as "the Night of Broken Glass." Synagogues were set ablaze, sacred scrolls profaned, and Jewish homes demolished. Thousands of Jewish men were dispatched to concentration camps, and approximately one hundred Jews murdered. Nazi policy aimed at harrying the Jews out of the country. In the wake of the Kristallnacht reign of terror, Jews faced additional human rights violations.

None of the foregoing, neither the aggressive Nazi foreign policy nor the homicidal bigotry on the home front, was deemed sufficient by the IOC to deny Hitler a chance to once again host the Winter Olympics in 1940. Although Montreal and Lake Placid were viable alternatives, the IOC made overtures to von Halt in May 1939. It offered the games to the Führer, who responded with alacrity.

Losing no time, the German Olympic triumvirate of Diem, von Halt, and von Tschammer visited the Führer at Obersalzberg on June 20 to officially inform him of the transfer of the Winter Games to Garmisch. Diem wrote to Baillet-Latour that Hitler had welcomed the news enthusiastically and promised his support.[26] He pledged a sizeable sum of his personal funds for the construction of a new pool, complete with saunas, and guaranteed all of the required appropriations. That very day, Hitler gave von Halt and von Tschammer full authority to bring about the cooperation of party, state, and armed forces for the Games.

The Games were scheduled for Garmisch from February 2 to February 11. Although they had only seven months to prepare, the Nazis had grandiose plans for a spectacle to rival 1936, and Hitler himself would play a central role. It was he who chose from twenty-five entries the logo for the worldwide publicity poster to be utilized for the Winter competition. Designed by a Munich artist, it consisted of two waving flags, the swastika and the five interlocking Olympic rings, set against the background of the breathtakingly lovely snowcapped Bavarian mountains.

While much of the Olympic infrastructure remained intact in Garmisch, additions and improvements were deemed necessary. A new Reich Sports Field was to be erected for winter sports, a facility that would be a "worthy companion" for the Berlin stadium built for the XI Olympiad.[27] The chancellor personally ordered the enlargement of the ice stadium. A second rink for hockey was to be built next to the first. There was to be a third unit, 400 meters in length, with artificial ice, so that contests would not be dependent on the weather. Newly constructed barracks, described to Baillet-Latour as "superb," would be available inexpensively for the Olympic Village.

Moreover, downhill ski courses were to be largely deforested and bobsled runs remodeled. To improve access to Garmisch, blueprints for new highways were drawn up, and telephone lines were to be added. Also envisioned was a skiers' torch relay to Garmisch from Chamonix, where the first Olympic Games had been staged in 1924. Messages of goodwill from French athletes would thus be conveyed. No resolution of the dilemma of the status of ski instructors seemed to be in the offing, so a ski demonstration involving 1,100 skiers from a variety of countries was contemplated. It was labeled a "ski festival." Overseeing this extravaganza would be the hastily formed organizing committee led by von Halt, who had served in the same post four years earlier.

As described by Diem, the Games would feature the tolling of Olympic bells and an Olympic trumpet flourish summoning the world's youth. De Coubertin's oft-cited words would be invoked: "The important thing in the Olympic games is not winning but taking part; the essential thing in life is not conquering but fighting well." Opening the Games would be Adolf Hitler, for whom, it is now obvious, the essential thing in life *was conquering*. Attendees would hear the Olympic hymn composed and directed by Richard Strauss, a Garmisch resident. Closing ceremonies would be a comparably "showy display" with skiers carrying the Olympic flag down from a summit.

By July 1939, seven countries had already accepted invitations to return to Garmisch. Von Halt was especially keen on having America represented and asked Brundage for his "precious assistance."[28] Brundage wasted no time. He told Frederick W. Rubien, secretary of the American Olympic Committee, to cable the Germans that the United States was willing to go to Garmisch, where they would be represented in every event.[29] Eighteen countries had been signed up by the time the Games were canceled.

Unlike 1936, there was no boycott movement, and the presence of Jewish athletes on the German team was not an issue. American Jews had much more serious concerns—rescuing their brethren. Kristallnacht had shown that their lives were in imminent danger, and the overwhelmingly unsuccessful July 1938 conference in Evian, France, revealed that most nations were inhospitable to the idea of admitting the threatened Jewish refugees from Germany and Austria. Delegates from thirty-two countries had met at the sumptuous mountaintop Hotel Royal in Evian, on the French side of Lake Geneva. FDR had taken the initiative to convoke a conference in the hope of relieving pressure on the United States to admit more refugees. With the notable and surprising exception of General Rafael Leonidas Trujillo's Dominican Republic, few havens materialized. Time was running out, and Jewish lives hung in the balance.[30]

None of the Nazi arrangements for Garmisch came to fruition. Using the flimsiest of excuses, on September 1, 1939, Hitler ferociously attacked neighboring Poland, thereby triggering World War II. Poland succumbed in three weeks. The war was to last almost six years and claim tens of millions of lives. Still, the IOC did not come to terms with the criminal reality that was the Third Reich. They took a wait-and-see attitude toward the belligerency in 1939.

On September 5, Diem reported that the Germans were still working feverishly around the clock to get ready for the games. One could literally see walls and stadium seats materializing, he told Baillet-Latour.

He claimed that on the very day that the Nazis launched their land and air assault on Poland, an order had been received from the Führer to push ahead with their labors at Garmisch.[31]

Only in late November did they cease their efforts. On November 22, because Britain and France had rejected proposals for world peace, hostilities would have to continue, declared von Tschammer and von Halt. Consequently, with reluctance, Germany officially announced that it had to surrender the Winter Games.[32] Baillet-Latour had anxiously awaited word from the German sports authorities and was crestfallen. How sad it was, he wrote to them, that all the wonderful work they had done in preparation had come to naught.[33] He had hoped for Games even more imposing than those in 1936. "The war has exacted a sacrifice in the history of the Olympic Games, and the world of sport has been deprived of an event which would have been a festival of peace and joy," opined Diem in the *Olympic Review*.[34] Of course, countless innocents were to sacrifice much more.

At their March 1938 executive session in Cairo, the IOC had forbidden the celebration of Olympic Games in a warring country, and it seemed most unlikely in the fall of 1939 that the war would be terminated in the near future. Nevertheless, the IOC did not call off the Games in Garmisch. Rather, it was Germany that took the initiative.

Despite the fighting, von Halt wrote Brundage in August 1940 that Germany was still complying with its international sporting obligations.[35] He hoped for a quick and complete victory, although the Third Reich was willing to continue the struggle for "any thinkable time." He looked forward to a "new Europe" that would provide a "better foundation for the Olympic movement."[36] A month later, Germany sent its athletes to Helsinki to compete in track and field against Swedish and Finnish squads.[37] By that time, the Nazis had taken over France, Belgium, the Netherlands, Denmark, and Norway.

In July 1940, with Hitler's blessings, Diem, von Halt, and von Tschammer traveled to Brussels to speak to Baillet-Latour. The *Sportfuhrer* informed the president of the IOC that "Germany, now as in the past, was prepared to promote and support the Olympic work."[38] The goal of the German delegation was, in reality, to reorganize the IOC with a view to augmenting German influence that had already been enhanced in recent years when the *Olympische Rundschau*, edited by Diem, absorbed the official bulletin of the IOC. Also, there had been the establishment of the International Olympic Institute in the German capital under the aegis of von Tschammer.[39] Now, in July 1940, the Nazis had their way. They wanted to nominate their own people to the IOC, which would abide by the nominations. Baillet-Latour offered no challenge.

Diem seemed mildly surprised that Baillet-Latour was not very resistant to the Nazi takeover of his country, Belgium. What concerned the IOC president, an enthusiastic and accomplished equestrian, was that the *Wehrmacht* then occupying his homeland would commandeer pedigreed horses.

When Baillet-Latour died a year and a half later, the Führer sent his widow a wire expressing sympathy. Von Halt and Diem attended the funeral. They may have recognized a kindred spirit, or, at least, a cooperative one.

How can we understand the determination of Brundage, Baillet-Latour, and their ilk to go to Berlin and Garmisch in 1936 and back to Garmisch in 1940? How could the Olympic power brokers not see Hitler's demonic deportment as an obstacle to hosting Olympic Games dedicated to international fraternity? Put simply, as political conservatives, they did not see his deportment as demonic. Whatever else he was, the Führer was a staunch anti-Communist, and, as such, he had something to teach the United States and Western democracies.

Speaking on "German Day" in New York in October 1936, Brundage eulogized Germany for its "remarkable recovery." Communism had been stamped out and the nation's foes interned or exiled. Communism was the greatest menace in the world for him and many of his colleagues.[40]

In addition to this sympathy for National Socialism, at the highest echelons of the Olympic Movement, antagonism toward Jews, Hitler's principal bête noire, was pronounced. Baillet-Latour wrote to Brundage that he was not "personally fond of Jews and of the Jewish influence."[41] In early December 1939, he recognized that the war was a calamity, but for him it was not Germany that was the chief villain: it was the USSR and Bolshevism that would benefit from the conflict. He wanted the world to march together against Communism, not Nazism. In the judgment of the count, who had attended a Nazi rally in Nuremberg in 1937, the Jews helped the Communists "with all their power and Poland served as the pretext."[42] It should be noted, in 1939, 3.3 million Jews lived in Poland. Less than 300,000 were alive in 1945.

Another voice expressing disdain for Jews was that of Baillet-Latour's deputy, Sigfrid Edstrom, a Swedish businessman, engineer, and, after 1937, an IOC vice-president. Newspaper agitation in the United States promoted by Jews made too much of the anti-jewish [*sic*] movement in Germany, he wrote in his capacity as president of the International Amateur Athletic Federation. He spoke derogatorily of "international" Jews and blamed anti-Jewish policies on the Jews themselves.[43] They took "a too prominent position in certain branches of life and have, as the Jews very often do when they get in the majority, misused their position."[44] In December 1933, he wrote hyperbolically to Brundage that while opposed to Nazi persecution of Jews, which was already much in evidence, he fully understood that a change had to occur in Germany because a "great part of the German nation was led by the Jews and not by Germans themselves." In Edstrom's blame-the-victim analysis, his language clearly indicated his prejudice, a staple among the Nazis, that German Jews were not authentic Germans, their centuries-old history in the country notwithstanding. Jews had lived in Cologne and other cities since the Roman era. Edstrom prophesied that one day the United States would have to "stop the activities of the Jews," whom he described as "intelligent and unscrupulous."[45] Lest Brundage consider him an anti-Semite, Edstrom, who was to become IOC president in 1942, issued a common disclaimer that "many of his friends were Jews."[46] Still, it was necessary to keep them within certain bounds.

Nazi anti-Semitism could only be understood if one lived in Germany. Jews were the majority in medicine and law, and Aryans were kept out of those fields, Edstrom claimed, quite inaccurately. Many were of Russian or Polish origin with minds entirely different from the Western mind. An alteration of these conditions was absolutely necessary if Germany should remain a "white nation," he told Brundage in 1934.[47] The Swede felt that the Nazi had acted too rashly and thereby incited opposition. Hitler, he believed, had been "unwise" in his persecution of the Jews—not evil, not immoral, but "unwise."

As for Brundage, his contempt for Jews was unmistakable in the fight over US participation in the 1936 Games. He may well have harbored ill will toward Jews even before the Olympic controversy, but it was very sharply intensified by the fact that Jews were in the forefront of the boycott effort. Brundage often equated Communists with Jews and virtually used the terms interchangeably.

In his correspondence, which may be found in the Avery Brundage Collection housed at the University of Illinois, he castigated New York newspapers, which he said were "largely controlled by Jews." They carried distorted pictures of conditions in Germany that "poisoned American public opinion against Germany," he told Baillet-Latour.

Perhaps, he mused, the "great Jewish merchant advertisers may have something to do with this."[48]

In his 1935 pamphlet, "Fair Play for American Athletes," Brundage talked of the oppression of German Jews as the "present Jew-Nazi altercation" and then conjured up a timeworn anti-Semitic stereotype by asserting, "Upon the altars of these peaceful Games, let no usury be committed."[49] To characterize Nazi oppression of German Jews, a helpless ethnic minority who constituted a mere 1 percent of the country's total population, as a "Jew-Nazi altercation" is to reveal Brundage's considerable antipathy to Jews. In addition, why did he use the medieval image of Jews as usurers in connection with the Olympics? It is no wonder that Gustavus Town Kirby, doyen of the Amateur Athletic Union (AAU), bluntly told Brundage that he was a "Jew hater and a Jew baiter."[50] Incidentally, Kirby disapproved of the 1936 boycott and concurred with Brundage that only sports discrimination fell within the Olympic purview.

Base motives were attributed by Brundage to those Christians who wanted the United States to give the 1936 Olympiad a wide berth. A case in point was Judge Jeremiah T. Mahoney, a Roman Catholic and long-time sports administrator. In his ad hominem attack on Mahoney, Brundage argued that Mahoney's position was shaped by his mayoral aspirations in New York City, where Jewish votes were critical for election.[51]

It is not surprising that Brundage also trivialized actions taken by the Nazis against the Catholic Church, whose loyalty to the regime was doubted. He chided Kirby for raising the Catholic question. "Hitler is a Catholic," he wrote disingenuously, and added so is almost half of southern Germany. In typical fashion, Brundage said it was the Jews who had tried to draw Catholics into the boycott debate. As far as Brundage was concerned, "[O]ur arguments shall be confined to the Nazi-Jew dispute."[52]

Brundage was enamored of Germany and sympathetic to Nazism. Of that there is no doubt. He was chairman of the Citizens to Keep America out of War Committee, and his support for Germany was consistent after 1936. For example, the following year, after the Austrian Handball Union concluded it was unable to organize the World's Field Handball Tournament scheduled for June 1938, Brundage wrote von Halt that he could think of no better venue for the event than Berlin.[53]

For their part, the Nazis were most grateful for his tireless efforts on their behalf. The "embassy affair" is illustrative of this appreciation. In February 1999, Robert Lipsyte, a veteran *New York Times* sportswriter, and the Simon Wiesenthal Institute in Los Angeles revealed that the lure of profit may have cemented the German-Brundage nexus.[54]

A new German embassy in Washington DC was on the drawing boards in 1938, and Brundage saw a golden opportunity to generate personal wealth. He wrote to his close friend, von Halt, a one-time German decathlon champion, and asked whether his Chicago-based construction firm could be considered for a contract to build the embassy.

In a "My dear Avery" letter dated August 17, 1938, von Halt informed Brundage that his chances were very good. He believed and hoped that Brundage would get the official charge to construct the project. To that end, he had written to Foreign Minister Joachim von Ribbentrop and spoken with von Tschammer.[55] The latter acted quickly and sent Brundage good news. Cognizant of his "friendly attitude toward German sports," the *Reichssportfuhrer* obtained approval for Brundage's bid from von Ribbentrop and from General Building Inspector Albert Speer, the Führer's personal architect and a key member of his inner circle. Both men were later convicted at Nuremberg. Von Tschammer wrote that he was "happy to have been able to help."[56]

Brundage looked forward to hearing from the German ambassador in Washington, but, with war clouds gathering over Europe and US-German relations deteriorating, the plans to construct a new embassy were postponed and eventually scrapped.[57] No one, certainly not the author, is suggesting that a Machiavellian and corrupt Brundage saw despotic Nazi Germany in a positive light for pecuniary reasons. Those reasons merely coincided with his Olympic ideology and political worldview.

On August 30, Brundage thanked von Tschammer and complimented him on the wonderful progress in sports that had been made in Germany under his administration. Said Brundage, "The advance had been phenomenal, and today in no other country is there more general interest in sport and the Olympic Games than in the Third Reich."[58]

In mid-1938, Brundage was also pleased that the recent track-and-field competition between the United States and Germany in Berlin in the Olympic stadium had been successful despite "opposition in certain quarters which it was necessary to overcome."[59] Brundage's crucial role in arranging that competition over the objections of many anti-Nazis, including Mahoney and Jewish Americans, won him accolades from von Halt, who sent him medals and badges for himself and AAU secretary Dan Ferris. Von Halt called the German-American match wonderful.

Brundage looked forward to a return match, but, as he wrote von Halt on February 7, 1939, "because of the manner in which the public attitude had been poisoned by Jewish propagandists, it would be very difficult to arrange such an event at this time."[60] Brundage pledged to do everything possible to bring a German team to America. In sharp contrast to Brundage, Mahoney wished to forbid competition with countries having totalitarian governments.

In December 1938, von Halt was still gushing about the German-US competition held earlier that year, but he was deeply distressed by the "defamation of Germany . . . in full swing in the United States." Anti-Nazi propaganda, he commented, "does not care for authentic reports."[61] He bemoaned the fact that in the United States, all happenings in German public life were seen from "a Jewish point of view."[62] Of course, for Brundage's attitude, there was only gratitude. It was that attitude that explained German willingness to enable Brundage to profit from the proposed embassy construction.

Even after the unprovoked Nazi blitzkrieg against Poland, the Brundage–von Halt correspondence continued with its warm tone. Von Halt wrote of his conviction that France and England labored under the delusion that they would be happier if "Germany would be cut to pieces."[63] Germany had no choice but to defend itself. The harsh truth that Hitler's aim was world domination seems not to have occurred to either von Halt or Brundage.

At war's end, von Halt fell on very hard times. In fact, when he was interned at Buchenwald by the Soviets, Brundage tried to secure his release. Von Halt survived and returned to sports administration in his native land. Brundage and von Halt remained close until the latter's death in 1964.[64] The former continued to feel an affinity for Germany, and as a widower in his mid-eighties had a December-May romance with a "German princess" almost half a century his junior. They married in 1973 in Garmisch, where they lived part of the year until Brundage's death there in 1975.[65]

In explaining the decision to go to Garmisch twice, one must also bear in mind that many of the movers and shakers in the IOC cherished the no-matter-what, "the games must go on," gospel. Brundage used those exact words when he spoke as IOC president in 1972 after eleven Israeli Olympians were slain by Palestinian terrorists at the Munich Olympics.[66]

According to the Olympic centennial volume, apropos of the Garmisch selection,

> The staging of the Games at any price and respect of the rules of sport were seen as primary objectives, while the defense of general humanitarian principles was pursued with lesser zeal.[67]

Brundage believed that regardless of the country where the Olympics were held, there would be some racial or religious minority that nursed a grievance and would register a protest. His belief was shared by several other Olympic grandees. Of course, this argument ignores the many gradations of evil. Some malefactors are worse than others. Oppression of minorities is more intense, more severe, more prolonged, and more ominous in some places. Some minority grievances are more justified than others. In addition, there have been democracies, however imperfect—Finland, Sweden, Norway, Iceland, and Estonia, to mention a few—that have aroused virtually no objections from the global community. They possess the requisite resources and capabilities to stage the Olympics.

Hosting the Olympics should be a reward, an honor, a prize to be earned. Apartheid South Africa, Stalin's Soviet Union, Mussolini's Italy, Mao's China, Hitler's Germany, and other tyrannical regimes belong in the undeserving category. Constructive engagement with a dictatorial Adolf Hitler was a shameful chimera in 1936 and a disgraceful pipedream by 1939.

Baillet-Latour and Brundage frequently reiterated that sport and politics ought not mix. However, to the extent that politics are intertwined with humanitarianism, morality, ethics, and human decency, they do mix, and they should mix.

Notes

1. *Official Bulletin of the International Olympic Committee* (October 1937).
2. Junko Tahara, "A Study of the Responses of Foreign Countries to the Cancellation of the Games of the XII Olympiad, Tokyo: Through the Analysis of the Documents in the Possession of the Diplomatic Record Office, the Ministry of Foreign Affairs of Japan," *Japanese Journal of Physical Education* 38 (July 1993): 87–98 (in Japanese). Admiral Yamamoto was killed in April 1943 when his plane was shot down over the South Pacific by American fighters.
3. Letter, Henry Nourse to Baillet-Latour, May 19, 1938, Baillet-Latour correspondence, IOC archives.
4. Ibid.
5. *New York Times*, June 20, 1938.
6. Ibid.
7. Letter, Changting T. Wang to Brundage, June 11, 1938, box 156, Avery Brundage Collection (hereinafter ABC).
8. See *Report of the Organizing Committee on Its Work for the XII Olympic Games of 1940 in Tokyo until the Relinquishment* (Tokyo: Organizing Committee of the XII Olympiad, 1940).
9. Letter, Baillet-Latour to Berdez, September 24, 1937, Baillet-Latour correspondence, IOC archives.

10. Telegram, Mayor Kobashi to Brundage, July 21, 1938, ABC, box 156. In October 1939, Brundage wrote that it was the Americans who exhibited hostility to Japan. The latter honestly wanted to be friendly. Guttmann, *The Games Must Go On*, 86–87.

11. Telegram, Matzuzo Nagai to Brundage, July 16, 1938, ABC, box 156.

12. Junko Tahara, "Count Michimasa Toyeshima and the Cancellation of the XII Olympiad in Tokyo: A Footnote to Olympic History," *The International Journal of the History of Sport* 9, no. 3 (December 1992): 48–471.

13. Christine M. Sell, "The 1940 Tokyo Games: The Games That Never Were— The Art Contests and the XIIth Olympiad," *Journal of Olympic History*, vol. 15, no. 2 (July 2007): 41, 42, 44.

14. *Official Bulletin of the International Olympic Committee* (October 1937).

15. Letter, Arnold Lunn to Lord Aberdate, December 3, 1937, Baillet-Latour correspondence, IOC archives.

16. Carl Diem, "The Meeting on the Nile," *Olympische Rundschau* (July 1938): 8.

17. Hajo Bernett, "Das Scheitern der Olympischen Spiele von 1940," *Stadion* 6 (1980): 282.

18. Lund to Aberdare, December 3, 1937, IOC archives, Folder 113.

19. Diem, "The Meeting of the Nile," 8.

20. Quoted in Allen Guttmann, *The Games Must Go On*, 126.

21. Letter, Baillet-Latour to an unnamed member of the FIS, December 1, 1938, Balliet-Latour correspondence, IOC archives.

22. Proces-Verbal De La Reunion De La Commission Executive, Londres, June 6, 1938, IOC archives.

23. Adolf Hitler, *Mein Kampf*, translated by Ralph Manheim (Boston: Houghton Mifflin Company, 1971), 3.

24. "A Conversation with Eric R. Kandel," *New York Times, Science Times*, March 6, 2012. Also see Eric R. Kandel, *In Search of Memory* (New York: W.W. Norton and Company, 2006), 394–395.

25. Lucy S. Dawidowicz, *The War against the Jews 1933–1945* (New York: Bantam, 1979), 134–139; Gerald Schwab, *The Day the Holocaust Began: The Odyssey of Herschel Grynszpan* (New York: Praeger, 1990).

26. Letter, Diem to Baillet-Latour, June 21, 1939, Baillet-Latour correspondence, IOC archives.

27. Winter Olympics, Garmisch-Partenkrichen Official Press Service, June 25, 1939.

28. Letter, von Halt to Brundage, July 1, 1939, ABC, box 57.

29. Letter, Brundage to von Halt, August 7, 1939, ABC, box 57.

30. Robert G. Weisbord and Thomas D. Morin, "The Caribbean Refuge," *Congress Monthly* (February 1977): 13–16. About 2,000 European Jews passed through the Dominican Republic. Several hundred went to Sosua on the northern coast where they established a flourishing dairy cooperative. Why did Trujillo, one of Latin America's most brutal dictators, make his generous offer to take in Jewish refugees? There were several reasons: He wanted to refurbish his international image, which had been badly tarnished in 1937 by the infamous massacre of Haitians. He wanted to establish a buffer near the border with Haiti and to whiten the Dominican population. In addition, he hoped to curry favor with President Roosevelt and, in return for his generosity, receive a larger sugar quota from the United States.

31. Letter, Diem to Baillet-Latour, September 5, 1939, Baillet-Latour correspondence, IOC archives.
32. Letter, von Halt and von Tschammer to Baillet-Latour, November 22, 1939, in *Vorbereitungen Zu Dem V Olympischen Winterspielen 1940*, Amtlicher Bericht, 1940, 8.
33. Ibid., letter, Baillet-Latour to von Halt and von Tschammer, November 24, 1939.
34. *Olympic Review*, July 1940.
35. Letter, von Halt to Brundage, August 28, 1940, ABC, box 57.
36. Ibid.
37. Bernett, "Das Scheitern," 277.
38. *Olympic Review*, January 1941.
39. *The International Olympic Committee: One Hundred Years—The Idea—The Presidents—The Achievements, 1894–1994*, vol. 1 (Lausanne: IOC, 1994), 217.
40. "German Day," speech, October 4, 1936, ABC, box 156.
41. Quoted in George Constable, *The Olympic Century: The XI, XII, & XIII Olympiads* (Los Angeles: World Sport Research and Publications, 1996), 105.
42. Letter, Baillet-Latour to Berdez, December 5, 1939, Baillet-Latour correspondence, IOC archives.
43. Letter, Edstrom to Baillet-Latour, December 6, 1933, Baillet-Latour correspondence, IOC archives; letter, Edstrom to Brundage, February 8, 1934, ABC, box 41.
44. Letter, Edstrom to Brundage, February 8, 1934, ABC, box 42.
45. Letter, Edstrom to Brundage, December 4, 1933, ABC, box 57.
46. Letter, Edstrom to Brundage, February 8, 1934, ABC, box 42.
47. Ibid. It was a monstrous distortion to claim that Jews excluded German Christians from careers in medicine or law. Jews constituted approximately 16 percent of the physicians and 10 percent of the lawyers—nowhere near a majority.
48. Letter, Brundage to Baillet-Latour, September 24, 1935, Baillet-Latour correspondence, IOC archives.
49. "Fair Play for American Athletes" (American Olympic Committee, 1935), 1.
50. Letter, Kirby to Brundage, May 27, 1936, ABC, box 29.
51. Guttmann, *The Games Must Go On*, 72.
52. Letter, Brundage to Kirby, November 11, 1935, ABC, box 29.
53. Letter, Brundage to von Halt, November 1, 1937, ABC, box 57.
54. Robert Lipsyte, "Evidence Ties Olympic Taint to 1936 Games," *New York Times*, February 21, 1999.
55. Letter, von Halt to Brundage, August 17, 1938, ABC, box 57.
56. Letter, von Tschammer to Brundage, August 13, 1938. Copy kindly provided by Robert Lipsyte.
57. Letters, Brundage to von Halt, September 13, 1938, and November 28, 1938, ABC, box 57.
58. Letter, Brundage to von Tschammer, August 30, 1938. Copy kindly provided by Robert Lipsyte.
59. Ibid.

60. Letter, Brundage to von Halt, February 7, 1939, ABC, box 57.
61. Letter, von Halt to Brundage, December 22, 1938, ABC, box 57.
62. Ibid.
63. Letter, von Halt to Brundage, nd, ABC, box 57.
64. Letter, Brundage to von Halt, October 6, 1955, ABC, box 57.
65. Guttmann, *The Games Must Go On*, 257–259.
66. Ibid., ix.
67. *International Olympic Committee: One Hundred Years*, 217.

4

Racism and the Olympics: Black Protest at the 1968 Mexico City Games

Late one fall afternoon in 2005, on the campus of San Jose State University in California, a 20-foot-high bronze sculpture was unveiled with much fanfare. The sculpture, portraying a pair of black athletes posed on a victors' podium, celebrated a seismic event that had occurred exactly thirty-seven years and one day earlier in Mexico City. It involved two African American world-class sportsmen, sprinters Tommie Smith and John Carlos. In 1968, they were reviled by many of their countrymen as un-American, disloyal, or worse; but on this day, October 17, 2005, they were honored at their alma mater as heroes in the never-ending struggle for racial equality and human rights. *New York Times* sports writer William C. Rhoden called the San Jose commemoration his "sports event of the year," although there was no running, jumping, kicking or shooting, no athletic activity at all.[1]

The genesis of the celebration was a brief, silent protest by the duo at the medal ceremony following their stellar performances in the 200-meter race at the 1968 Games of the XIX Olympiad. Smith had won the gold medal in record time, Carlos the bronze. While the "Star-Spangled Banner" played, they stood with their heads bowed, each with a black-gloved, clenched fist raised aloft. Jeers, whistles, and some cheers filled the Estadio Olimpico. Almost immediately, their action became a cause célèbre. The photograph of the protest soon achieved iconic status, and their deed is considered one of the most memorable in the history of twentieth-century sports. Peter Norman, the Australian physical education teacher who was the surprise winner of the silver medal, observed in 2005, the year his death, that, "It was like a pebble in the middle of a pond, the ripples are still traveling."[2]

The Smith-Carlos phenomenon occurred in a specific historical context, that of the turbulent 1960s. Along with the Vietnam quagmire, America's racial dilemma was center stage. Despite several Supreme Court decisions recognizing hitherto denied legal rights for African Americans, culminating with the landmark 1954 *Brown vs. Board of Education* case, and the passage of civil rights laws in 1964, 1965, and 1968, the United States, as the Kerner Commission stated in 1968, was becoming two societies, one black and one white, separate and unequal. Gross disparities existed between the white and black communities. Black longevity trailed that of whites by a wide margin. Black American maternal mortality statistics compared unfavorably with countless countries, developed and developing alike, and so did infant mortality. Black income and black wealth were much lower than that of their white countrymen. Black unemployment was twice that of whites. Dilapidated housing was the rule rather than the exception in American's ghettoes.

Assassinations of black leaders, such as Mississippi's NAACP official Medgar Evers, was the response of diehard white supremacists to black demands for change. Atrocities shocked the conscience of the nation and galvanized blacks determined to win long overdue freedom for their race. Birmingham, Alabama, provides a case in point. In September 1963, four black girls, ranging in age from eleven to fourteen, were killed when their church, the 16th Street Baptist Church, was bombed by white bigots infuriated by the recently court-ordered school integration.

Peaceful marches, boycotts, sit-ins, and freedom rides were the main tactics of the civil rights movement, but black rage could not be contained. Urban convulsions erupted in cities throughout the country. These so-called race riots were completely different from the civil disorders, or *pogroms*, early in the century, when mobs attacked black communities. In the mid-1960s, frustrated blacks who typically lived in badly overcrowded conditions went on rampages—looting, stoning, sniping, and torching. "Burn, baby, burn," was their mantra. Allegations of police brutality frequently touched off the violence. Such was the case in the Watts section of Los Angeles in 1965. Cities, large and small, witnessed conflagrations—Newark, Chicago, Cleveland, Boston, New Haven, Cincinnati, and Providence. Detroit was the most deadly in 1967, which was a particularly bloody year.[3] The assassination of Dr. Martin Luther King Jr., the apostle of nonviolence, in Memphis in April 1968, was the catalyst for a new cycle of urban violence. That tragedy, which intensified racial and political awareness among African American athletes, preceded the Mexico City Games by just six months.

In the racially charged atmosphere of the 1960s, restiveness on the part of black athletes had burgeoned. A number of protests that targeted Utah's Brigham Young University, a symbol of the Church of Jesus Christ of Latter-day Saints, popularly known as the Mormons, were much publicized. Their theology was clearly laced with racism. Because they supposedly bore the "mark of Cain," blacks were barred from the Mormon priesthood and could not become full and equal members of the church. Moreover, interracial marriage was deemed sinful and was actively discouraged. The notion that people of African descent were diabolical was widely accepted in the religion.

Long jumper Bob Beamon, a future Olympic gold medalist, and seven other African American athletes at the University of Texas at El Paso opted to boycott a track meet against Brigham Young University to assert their opposition to Mormon racial policies. Beamon forfeited his scholarship for his convictions. Their ire raised, other black athletes at several schools staged protests against Brigham Young University. Fourteen football players from the University of Wyoming planned to wear black armbands to signal their objections. They were dismissed from the team.

In 1978, the president of the Mormon Church, Spencer Kimball, opened the priesthood to black males, a dramatic volte-face that he attributed to divine revelation. There is no doubt that it was the negative publicity generated by Beamon and the University of Wyoming "fourteen" as well as the unwillingness of new African states to admit Mormon missionaries that convinced the Latter-day Saints to alter their racial practices.

One year before the Mexico City Olympiad, Harry Edwards, a sociologist and former athlete himself, then teaching at San Jose State and an African American activist, was instrumental in forming the Olympic Project for Human Rights. Its principal goal was to organize a boycott of the Mexico City Olympiad as a way of crying out against the subjugation of black people in American society and specifically the exploitation of black athletes.

Edwards did not originate the idea of an Olympic boycott. Comedian and social critic Dick Gregory had favored it, as did Olympian Mal Whitfield. Edwards, the erstwhile junior college discus-throwing champion, was of the opinion that, "Grinning black faces atop an Olympic victory stand only mock kids smothering in slums, old women dying of malnutrition, bombed out churches, the bodies strewn along the path of riot."[4]

In 1968, the New York Athletic Club was marking the centennial of its initial indoor track-and-field meet. Support for boycotting this event came from a variety of athletes, including Tommie Smith, John Carlos, Lee Evans, and even O. J. Simpson, known then for his scintillating gridiron exploits. Although the meet organizers sold out Madison Square Garden, adverse news reports left the arena half empty. Only a small number of black athletes appeared. Some sympathetic white competitors were also no-shows. Several university and club teams stayed home, and the Russian national contingent belatedly decided to give the meet a wide berth. The sparsely attended meet was adjudged a triumph for Edwards and the Olympic Project for Human Rights and a dismal failure for the New York Athletic Club.[5]

In the Olympic Movement, anxiety was growing for a number of reasons, and not just race. Student unrest was proliferating in 1968. It was found in the United States, France, and Peru. Students in the Mexican capital understood that with the Olympics soon to take place, the time was propitious for venting their grievances. Strikes involving a quarter of a million students were followed by protests and then pitched battles with the Mexican military. Thousands marched against the military occupation of the national university, Latin America's largest. Rioting broke out, and rooftop snipers contributed to an air of anarchy, which seriously jeopardized the upcoming Games.

In early October, a week before the scheduled opening, the military fired at throngs of protesters in the Plaza of the Three Cultures in what has come to be called the Massacre at Tlatelolco.[6] There are no accurate statistics on the number of civilians killed. Estimates of fatalities run as high as five hundred students and bystanders. Perhaps in excess of a thousand were wounded. But order was restored, and the government was determined that the Olympics would proceed. The full story remains to be told. Pedro Ramirez Vasquez, chairman of the Mexican Organizing Committee, gave assurances that the Games would move forward with the safety of spectators and athletes guaranteed. This was to be the first Olympiad held in a Spanish-speaking land and the first in a third world country.

Many students wanted to know how the country could afford to host the Olympics but claimed that it lacked the funds to ameliorate the grinding poverty of the Mexican masses. John Carlos has written in recent years that black American Olympians, in concert with Harry Edwards, had planned to "hook up" with the disgruntled Mexican students. That did not happen.[7]

US federal agencies—the Department of Defense, the CIA, the FBI, and even the White House—closely monitored Olympic-related activities. They were vigilant, even paranoid, about the possible Communist role in the student convulsions in Mexico City and the potential for the disruption of the Games. Race was very much on the minds at the FBI. An FBI agent in Dallas reported to J. Edgar Hoover, the infamous director of the bureau, that there were two men en route to the Olympics in the Mexican capital. Supposedly, the two were armed with "bull whips, machettes [sic] and literature concerning black power."[8]

With the journeys of Columbus as an inspiration, the Olympic torch took a circuitous route from Greece, the site of the ancient Games, to Mexico. After being lit at Mount Olympus, the flame was carried by runners to the port of Piraeus and then traveled by sea to Genoa, the Italian city associated with Columbus. Next it was transported to Barcelona and afterward to Madrid. It was then placed on board a Spanish vessel, which sailed to San Salvador, Columbus's first landfall in 1492. A Mexican ship took the torch to the port of Vera Cruz, and runners carried it to the pyramids of Teotihuacan.

On October 12, before a crowd of approximately one hundred thousand, the Games were officially opened in the refurbished Estadio Olympico by President Gustavio Diaz Ordaz. For the first time in Olympic history, a woman, Enriqueta Basilio Sotelo, a Mexican hurdler, brought the torch into the stadium. For the next twelve days, Mexico City would be the sports capital of the world; 7,639 athletes from 110 countries would take part. World and Olympic records would be broken, and the Games would feature several superhuman athletic performances such as that of Bob Beamon, the American long jumper. But it would be the names of Tommie Smith and John Carlos that would be inextricably and controversially linked with Mexico City.

As early as March 1967, the United States Olympic Committee saw trouble on the horizon, and Tommie Smith was viewed as a major troublemaker. Precisely what was said about him at the executive board meeting of March 23 is not known. Much of the board's discussion was put off the record, which is full of lacunae as a consequence.[9]

Smith had previously issued a personal statement in which he described his discomfort competing for a country in which the "vast majority of black people suffer from unthinkable discrimination and racism." He said it was his obligation "as a black man to do whatever is necessary . . . to aid my people in obtaining the freedom that we all seek. If I can open a single door that might lead in the direction of freedom for my people, then I feel that I must open that door."[10]

Smith added that he was prepared to bypass the Olympics and was even willing to give up his life for the cause. But after the summer of 1968, talk about a boycott diminished among black athletes. Too much was at stake. Many, even some of those most committed to striking a blow for black freedom and equality, understood that their careers in track and field and possibly professional football were endangered if they passed up Mexico City. Lucrative endorsement opportunities surely entered into their decision-making processes.[11] Also, protest was potentially more effective and less risky than simply ignoring the Olympics and staying home.

Precisely what the African American athletes would do was a matter of conjecture. Several days before the Games commenced, there was an impressive US flag–raising ceremony in Mexico City. All of the black members of the team attended. They saluted the flag, sang the "Star-Spangled Banner," and politely listened to a speech by the US ambassador to Mexico, Fulton Freeman. However, the confident, even cocky, verbose, and volatile, John Carlos announced that blacks would demonstrate in some fashion. There was no agreement on the form the demonstration or demonstrations would take. "The collective decision," according to Carlos, writing in 2011, "was that we would go to the games and each person would do their own thing. Whatever they felt was the right thing to do would get done and we'd have each other's back. That was the last word." However, once in Mexico City, planning on the part of Carlos and Smith led to controversial medal stand symbolism.[12]

For African American track-and-field athletes, their bête noire—to be more precise, their bête blanche—was Avery Brundage, an Olympic pentathlon competitor in 1912 who had been elevated to the presidency of the International Olympic Committee in 1952 after serving as the head of the United States Olympic Committee for a quarter of a century. Imperious, intransigent, pugnacious, distant, and condescending, Brundage had been engulfed in controversy for most of his tenure as an Olympic sports administrator. Then at eighty-one years of age, he was reelected president of the IOC on the eve of the Mexico City Games. He was consistently patronizing in his dealings with blacks and was anathema to those who favored a boycott and those who opposed a boycott, to those who supported a protest and those who opposed it.

Among black track-and-field athletes, there was a consensus that if they should win medals in Mexico City, they wanted someone other than "slavery Avery" to present them with their medals. They also balked at shaking hands with him. He was as much a satanic figure for blacks in 1968 as he had been for Jews in 1936 at the time of the Berlin Olympics when he minimized Hitler's persecution. Tommie Smith had retrospectively observed that in Harry Edwards's eyes, Brundage was "our version of Bull Connor," a reference to the public safety commissioner in Birmingham, Alabama, during the civil rights era who employed dogs and fire hoses to preserve racial segregation. Smith added, "I say he was our Hitler."[13]

Smith's backbreaking labor in the cotton fields as a young man had fired his ambition to escape a life of grinding poverty. Athletic excellence would make possible a college education that would enable him to do just that. On October 16, he had reached the pinnacle of success. He held no fewer than eleven world records, a unique achievement, and had just won the Olympic 200 meters in record-shattering fashion. What now?

In his years at San Jose State, except for his involvement with the Olympic Project for Human Rights, Smith, a sociology major, was not immersed in radical politics. He was not a Black Panther, rumors to the contrary notwithstanding. In fact, he was studious, a person of faith, and even a member of ROTC (Reserve Officers Training Corps), the symbol of the political establishment on university campuses. Nevertheless, he and John Carlos, a product of the mean streets of Harlem, committed themselves to sounding a clarion call on behalf of their downtrodden brothers and sisters in their moment of triumph. The walk to the medal award ceremony was as long as the path to the cotton fields he had trod so often, Smith said.[14]

Thirty minutes after their electrifying track performance, Smith and Carlos received their medals. As the melody of the US national anthem wafted throughout the stadium, Smith wore a black glove on his right hand, which he pointed skyward. It represented black power in America. Carlos's black-gloved left hand also lifted toward the heavens, representing the unity of Black America, it was later explained. They were fists for freedom, and together "they formed an arch of unity and power," Smith told sympathetic commentator Howard Cosell.[15] Around Smith's neck was a black scarf, symbolizing black pride. Both men were shoeless, emblematic of African American poverty. They wore black socks, which were purchased for eighty-nine cents a pair and now reside in the National Track & Field Hall of Fame in Indianapolis. Both Smith and Carlos looked at the ground almost prayerfully.[16]

Even before the Games got underway, Smith had received death threats. Given the killings of Dr. King and other "uppity" blacks who had the temerity to challenge the racial status quo, the threats were very credible. In his recently published memoir, Smith recalls his thoughts and his emotions:

> [I]nside that bowed head, I prayed that the next sound I would hear, in the middle of the Star Spangled Banner, would not be a gunshot and prayed that the next thing I felt would not be the darkness of sudden death. I knew there were people, a lot of people, who wanted to kill me for what I was doing.[17]

For his part, Carlos was acutely aware of the danger while standing on the dais. He has written that at that moment he felt that out of the five billion people on earth, God had selected Smith and himself to make a silent protest: "I was at peace in the middle of America's nightmare. I was ready to die!"[18]

For the United States Olympic Committee, the Smith-Carlos drama, which unfolded on October 16, constituted a major crisis, and the following morning, a special meeting was called by USOC president Douglas Roby for 10:00 AM. Without hesitation, it was decided that the "accused" were not entitled to a hearing or a fair trial before action was taken against them because the facts were not in dispute. Their behavior on the victory stand had been seen by the vast audience in the Olympic stadium and by millions watching on television. Published photographs appeared the next day in newspapers around the world.

A swift response was deemed essential, especially in view of IOC pressure. Brundage and the executive board of the world body indicated to the USOC that if "rigid punitive action" was not taken, the entire US team could be precluded from further competition in the Games.

The USOC responded with alacrity. A public statement was issued forthwith, one that expressed its embarrassment and its regret for the Smith-Carlos misdeed to the IOC, the Mexican Organizing Committee, and the Mexican people.[19] There is scant evidence that the Mexicans felt insulted. The USOC also asserted its determination to strongly punish those who committed comparable offenses in the future.

Brundage and England's Lord Exeter informed Roby that the statement was "too mild and appeasing." Lord Exeter, a member of the IOC executive board, wanted Smith and Carlos to be immediately removed from the team, sent home, and prevented from participating in future Olympic competition.[20]

Never one to mince words, Brundage rebuked the USOC for insufficiently disciplining the American team. It was their duty to shield the IOC from humiliation and the "flouting of Olympic ideals and principles," he said. "If you don't do something to rectify it, the IOC will do something." Brundage had insisted for decades that politics had no place in Olympic sports, and what Smith and Carlos had done was politics, pure and simple.[21]

In the face of his thinly veiled threat, the USOC consulted for an hour and returned with a slightly revised declaration. It apologized for the athletes' rudeness and said their "untypical exhibitionism violates the basic standards of sportsmanship and good manners . . . so highly regarded in the United States."[22]

Consequently, the two men were immediately suspended from the American squad and ordered to leave the Olympic Village. In point of fact, Smith and Carlos had already departed the village. The former relocated to the Hotel Diplomatico, the latter to the Hotel Reforma. Still, the USOC was apprehensive about the prospect that there would be repeat demonstrations.

To discourage imitations of Smith and Carlos, Jesse Owens was sent to speak to the more defiant and dissatisfied black athletes. Owens, of course, was the legendary "Negro" sprinter and long jumper who had won four gold medals in Berlin at the "Nazi Olympics." But his pitch for restraint and moderation was soundly rebuffed by athletes in no mood for submission. President Roby himself went to speak to the three African American finalists slated to run in the 400-meter race that very afternoon.[23]

Lee Evans was the object of particular concern and scrutiny. The California-born Evans was reputed to be one of the most militant black athletes. He was a teammate of Smith and Carlos at San Jose State and a close friend of both, and he was livid about their shabby treatment at the hands of the USOC. Because he had been threatened by the Ku Klux Klan and believed for good reason that his life was in jeopardy, Evans, emotionally distraught, found himself in a quandary. Should he run? If so, and if he won, which was likely, should he protest? If yes, how?

In accordance with the USOC, Roby, an affluent businessman, along with USOC bigwigs and the African American track-and-field coach, Stan Wright, approached Evans just before he was about to compete in the finals of the 400. To hear Vince Matthews, another black track star, tell it, Roby nervously stammered that no demonstration whatsoever would be tolerated. Villanova's Larry James, who was about to run, then lost his composure and told Wright, referring to Roby, "You better get this sonofabitch out of here or I'll punch him in the mouth."[24]

Evans, despite his highly unorthodox running style—he was described as a "drunk on roller skates"—or because of it, won the 400 meters in record time.[25] On the victory podium, Evans; Larry James, who finished second; and Ron Freeman, a third African American who won the bronze, wore black berets, but doffed them when the national anthem was played. They did not bow their heads. Afterward, they smiled broadly and raised their fists. Relatively few objections were heard. Even the USOC, which feared the worst, believed that they had shown proper respect. Some black militants had hoped for a more obvious protest.[26]

Following the American triumph in the 4 × 400 relay final, Matthews, Freeman, James, and Evans as the anchorman made a comparatively mild gesture once again. They received their medals and then assumed a casual stance instead of standing stiffly at attention during the playing of the national anthem. In his memoir, *My Race Be Won*, Matthews described it as a hands-behind-the-back at-ease posture, which was met by a chorus of boos.[27] All were surely worried about their futures in athletics, but at the same time, they seethed over the plight of America's blacks and what was transpiring in Mexico City. Matthews characterized his fury over the Smith-Carlos expulsion in the following words: "I angrily pulled the sheet off my bed, found some black liquid polish, painted the words, 'Down With Brundage' on the sheet and put it outside my window for the world to see."[28]

Before the Games ended, there were several other manifestations, but nothing as dramatic as that of Smith and Carlos. One involved Bob Beamon, who long jumped twenty-nine feet, two and a half inches, breaking the world record by almost two feet! His feat has been called the "most superlative accomplishment in the history of recorded sports" by Arthur Ashe, "a once-in-a-million event."[29] Impelled to bring about racial change at home and desirous of expressing his solidarity with the banned sprinters, Beamon donned black socks for a second jump. He rolled up his sweatpants to make the hose easier to see. Ralph Boston, the winner of the bronze medal, also was shoeless during the same medal ceremony. It was his statement against the ouster of Smith and Carlos, Boston, an early and vocal critic of an Olympic boycott, explained. He reiterated that he did not wish Brundage to give him his medal.[30]

Jimmy Hines of Oakland, California, the gold medalist in the 100 meters; Jamaican Lennox Miller, the silver medalist; and the third-place finisher, Charlie Green of Seattle, all balked at receiving their medals from Brundage. Instead, the Marquess of Exeter did the honors.[31]

A possible pro-black demonstration by members of the all Caucasian Harvard rowing team was also very much on the minds of the USOC in the wake of the Smith-Carlos contretemps. Along with seven other Harvard rowers, Paul Hoffman, coxswain of the rowing crew, had written to the USOC on September 17, expressing sympathy for the predicament of African Americans so little understood by whites. Communicating black displeasure was the main purpose of the black athletes' behavior, and the Harvard oarsmen did not see it as contrary to the Olympic spirit, "for it is in the interests of brotherhood and understanding among men."[32]

Of course, the USOC viewed the situation differently and was fearful that the crews were planning a racially oriented action. On September 22, a letter written on USOC stationery and signed by rowing officials was sent to all members of the US rowing team, requiring each to sign a statement declaring "if he personally intended to take part in such a demonstration that he immediately give up such plans and activities."[33]

Afterward, the USOC alleged that the rowing squad had spent considerable time in Gunniston, Colorado, where they trained, and in Mexico City attempting to organize a demonstration, distributing OPHR protest buttons, and writing to members of the Olympic team soliciting their support in a proposed action "to cast contempt upon the United States and the flag."[34] Indeed, Hoffman did pass buttons to Carlos, Smith, and Peter Norman on the victory stand.

The USOC contemplated suspending Hoffman, but the rowing coach said that in such an eventuality, "we might as well not row. It is too late to adjust to a substitute coxswain."[35] Appearing in person at the Hotel Reforma, the USOC headquarters, Hoffmann testified that at first he had no intention of giving Smith and Carlos buttons and did so only when the medalists requested them. He played no role whatsoever in planning their demonstration, to which he was sympathetic, but believed it to be too theatrical. Hoffman was prepared to pledge that Harvard's crew would not demonstrate at the upcoming rowing competition. There was some sentiment in favor of meting out to Hoffman the same penalty given to Smith and Carlos, but the motion to that effect lost fourteen to two.[36]

There were some at the time who found the hard-line "no politics" policy regarding Smith and Carlos to be hypocritical given the unwillingness of the US contingent to dip Old Glory when it passed before the reviewing stand in the opening ceremonies. It supposedly slighted the Mexican president. Other nations cherished their colors, yet they were willing to lower their flags as a courtesy.

The failure to dip the Stars and Stripes when passing before the English sovereign, Edward VII, at the 1908 London Olympiad had been chided by some as rudely chauvinistic and hailed by others as true patriotism. In Berlin, in 1936, the standard-bearer failed to lower the flag when the US team passed before Chancellor Hitler, but not out of contempt for the Nazi dictator. At that juncture, the matter was taken to the Department of State, which informed Frederick W. Rubien, secretary of the American Olympic Committee, as the USOC was then known, that army regulations provided that, "The National flag will not be dipped by way of salute or compliment." A War Department advisory cautioned against dipping the flag "to any person or any thing."[37]

One Los Angeles–based attorney wrote to the USOC following the Mexico City Games, opining that a way should be found to modify the practice, perhaps through a White House proclamation. The writer felt that given the ideological standoff between the United States and the Soviet Union, the American no-dipping tradition put the United States at a distinct disadvantage. "Did the United States make a lot of friends by pompously and arrogantly refusing to dip their flag?" he asked. The Russians in sharp contrast, lowered their colors, and every member of their team waved little Mexican flags at the huge audience in the stadium. He saw the American practice as a public relations blunder.[38] However, the USOC Board of Directors was opposed to seeking enactment of a new law or a presidential decree to allow dipping, and the tradition continues to this day.[39]

In his long stewardship of the American Olympic Committee, Brundage, despite his vehement opposition to politics in the Olympics, acquiesced. It is also noteworthy that back in 1936, when German medal winners gave the stiff-armed political salute "heiling" Hitler, Brundage never uttered a word of disapproval.

Inconsistency was also charged against Brundage and USOC authorities because they neglected to object to what was plainly a symbolic protest by Vera Caslavska, a Czech gymnast who earned seven gold medals in Mexico City. On the dais with her Soviet rival, with whom she shared the gold in the women's field exercises, Caslavska defiantly lowered her head when the Soviet national anthem was played. Her action was blatantly political. Her motive was unmistakably to show her antipathy to the Soviet Union for its August invasion in concert with East Germany of her homeland to suppress its Prague Spring freedom movement.[40] Caslavska was no stranger to political activism. Several months before the Olympics, she had signed the "Manifesto of 2000 Words," an historic document expressing dissatisfaction with Soviet rule. She was forced to go into hiding and was compelled to train under primitive circumstances.[41]

So great was the tension between the Czech and Soviet teams in the Olympic Village that they had to take their meals separated from one another. The Czech team was extremely popular in Mexico City and received thunderous applause at the opening ceremonies and were cheered whenever they appeared. Caslavska, with her golden tresses and phenomenal gymnastic talent, was a personal favorite of the Mexican fans. When she performed her floor exercises to the strains of the Mexican hat dance, she further endeared herself to the home crowd. Her wedding to a teammate before leaving Mexico received the kind of attention usually reserved for a national celebrity.

Caslavska's political gesture detracted not one whit from her popularity, and probably enhanced it. Brundage conveniently claimed that he did not see Caslavska incline her head on the podium. In any event, he thought it "quite a different thing from the belligerent attitude of the two sprinters."[42] In a USOC newsletter, special mention was given to twenty individual gold medal winners from a variety of countries. Caslavska was included, while Smith and Carlos were excluded.[43] Critics could say with justification that it all depended on whose ox was being gored, or on which country was being rebuked. In the Caslavska case, if Russian pride was wounded, so much the better.

Then there was the matter of nineteen-year-old pugilist George Foreman, who decisively defeated his more experienced Soviet opponent by technical knockout in the second round to capture the gold medal in the heavyweight boxing competition. The ebullient Foreman proceeded to prance around the ring waving a small American flag. To what extent was this exhibition planned? Foreman told Howard Cosell that he had carried the flag to the arena himself because he wanted people to know which country he represented, something that would have been evident to all in the absence of the flag. Foreman denied it was a show of patriotism or a response to the Smith-Carlos protest. The future professional heavyweight champion of the world was quoted by Cosell as insisting, quite implausibly, "I just do my own thing . . . and make sure of one thing, I'm no Uncle Tom."[44] One can justifiably ask whether Foreman was politically innocent or whether he was trying to curry favor with sports authorities, Olympic and other.

His little exhibition elicited no condemnation from jubilant American Olympic officials, who swelled with pride. It was surely perceived as Americanism at its best, not an unwarranted injection of politics into sports. In fact, Foreman was used by Brundage and others as a counterpoint to Smith and Carlos. In contrast, he was chastised by Harry Edwards as the "good Negro," one who appeased whites to the detriment of blacks.[45]

Foreman was hailed by many white Americans for his flag waving. "God bless George Foreman," one woman wrote to Brundage. She added that there was no place for politics in the Olympics![46] Expressions of pro-American sentiment were nonpolitical, whereas what was construed as negative criticism of America was political and therefore objectionable.

For many African Americans, Foreman's conduct in the Mexico City ring earned him the pejorative sobriquet "Uncle Tom," which endured. He quickly became an object of derision, and when, as a professional, he was thoroughly thrashed by Muhammad Ali in their 1974 Congo clash, the famous "rumble in the jungle," black Americans, by and large, were exhilarated. Ali had come to embody black pride. He was the assertive "field Negro," whereas Foreman was still seen as the subservient "house Negro."

Racial happenings at the Mexico City Olympiad, especially the Smith-Carlos gesture, which was interpreted by some as tantamount to sedition, brought to the surface ugly racial sentiments. Voluminous correspondence in the Avery Brundage papers and in the records of the USOC make this abundantly clear. "Treasonable black rats" was the venomous term used by one writer to characterize them.[47]

An Omaha woman believed that the "white man owes the Negro nothing. Let some of them return to the stone age delights of tribal Africa.... [T]he Negro race is the only race to have contributed nothing toward civilization." However, the writer did allow that they excelled in motor coordination.[48]

There were others who felt that blacks, owing to their "jungle ancestry," had a distinct advantage over white runners. Henceforth blacks ought to be permitted to only race against other blacks. Alternatively, white athletes ought to be given an advantage.[49]

Many letter writers wanted Smith and Carlos to forfeit their medals. There were those who wished them to be banished from the Olympic Movement and also banned from professional sports. One letter to the USOC suggested that future US entrants in the Olympics be required to take a loyalty oath to the United States of America.[50] Another correspondent advocated deporting the "revolutionaries," for, in effect, "they have renounced their citizenship."[51] An undated note stapled to a picture of Smith and Carlos at the Olympics wanted them to be put in jail.[52] Offensive racial terminology was often included in the letters.

Smith and Carlos were frequently equated with Nazis. One woman wired Brundage, "Let's have no more Hitler-like salutes or black glove nonsense." Such equations were even found in the press. One day after the protest, Brent Musburger wrote in his sports column that Smith and Carlos looked like "black-skinned storm troopers." Theirs was no more than a "juvenile gesture by a couple of athletes who should have known better."[53] A letter to the *Chicago Tribune* alluded to their "Communist salute."[54]

Newsweek magazine had dispatched a raft of reporters to Mexico City. One piece informed readers that Smith and Carlos had appeared at preliminary races "wearing long black socks called 'pimp socks' in the ghetto."[55]

Letters and telegrams deluged the IOC and the USOC from the other side of the racial divide. Many, maybe even a majority, aligned themselves with Smith and Carlos. Some of the correspondents were African Americans, some Caucasians. In many cases, the race of the writer cannot be ascertained.

A number of the writers wanted the sprinters reinstated. They saw the protest as completely justified and found the USOC reaction childish and vindictive.[56] Excluding South Africa from the Games (a move that Brundage strongly opposed but could not prevent) and then penalizing Smith and Carlos for highlighting American apartheid was thought hypocritical. Some urged that the points earned by the pair be deducted from the overall US tally, given their removal from the team.

A telegram sent to Brundage took the position that so long as winners were recognized by national flags and anthems rather than by simply announcing individual triumphs, the Olympic authorities themselves had introduced political questions into the Games. Rescinding the expulsion verdict was called for.[57] A union official in California believed the exclusion was an "affront to athletes throughout the world and in particular to those from populations considered non-Caucasian."[58] A white Seattle resident found the IOC action "disgusting, uncalled for, narrow-minded, and indicative of your prejudice against black people."[59]

Brundage's file even included telegrams meant for Smith and Carlos. One came from Jesse Jackson and congratulated them for "expressing to the world the gift of Black soul and talent. . . . We can no longer abuse and refuse to use privileges and platforms to communicate our plight to the world." Jackson, who had been aide to the late Dr. King, added, "You may have been on the wrong side of the Olympic Committee but on the right side of history."[60]

Support also came from abroad. For example, a telegram from Nigeria saw disciplining Smith and Carlos as a violation of the athletes' freedom of speech.[61]

America's racial schism was spotlighted by the controversy as was the USOC's misunderstanding of the mentality of black athletes in a tempestuous era. That was apparent when Smith and Carlos were approached in the Olympic Village by Patrick H. Sullivan, counselor and ex-officio member of the Executive Committee of the USOC. Sullivan later reported that he had made the grave error of saying, "You boys know why you did it." Smith snapped, "Man, we ain't no 'boys.'"[62] When Sullivan recounted the exchange at a meeting of the Executive Committee on December 1, 1968, Robert Kane, secretary of the USOC board, explained that the appellation "boys" in modern American discourse meant "come here, boy, get my shoes or shine my shoes." President Roby added that the question of language had arisen even earlier, "I was down presenting the medals on one occasion and there were three Negroes and I said 'Boys.' The athletes retorted, 'We ain't boys, we ain't boys' and they were mad."[63]

Several members present had not understood that blacks had been infantilized ever since slave days, when whites would not address persons of African descent as equals and would not employ the term of respect "mister" but insisted on addressing and referring to blacks either by their first names or as "boy," regardless of age. Brundage had habitually talked of the "boys" going to Mexico City and so demeaned Jesse Owens when he was a man in his fifties. Perhaps in this respect, the Mexico City Olympiad was a learning experience for at least some sports administrators.

Months after the closing ceremonies, these remained thorny issues to be resolved. One that split the USOC was whether Smith and Carlos were entitled to commemorative rings. They did not receive ring measurement applications, inasmuch as they had been suspended. President Roby twice suggested to the athletes that they file an appeal, but the two flatly refused.

Clifford Buck, first vice-president of the USOC, wanted the other members of the 1968 Olympic team to make the decision. He was personally opposed to awarding the rings. Before their suspension, they were entitled to their medals, he argued. To give the rings after would "not only be unfair to the team members, but would make a travesty of Olympic rules and principles." He frowned on a "policy of appeasement or preferential treatment toward a very small militant minority which would invite future confrontations."[64]

Kane sharply disagreed. His contention was that Smith and Carlos had legally competed: "Whatever action for suspension that was taken occurred after they competed in the two hundred meter dash." Their suspension, Kane wrote, ought not go on forever.[65]

One of the strongest statements in support of Smith and Carlos came from long jumper Ralph Boston in April 1969, when he was assistant dean of student development at the University of Tennessee. He had visited Carlos the previous weekend and was taken aback to learn that Carlos had still not received an application to obtain an Olympic ring. Boston subsequently wrote to Arthur G. Lentz, executive director of the USOC, deploring the committee's "hands-off" policy. Had Smith and Carlos not earned the rings? he inquired. Additionally, why had they been excluded from such USOC functions as the "Olympic meet" at Madison Square Garden? Boston thought the committee's policy was petty. If it continued, an investigation was warranted.[66]

On June 2, Lentz replied that it was nonsense that because they had been suspended they were ineligible for post-Olympic awards. "Both men won their places on the team, both competed successfully and neither was a professional at the time of their Olympic competition," he declared.[67] They deserved the rings, and Lentz pledged that they would receive them. They did. In this instance vindictiveness was overcome by a sense of fairness on the part of some USOC members.

In President Roby's summary of the Games, there was a brief, vague reference to "one serious form of demonstration which took place during a victory ceremony." Because of their "disrespectful" actions, the two athletes were suspended, he reported. Roby could not bring himself to mention the names of Smith and Carlos.[68] It was as if the USOC was still seriously threatened. This was especially true of Brundage. Having been unable to prevent the black athletes' stand, Brundage was adamant about minimizing its significance. Eradication of its memory would have been ideal. When footage was included in the official film of the XIX Olympiad, a livid Brundage objected strenuously to "pictures of the nasty demonstration against the United States flag by negroes." He informed Pedro Ramirez Vasquez that the Smith-Carlos portion of the film would create "needless resentment among Olympic followers all over the world." In his acerbic communication with Ramirez Vasquez, Brundage argued angrily that it "had nothing to do with sport, it was a shameful abuse of hospitality and it has no more place in the record of the Games than the gunfire at Tlatelolco. Should the Mexican flag and the Mexican athletes have been involved, I am sure it would not be featured."[69] To eliminate the possibility of protest, IOC approval ought to be made mandatory for future Olympic films.[70]

Forty years later, there is still lingering resentment toward Smith and Carlos in Olympic circles. At the American Olympic Hall of Fame, located on the premises of the USOC in Colorado Springs, Colorado, a number of standouts from Mexico City are honored. Bob Beamon and Ralph Boston are there as well as Lee Evans and Dick Fosbury, who revolutionized high jumping, and swimmer Debbie Meyer. Smith and Carlos are nowhere to be found.

Smith and Carlos have paid a very high price for their epic idealistic spectacle, for their rebellion against injustice. It is not too much to say that their sacrifice was monumental. Their personal lives were badly damaged. Smith has written that not just he but his family members were subjected to continuing threats. It killed his mother, he said, and heightened Olympic-related stress contributed to his marital discord, which ended in divorce.[71] Carlos's wife committed suicide ten years later.

Their professional lives were adversely affected as well. Jobs were hard to obtain, their illustrious sports accomplishments notwithstanding. They found it difficult to surmount vocational hurdles. For a while, Smith had to wash cars to keep body and soul together. Corporate sponsorships were mostly unattainable, the lost revenue incalculable. Both speedsters tried professional football, but their careers were abbreviated. Eventually, they did secure positions in education. For a time, Smith served as athletic director at Oberlin College in Ohio.

Regrettably, chilliness came to pervade the relationship between the two men. A major contributor was Carlos's claim that he had wanted Smith to have the gold medal and had allowed him to finish first in Mexico City: "I had the ability to win the race. But I chose not to."[72] Despite the schism, the two Olympic medalists will forever be bonded to one another in the annals of sports and the popular imagination.

In hindsight, it is worth remembering that Smith and Carlos did not disrupt the Mexico City Olympiad, nor did they delay the Games, not for one minute. Their gesture, simultaneously stupendous and subdued, was both eloquent and poignant. It is hard to imagine a more dignified protest. It was no more political than countless others that punctuate quadrennial Olympics, including the 1968 competition. In fact, theirs was a moral statement as well as a political one.

Their real offense was to focus global attention on racial inequality in their own country in the midst of the Cold War with the Communist world, to graphically tell the truth about the plight of blacks in the United States, a truth belied by their prominence in athletics, a truth that subverted the myth that their nation was the land of the free and the home of the brave with liberty and justice for all, black as well as white. To have the United States humiliated by two of its own citizens was intolerable for many. That is what prompted the cascade of invective aimed at them.

With the passage of time, appreciation of the courage shown by Smith and Carlos has grown. The Nike company has chosen their gesture as one of half a dozen pivotal Olympic happenings.[73] Understanding of their sacrifice and suffering has deepened. It is no exaggeration to say that they are increasingly recognized as bona fide members of the pantheon of human rights champions. They were patriots in the best sense of the term. They and their demonstration were American to the core.

Racial Protest Reprise—Munich 1972

Munich was chosen as the location of the Summer Games of the 1972 XX Olympiad, the first to be held on German soil since the "Nazi Games" thirty-six years earlier. Unlike Berlin, the Bavarian city had been one of the Führer's favorites; he had lived there as a young man, and it had been the site of the so-called Beer Hall *Putsch*, his 1923 unsuccessful bid for power. Now, West Germany's government wanted to dramatize the fact that Nazism was dead and buried and the nation was a flourishing democracy that had tried to atone for the Holocaust in the twenty-seven years since World War II ended. Echoes of the genocide could be silenced, it was hoped.

In an ironic twist of fate, the Games are most remembered for the appalling murder of eleven Israelis, Olympic athletes and coaches, by Palestinian terrorists, members of the Black September guerrilla organization who had invaded the Olympic compound. Some of the Israelis were butchered in the village. Others, who had been seized as hostages, were slaughtered in cold blood amid a shootout between German police and the Arab fedayeen at the nearby NATO air base.[74] Once again, to the chagrin of the German government and populace, Germany was stained with Jewish blood. What had been planned as a national renaissance festival quickly became a national catastrophe.

On September 5, the day of sanguinary infamy, the Olympic proceedings, which were already underway, were halted by the International Olympic Committee, an action without precedent in modern Olympic history. Immediately, questions were asked. Would the Games continue? Should they continue? There was no agreement inside or outside Olympic circles.[75] A memorial service with more than eighty thousand in attendance was quickly conducted. Avery Brundage and the executive board, that is, the Olympic hierarchy, were determined that the Games would go on. The very next day, September 6, even before the bodies of the Israelis could be interred in the Jewish state, the Games resumed.

Because of the killing, which was front-page news around the globe, a racial protest reminiscent of the Smith-Carlos incident received comparatively little attention at the time, and it is largely ignored today. Teammates Vince Matthews and Wayne Collett were the gold and silver medalists, respectively, in the 400-meter event. At the awards ceremony, while the American national anthem played, the two African American quarter milers turned away from the flag and assumed a casual stance, arms akimbo. Olympic etiquette called for them to stand erect, still, and silent. Instead, they chatted. Matthews twisted his golden prize and stroked his beard. Their jackets were open, and Collett was barefoot. After leaving the victory stand, he gave what the press described as a black power salute. If there were any cheers from the hostile capacity crowd, they were drowned out by jeers, whistling, hooting, boos, and catcalls.[76] With whiplash speed, Brundage removed them from the team.

Why did they do it? Collett, a product of UCLA, told the media that his actions "mirrored the attitude of white America towards Blacks." He explained, "They treat us in a casual manner as long as we don't embarrass them."[77] Matthews denied, somewhat disingenuously, that any protest gestures were intended. In a short article he wrote for the *New York Times*, Matthews, a twenty-four-year-old youth worker from New York, expressed surprise at the brouhaha he had ignited. "On the victory stand I was standing there just the way I would be standing at a baseball game or a flight. I never stand at attention," he explained. Had he been requested to stand at attention, he would have complied, "but it wouldn't be me and I was led to believe that the Olympics was for athletes."[78] He was an athlete, not a politician, he declared. Both men clearly understood their actions.

Elaboration came in Matthews's autobiography, published in 1974. He discussed his interview in Munich with Howard Cosell. Matthews had not intended to protest: "Wayne and I have both seen protests, and if we had meant to stage any kind of protest, it wouldn't have come out like that." However, Matthews, who was chastised by his distraught mother right after the ceremony, implied that he had race on his mind. He said he was thinking about his great-grandmother and the fact that "she just missed slavery by a couple of year[s]." Matthews noted that only a few generations separated him from bondage.[79]

Collett was more forthcoming about his motives. Speaking about the award ceremony, Collett said, "It was just me standing up for the national anthem, and I couldn't stand there and sing the words because I don't believe they are true. I wish they were. I think we have the potential to have a beautiful country, but I don't think we do."[80] To Brundage, it was Smith-Carlos redux.

Shortly after, track legend Jesse Owens approached the two athletes. He wanted them to apologize for their dais antics lest the anticipated victory of the US relay team in the upcoming 1600 meters be imperiled. Matthews and Collett adamantly refused to back down, nor would they permit Owens to be their surrogate before the IOC. In a last-ditch effort to mitigate the seriousness of the situation, Owens dangled the possibility of future corporate employment. The proviso was that Matthews and Collett concede that they were not fully cognizant of their wrongdoing.[81] They remained unmoved by the blandishment of Owens, who was seen less as a brother than as a stalking horse for the white athlete establishment.

When Matthews and Collett were interrogated by the USOC, Owens was still hoping that they would be conciliatory—but to no avail. Brundage's letter of September 8 that eliminated them from current and future Olympic competitions was read at the meeting. The die had been cast as far as Matthews and Collett were concerned. Matthews discovered that his dormitory room had been cleaned out and his clothes placed in storage. He was informed by a USOC functionary that he was no longer welcome in the Olympic Village.[82] Because of their ouster, the United States was unable to enter the 4 × 400 relay. Indeed, Matthews was of the opinion that Brundage had acted with great haste to keep them out of the trials for the relay.

A jurisdictional dispute between the IOC and the USOC erupted almost immediately after the medal ceremony on September 7. Brundage wrote to Clifford Buck, then president of the USOC, that the entire world had seen the "disgusting display of *your two athletes* [emphasis mine] when they received their gold and silver medals for the 400 m.

event yesterday."[83] It was the second time that the USOC had "permitted" such spectacles, asserted Brundage, an obvious reference to the Smith-Carlos imbroglio four years earlier. Never again would Matthews and Collett participate in Olympic contests. If it happened again, Brundage threatened, medals would not be granted to the malefactors.[84]

Without losing a moment, Buck replied with obvious annoyance. He chided the IOC for not giving his organization the chance to exercise its responsibility and to gather relevant facts so that it could decide on the appropriate course of action. He wanted the IOC to rescind its decision. A USOC hearing was already scheduled for that very next day.[85]

Indeed, a day later, Buck sent a letter to Matthews about his "flagrant disrespect" for the American flag, which had brought dishonor to the whole US Olympic team. Therefore, he was ineligible to wear any insignia of the USA Olympic team. Matthews was requested to "remove all Olympic patches and insignia from your clothing and competitive apparel."[86]

Less than a week later, Buck, still fuming, issued a strong statement declaring that the IOC owed the USOC the opportunity to carry out its duty to impose stern disciplinary actions "which we were within 30 minutes of announcing when we learned that the IOC had announced its ruling without awaiting ours."[87] He pointed out that his committee's penalties were more draconian than those of the IOC. Buck was trying to counter reports in the press that he condoned the behavior of Matthews and Collett. A letter sent to the USOC accused it of coming to the aid and support of the runners whose deportment was characterized as "boorish."[88]

On September 11, Brundage claimed that the decision to disqualify Matthews and Collett had been taken at the suggestion of the International Association of Athletics Federations (IAAF), which was in charge of the track-and-field program. Trying to smooth over differences, Brundage, a man of overwhelming pride and czarist proclivities, uncharacteristically wrote to Buck, "We understand the reason for the delay by the USOC, and we believe that at the first meeting similar action was taken."[89] That was as close to an apology as the imperious Brundage was capable of voicing.

Red Smith, arguably the preeminent sports columnist of the day, had found fault with Brundage's handling of the Matthews-Collett matter. They had been banished without the "pretense of a hearing, without the courtesy of prior notice to the American Olympic Committee . . . without asking for an explanation, hearing witnesses or consulting officials responsible for the behavior of the Olympic teams."[90] Even Brundage's supporters would not contend that due process was his strong suit.

The incident drew a substantial volume of correspondence directed to Brundage. It is preserved in his papers at the University of Illinois. As had been the case with the Smith-Carlos affair, thinking was sharply split and vehemently expressed. One Californian, referring to the "Matthews-Collett malignity," agreed with Brundage's position that "the winners' dais is not a political forum."[91] Another correspondent, much more vitriolic, called their behavior disgraceful and lamented that they had not been shot but merely booed.[92] Sportswriter Gene Ward, in his "Ward to the Wise" column, called them "ugly Americans" and decried their "insensitivity." They had damaged the cause of understanding and peace and had sowed the "seeds of discontent and animosity." Incredibly, Ward wrote that "what Matthews and Collett committed, in its context of time and place and the sequence of horror, was a form of violence." It was as if they had "toted guns to the podium."[93]

More often than not, correspondents saluted Brundage and upbraided the black athletes. If they represented their race, not their country, why should they retain their medals, asked the senders of a telegram.[94] A resident of Skokie, Illinois, also urged revocation of the 400-meter medals and disqualification from future competitions.[95] Several people regarded the Matthews-Collett "slovenly" disdain for the flag and national anthem as unpatriotic and insulting to the country. Calls for the de-emphasis of flags and national anthems in some quarters elicited this sarcastic rebuttal: "[W]hen we do that, we also set fire to Independence Hall, burn all the historical documents that set this nation apart and quietly surrender to Jane Fonda," referring to the Hollywood star who was pilloried for supporting the North Vietnamese cause.[96]

A minority of telegrams and missives backed Matthews and Collett. One, for example, which emanated from the staff of the Pittsburgh office of the Human Relations Commission, lashed out at the "racist, arbitrary and capricious disqualifications."[97] A second, sent by a professor of pediatrics at UCLA, found the IOC decision "outrageous" and asserted that the athletes' demeanor reflected white America's "disrespect to blacks from childhood not their disrespect to Olympics."[98] A third felt that their banishment was "tyrannical, racist and political."[99] Several saw misplaced jingoism in the Matthews-Collett matter. "Proof of skill is the purpose of Olympic competition not show of USA allegiance," read a telegram.[100] One that asked that the "obscene compulsive decision" be revoked was more emotional: "Good Americans can handle constructive criticism if nationalist pigs can."[101] More tempered approval came from the black newspapers published in major American cities.

By the time of the 1972 Olympiad, race relations had incrementally improved, owing to sundry Supreme Court rulings and civil rights laws enacted on the federal and state levels. Greater numbers of African Americans enjoyed equal rights before the law, but economic progress was halting at best. True equality in housing, employment, education, income, and personal wealth remained a hope rather than a reality. Widespread discrimination and deep-seated prejudice could not be made to vanish at the blast of a trumpet. Unfinished racial business, the deferred dreams of which Martin Luther King Jr. spoke, spawned the black demonstrations in Mexico City and Munich. With the civil rights movement in decline and black power little more than a rarely heard slogan, nothing comparable occurred at subsequent Olympiads.[102]

Notes

1. William C. Rhoden, "Vilified to Glorified: Olympic Redux," *New York Times*, October 17, 2005.
2. *New York Times*, October 4, 2000.
3. Harvard Sitcoff, *The Struggle for Black Equality 1954–1980* (New York: Hill and Wang, 1981), 200–203; Robert Weisbrot, *Freedom Bound: A History of America's Civil Rights Movement* (New York: Plume, 1991), 262–264.
4. Amy Bass, *Not the Triumph but the Struggle: The 1968 Olympics and the Making of the Black Athlete* (Minneapolis: University of Minnesota Press, 2002), 87; Kevin B. Witherspoon, *Before the Eyes of the World – Mexico and the 1968 Olympic Games* (De Kalb: Northern Illinois Press 2008).
5. Harry Edwards, *The Revolt of the Black Athlete* (New York: The Free Press, 1969), 68.
6. *Chicago Tribune*, August 29, 1968 and September 26, 1968; *Chicago Sun-Times*, September 26, 1968; *Chicago Daily News*, October 3, 1968. Also see Elena Poniatowska, *Massacre in Mexico* (New York: The Viking Press, 1975) and *La Noche de Tlateloco: Testimonios de Historia Oral* (Mexico City: Biblioteca Era, 1981).
7. John Carlos and Dave Zirin, *The John Carlos Story: The Sports Moment That Changed the World* (Chicago: Haymarket Books, 2011), 107.
8. "Criminal Activities at the 1968 Olympic Games in Mexico City, Foreign Police Cooperation, George Washington University," National Security archive, FBI report, document 94, September 6, 1968.
9. Executive committee meeting transcript, March 23, 1968. United States Olympic Committee archives, Colorado Springs, Colorado.
10. Edwards, *The Revolt of the Black Athlete*, 63–64.
11. Tommie Smith and David Steele, *Silent Gesture: The Autobiography of Tommie Smith* (Philadelphia: Temple University Press, 2007), 166–167. Nevertheless, superstar Kareem Abdul-Jabbar boycotted the Olympic trials.

12. Carlos, *The John Carlos Story*, 103, 109–110.
13. Smith, *Silent Gesture*, 165.
14. *Stride to Glory*, produced by Rich O'Connor, Bob Oliver, and Martin Callanan (Warner Vision Australia, International Olympic Committee, and Trans World, 1966), film.
15. Smith, *Silent Gesture*, 173.
16. Ibid., 28, 173.
17. Ibid., 1.
18. John Carlos and C. D. Jackson Jr., *Why?: The Biography of John Carlos* (Los Angeles: Milligan Books, 2000), 207.
19. Minutes from meeting of the administrative board at Mexico City, Hotel Reforma, October 17, 1968. USOC archives, Robert Kane Papers, box 12, Board Minutes and Reports, folder 12-179.
20. Minutes from meeting of administrative board, October 17, 1968. In an unpublished manuscript, Brundage spoke of "some feeble demonstrations on the victory stand" and chided the USOC for having brought competitors of "such warped mentality and so little appreciation of Olympic principles and the dignity of the Games." Chapter 15 in "Olympic Story," box 330, Avery Brundage Collection (hereinafter ABC), University of Illinois.
21. Ibid.
22. Ibid.
23. Ibid. The meeting was reconvened on the morning of October 18, 1968.
24. Vincent Matthews and Neil Amdur, *My Race Be Won* (New York: Charter House, 1974), 198.
25. Frank Murphy wrote that one sports journalist said that Evans "ran like a man struggling out of a corset." Frank Murphy, *The Last Protest: Lee Evans in Mexico City* (Kansas City: Windsprint Press, 2006), 11.
26. Douglas Hartmann, *Race, Culture and the Revolt of the Black Athlete: The 1968 Olympic Protests and Their Aftermath* (Chicago: The University of Chicago Press, 2003), 162–163. Also see Smith, *Silent Gesture*, 170–171.
27. Matthews, *My Race Be Won*, 205.
28. Ibid., 197.
29. Arthur R. Ashe Jr., *A Hard Road to Glory: A History of the African-American Athlete since 1946* (New York: Amistad Press, 1993), vol. 3, 177. Also see Smith, *Silent Gesture*, 174.
30. *Los Angeles Times*, October 18, 1968.
31. A petition calling for the removal of Brundage as head of the IOC was submitted by black American athletes even before the Games began. *Chicago Sun-Times*, September 25, 1968.
32. Letter from Paul Hoffman et al. to USOC, September 17, 1968. 1968 post-Olympic file, letters on Smith-Carlos incident, USOC archives.
33. Ibid. Letter from John A. Bergen, member of the US Olympic Rowing Committee et al. to all members of the United States Olympic rowing team, September 22, 1968.
34. Jack Sulger, member, board of directors, USOC, 1968 report, Robert Kane Papers, box 12, 12-182 USOC archives.
35. Minutes of the USOC administrative board at Mexico City, Hotel Reforma, October 18, 1968.
36. Ibid.

37. Letter from J. C. Holmes to Frederick W. Rubien, secretary, American Olympic Committee, Robert Kane Papers, box 4a, 4-38 USOC archives.
38. Letter from Lee B. Wenzel to USOC, November 15, 1968, USOC archives.
39. Letter from Arthur G. Lentz to USOC officers, designates, and counselors, March 14, 1969; Letter from Arthur G. Lentz to Leonard C. Meeker, legal adviser, Department of State, May 5, 1969, USOC archives.
40. *New York Times*, October 26–28, 1968, and October 27, 1968 (Sports). Journalist Richard Hoffer wrote that Caslavska lowered her head not once but twice at two different podium presentations. American television on the ABC network commented on her gesture of contempt toward the Soviets. Richard Hoffer, *Something in the Air: American Passion and Defiance in the 1968 Mexico City Olympics* (New York: Free Press, 2009), 225.
   Head bowing as Olympic political protest was nothing new in Mexico City. In Berlin, in 1936, a Korean marathoner, Sohn Kee-chung, established a new Olympic record. Sohn had been required to compete for the empire of Japan rather than for his native land, which the Japanese had conquered twenty-six years earlier. Thus, it was the flag of the Rising Sun that was raised in the Olympic stadium and the Japanese national anthem that was played when Sohn stood on the victor's podium. Sohn, who had been coerced into running under his adopted Japanese name, was a fervent Korean patriot and deeply resentful of the Japanese occupation of his homeland. In his moment of triumph, Sohn was banished from competitive track for life. David Clay Large, *Nazi Games-The Olympics of 1936*, (New York: W. W. Norton and Company, 2007) 257–59; Jeré Longman, "Reaching Back 73 Years for Inspiration," *New York Times*, November 15, 2009.
41. Bass, *Not the Triumph*, 281.
42. Letter from Brundage to A. Gilbert Belles, November 18, 1968, ABC, box 179.
43. *USOC Newsletter* 4, no. 6 (December 1968).
44. Howard Cosell, *Cosell* (Chicago: A Playboy Press Book, 1973), 64.
45. Harry Edwards, *The Struggle That Must Be: An Autobiography* (New York: Macmillan, 1980), 204.
46. Letter from Mrs. Elmer T. Carr to USOC, November 1, 1968, ABC, box 179.
47. Letter from Richard T. Poling to Avery Brundage, October 24, 1968, ABC, box 179.
48. Letter from Edna Howl to Avery Brundage, October 21, 1968, ABC, box 179.
49. Unidentified flier, nd, ABC, box 17.
50. Letter from Mrs. Fred Hamby to USOC, October 18, 1968. 1968 post-Olympic letters on Smith-Carlos, USOC archives.
51. Letter from John C. Norris to USOC, nd, 1968 post-Olympic letters on Smith-Carlos, USOC archives.
52. Telegram from Mrs. Bruce Johnson to Avery Brundage, nd, ABC, box 179.
53. Brent Musburger, "Bizarre Protest by Smith, Carlos Tarnishes Medals," *Chicago American*, October 19, 1968.
54. Letter from Thomas J. Dunne to the "Voice of the People," *Chicago Tribune*, nd, ABC, box 179.
55. "The Olympics' Extra Heat," *Newsweek*, October 28, 1968.
56. Telegram from L. H. Hall to Avery Brundage, October 20, 1968, ABC, box 179.

57. Telegram from J. Geoffray Tootel to Avery Brundage, October 20, 1968, ABC, box 179.

58. Letter from Mrs. Wanonah Drasnin to Avery Brundage, October 20, 1968, ABC, box 179.

59. Letter from Mrs. George A. Johnson to IOC, nd, ABC, box 179.

60. Telegram from Jesse Jackson to Tommie Smith, care of IOC, October 23, 1968, ABC, box 179.

61. Telegram from Welfare Association of Nigeria to IOC, October 20, 1968, ABC, box 179.

62. Meeting of the executive committee of the USOC in meeting minutes for the XIX Olympiad, vol. 19, no. 10, March 23, 1968, to December 1, 1968.

63. *New York Times*, June 7, 1970, citing a paper written by a Harvard senior, a member of the Harvard rowing team in Mexico City, who said that many athletes left the sole team meeting in the Mexican capital when President Roby began his remarks with the words, "Boys and girls, I want to . . .."

64. Buck memo to all USOC officers, Counselor Sullivan, and Arthur Lentz, May 13, 1969. Robert Kane Papers, box 4a, folder 4-38, USOC archives.

65. Ibid., letter from Kane to Lentz, May 9, 1969.

66. Ibid., letter from Ralph Boston to Arthur Lentz, April 21, 1969.

67. Ibid., letter from Arthur Lentz to Ralph Boston, June 2, 1969.

68. Ibid., "Quadrennial Review of Activities 1965–1969," presented at the Quadrennial Meeting of the USOC, Denver Hilton Hotel, Denver, Colorado. April 18–20, 1969.

69. Letter from Avery Brundage to Pedro Ramirez Vasquez, August 19, 1969, ABC, box 179.

70. Letter from Avery Brundage to Marquess of Exeter, March 19, 1970, ABC, box 51.

71. Smith, *Silent Gesture*, 144, 210, 217.

72. Carlos, *Why?*, 198, 200.

73. William C. Rhoden, "Enduring Image Coupled with an Enduring Dispute," *New York Times*, February 22, 2008.

74. Serge Groussard, *The Blood of Israel: The Massacre of the Israeli Athletes, the Olympics, 1972* (New York: William Morrow & Co., Inc., 1975).

75. Among the naysayers was the black press, which had long loathed Brundage. The *Amsterdam News* editorialized as follows:

> The continuation of the Olympics in the face of such a tragedy, is offensive to the spirit of peacefulness and international friendship and humanity for which the games have become symbolic.
>
> It requires a painful twisting of morality, indeed, to justify the continued games as a tribute to the slain Olympic competitors. The Olympic games should have ended yesterday. This would have been a more fitting tribute to the murdered Israeli athletes.

New York Amsterdam News, September 9, 1972.

76. *New York Times*, September 8–9, 1972. Dave Wottle, a white American middle distance runner, captured the gold medal in the 800-meter event and was inadvertently caught up in a minor fracas. While on the victory stand, Wottle failed to doff his signature golf cap during the playing of the "Star-Spangled Banner." A few in the press corps also wondered when Wottle

unconsciously covered his USA team patch when he put his hand over his heart. It should have been apparent that Wottle did not intend to protest anything. His failure to remove his head covering was due to a lapse of memory in what must have been an exhilarating moment. Interviewed by the ubiquitous Howard Cosell, Wottle set the record straight and apologized for any offense he may have given. Telephone interview with Dave Wottle, May 26, 2010.

77. *New York Times*, September 9, 1972.
78. Ibid.
79. Matthews, *My Race Be Won*, 353.
80. Ibid., 356.
81. Ibid., 357.
82. Ibid., 363.
83. Letter from Brundage to Clifford Buck, September 8, 1972, ABC, box 183.
84. Ibid.
85. Letter from Buck to Brundage, September 8, 1972, ABC, box 183.
86. Letter from Buck to Matthews, September 9, 1972, ABC, box 183.
87. Statement by the president of the United States Olympic Committee, September 15, 1972, ABC, box 183.
88. Letter from Frank Dowd Jr. to the USOC, September 12, 1972, ABC, box 183.
89. Letter from Brundage to Buck, September 11, 1972, ABC, box 183.
90. Red Smith, "Sports of the Times," *New York Times*, September 1972.
91. Letter from Gordon Shaw to Brundage, nd, ABC, box 183.
92. As he always did, Brundage thanked the writer for his "kind and friendly words." See letter from Brundage to Robert A. Kantz, September 29, 1972, ABC, box 183.
93. Undated column, Ward was a long-time columnist for New York's *Daily News*.
94. Telegram from the Schu family to Brundage, September 12, 1972. Scribbled on a copy of the Matthews-Collett victory ceremony photograph were the words, "They can go to Africa—the best thing." The sender did not identify himself/herself. ABC, box 183.
95. Telegram from Paul D. Keller, nd, ABC, box 183.
96. Letter from Regina A. Chapman to the American Broadcast Company, September 17, 1972. The writer indicated that her letter was really intended for Brundage.
97. Telegram from the Pittsburgh regional office of the Human Relations Commission to Brundage, nd, ABC, box 183.
98. Telegram from James Yamazaki to Brundage, nd, ABC, box 183.
99. Telegram from Mignon Anderson to IOC, nd, ABC, box 183.
100. Telegram from Patricia Madsen to Brundage, nd, ABC, box 183.
101. Telegram from Frank Wasp to IOC, nd, ABC, box 183.
102. Hartmann, *Race, Culture and the Revolt of the Black Athlete*, 243.

5

Apartheid and the Expulsion of South Africa from the Olympics

The word *apartheid* is the most recognizable contribution made to the global lexicon by the Afrikaans language, a tongue that evolved from Dutch in South Africa after the arrival of Hollanders in the seventeenth century.[1] Apartheid means apartness or separateness, of course, and refers to the malignant policy of racial segregation fashioned mainly by the dominant Boer or Afrikaner community and officially and strictly implemented following the electoral triumph of the National Party in 1948.

An understanding of South Africa's demography and troubled history are essential for an appreciation of why apartheid was the cause of the nation's protracted Olympic tribulations. South Africa is a truly multiracial nation, a mélange of ethnicities, a mosaic of tribes. Bantu people vastly outnumber whites. Zulus and Xhosas are the largest tribes. In addition, there are Swazis, Sothos, Tswanas, Vendas, and many others, each with its own language, culture, customs, and myths. To justify their Bantustan policy, the apartheid government spoke not of tribes but of nations, each with its own homeland. Apartheid was often euphemistically referred to as "plural democracy." South Africa, it was claimed, was "developing the various territories occupied by the different black nations into independent nation states."[2] As to those blacks resident in South Africa, many of whom were born there and had never laid eyes on their so-called homelands, nor desired to, "separate facilities are provided for different race groups for the sole reason of diminishing race friction."[3] This was a transparent, self-serving untruth.

Coloureds concentrated in the Cape region, are not a tribe but a racially heterogeneous ethnic group whose ancestors were indigenous Hottentots, Malay slaves, and whites. They speak Afrikaans or English

103

or their own patois based on those two languages. They do not have their own religion.

Living in the main in the vicinity of Durban is the Indian population. Durban—the name honors a nineteenth-century governor of the Cape Province—is a city replete with temples and mosques that could easily be mistaken for a population center on the Indian subcontinent. The Indians are descended from indentured laborers who toiled in the sugar fields, mostly Hindus or Muslims.[4] They ordinarily spoke English as their first language. They too were subjected to apartheid and its attendant abuses.

Although he is usually associated with India's struggle for independence, Mahatma Gandhi, as a young British-trained lawyer, traveled to South Africa in the 1890s to fight for basic rights for the Indians there. He failed. In fact, at one point, as a brown "coolie," he was unceremoniously ejected from a train when he defiantly refused to travel in a compartment reserved for Indians.[5]

Of course, the political and economic wielders of power in South Africa were the Whites—Afrikaans speakers and English speakers. European immigrants such as Greeks, Portuguese, or Lithuanian-born Jews were incorporated into the English-speaking community and enjoyed rights on the very day of their arrival that blacks, who had been on the scene for centuries, were systematically denied. All told, the "White Nation" constituted no more than a sixth of the entire population living in South Africa in the 1960s.

Not only did the Afrikaners see themselves as defenders of civilization, they believed that their presence in South Africa was divinely conceived. They were "chosen," a notion inculcated by their Dutch-reformed churches. With the passage of time, their connection to the Netherlands became increasingly tenuous. There was no mother country for the Afrikaners in the sense that whites in Kenya or Rhodesia had Britain.

What of the British role in the making of South Africa? Lest the Cape fall to France in the Napoleonic Wars, British naval forces were dispatched, and they forced the Dutch to capitulate in 1795. British rule was not finalized until the Congress of Vienna in 1815. Briton and Boer would henceforth occupy the Cape, but not in equal measure and rarely in a fraternal manner.

When, in 1807, Britain abolished the slave trade throughout their vast empire, relations with the Boers were exacerbated. The killing of a Boer who had been arrested for abusing a black sparked a small-scale uprising. In 1815, seven Boer rebels were hanged in what became a cause célèbre—Slachter's Nek (Butcher's Neck), the Boer equivalent of the Boston Massacre. British missionaries afforded nonwhites some protection. Thus they were seen by the Boers as their nemesis. British immigration in the 1820s, the official replacement of Dutch by English for judicial and other purposes, and the adoption of English currency all added to the tensions between the two European peoples.[6]

In 1834, a landmark statute enacted at Westminster emancipated slaves throughout the British Empire. Dutch farmers' anger toward the British grew immeasurably as a result. In effect, Parliament was buying the slaves' freedom from their owners, but the compensation was deemed unsatisfactory by the Boers and, for that matter, slaveholders in the West Indies and elsewhere. More and more Boers felt that their way of life was being undermined.

Clashes between the Bantu and the whites on the frontier made an already precarious situation worse and set the stage for a milestone in South African history—the Great Trek, a large migration into the hinterland during the course of which blacks and pestilence took their toll on the Boers. The Great Trek has been called the central event in the history of South Africa, comparable to the ancient Israelites' flight from Pharaoh's Egypt or the epic westward migration of Mormons in mid-nineteenth-century America.[7]

It became traditional for those of Dutch extraction to commemorate the courage, fortitude, and suffering of their ancestors every December 16. It was on December 16, 1838, in the Battle of Blood River, that the Zulus were defeated in a major confrontation. The battle followed the entrapment and murder of Voortrekkers by the Zulu chieftain Dingane.[8] On December 16, Afrikaners still gather at the Voortrekker Monument near Pretoria, which became a shrine. After their battlefield victory, the Boers created an independent political entity, but British military forces quickly seized control and annexed Natal to the Cape Colony.

Turning their back on the British Empire and on the European enlightenment, some recalcitrant Boers moved farther into the interior. The Orange Free State and the Transvaal came into being as Boer republics. Diamonds were discovered in 1868. Then the discovery of gold in the Witwatersrand in 1886 raised the stakes in the conflict between the Boers and the Britons. The gold fields were truly a bonanza. Nothing on that scale had ever been found before.

Inspired by their Old Testament faith, Boers believed that they had a God-given right to their South African land and a God-given right to enslave the Bantu, whom they referred to as "Kaffirs," a pejorative term drawn from Arabic, meaning "infidel."

Given their newfound mineral wealth and Boer expansion, a clash with the British was inevitable. Cecil Rhodes and Paul Kruger, the president of the Transvaal, were the main protagonists in the drama that would reach its denouement in what the British called the Boer War. It was more objectively called the Anglo-Boer War or, better still, "the South African War." The fray was nothing less than a showdown between Afrikaner nationalism and British imperialism at its zenith.

During the war, from 1899 to 1902, which can be largely ascribed to Britain's eagerness to possess the mineral riches of the Transvaal, thousands of Boer men were deported. Women and children were consigned to concentration camps under unsanitary conditions where the mortality rate was frightening owing to rampant disease and starvation. Cattle were killed and farm buildings burned, leaving a residue of bitterness.

England's cause was globally unpopular in general. Its empire was already so large that it could be rightly said that the sun never set on the British Empire, perhaps because, as one wag observed, God did not trust the British in the dark. However, the white dominions did provide much support to the war effort.

Boer resentment was slow to dissolve, but by May 1910, the union of South Africa was proclaimed, encompassing the Cape, Natal, the Transvaal Republic, and Orange Free State. What was created was a unitary state, not a federation such as the United States. The franchise was a very thorny, contentious issue. In the end, the two former Boer republics clung to white manhood suffrage. Only in the Cape Province was white skin color not required to exercise the franchise.[9] It is no exaggeration to say that the Afrikaner character and world outlook were, to a considerable extent, forged by the struggle to avoid British domination and simultaneously to dominate the "lowly" Bantu.

While the Boer anguish during the war received much popular and scholarly attention, black agony has been largely ignored. Recent scholarship has provided a corrective. We now know tens of thousands of blacks were included in the war. Britain operated concentration camps for them also, and over twenty-five thousand perished. Outside the camps, Afrikaners often shot and killed blacks with impunity, so the Anglo-Boer war was by no means an all-white conflict.[10]

Over the decades, a popular South African propaganda chestnut held that the original Dutch settlers had displaced no blacks. In explaining his nation's policy of apartheid in London in 1961, Dr. H. F. Verwoerd, the prime minister, observed, "More than 300 years ago two population groups, equally foreign to South Africa, converged in rather small numbers on what was practically empty country. Neither group colonized the other's country or robbed him by invasion and oppression."[11] The South African government and its apologists had long claimed that when the original Dutch settler, Jan van Riebeeck, arrived in Table Bay on April 6, 1552, South Africa's population consisted of only "a few wandering Hottentots and Bushmen."[12] It was their contention that when, after van Riebeeck established his supply station at the Cape and the settlers started to move from one fertile valley to the next, they met with no other indigenous people. "All was empty. All was no man's land."[13] Supposedly, the Bantu people, whose descendants now constitute the vast majority of the South African population, were only then beginning their own great trek to the south.[14] Addressing himself to this very point in 1959, Eric Louw, then foreign minister, noted "that the Bantu began to trek from the North across the Limpopo when van Riebeeck landed in Table Bay."[15]

The reiteration of this version of early South African settlement, a historically inaccurate one to be sure, is not coincidental. Its purpose was to convince the world, and probably the white South African himself, that the blacks of South Africa, no less than the whites, are immigrants.[16] In this view, South Africa is not a case where the white man dispossessed the black man.[17] Parts of the country, allegedly uninhabited, were settled by Europeans by right of first occupation. At the same time, more or less, other tracts were settled by the Bantu, also by right of first occupation. Therefore, neither the Bantu nor the Europeans have a prior claim to the whole of South Africa. No colonialism occurred. Rather, there was a historical encounter in the 1700s in what shortly before had been virtually vacant land. This, briefly, is the South African case.

For quite some time, the Bantu migrations have been a source of fascination and conjecture to scholars. One formidable task that has confronted them has been to determine the region from which the Bantu-speaking peoples began their migration southward. Fortunately, research in linguistics and history has made possible a reconstruction of African history in the forest belt and savanna regions. Until recently, the prevailing view was that the Bantu had originated in the Great Lakes area of East Africa. However, the preponderance of available linguistic evidence strongly points to Nigeria and the Cameroons as the first Bantu homeland, and it is this latter view that has now gained general acceptance.[18]

Significantly, many supporters of the white South African regime adhered to the Older Great Lakes theory. Perhaps this adherence is one aspect of a general orientation that would, as Joseph Greenberg put it, "attribute virtually all the seminal events of African history to the stimulus of incoming superior Caucasoids, both Semites and Hamites, as they exercised their influence on an indigenous, culturally passive Negroid population."[19] According to his interpretation, the Bantu languages resulted from contact between a Hamitic people and a Sudanic-speaking Negro group.

The beginnings of the Bantu dispersal are now dated by most authorities within a few hundred years of 300 BC.[20] Nigerian ironworking has also been traced to approximately the same period. Possessing the skills of both ironworking and agriculture, the Bantu were able to move south from the edge of the Sudanic belt into areas theretofore only sparsely occupied by people at the hunting stage of development. The indigenous hunters were either absorbed or pushed farther south, where their descendants, pygmoid peoples and Bushmen, are found today. From among captive Bush people, the conquering Bantu selected women to be slaves, concubines, and even mothers. This race mixing of Bantu and Bushmen, in addition to the intermarriage of Bantu and Hottentot and of Nguni and Sotho, different Bantu subgroups, further complicates the issue of primary rights.

But when did the Bantu finally arrive in southern Africa, or, more specifically, in the area corresponding to the present-day Republic of South Africa? Theoretically, this remains the crucial question. Was it at about the same time as the first Dutch settlers in the mid-seventeenth century?

Monica Wilson, a South African anthropologist, marshaled a wealth of data to indicate that it was, in fact, considerably earlier.[21] Her evidence is drawn from three sources: archeology, oral tradition, and the accounts of shipwrecked Portuguese seamen. Of the three, the last is by far the most conclusive. Wilson quotes from the accounts of survivors of a number of sea tragedies to support her thesis that there were Bantu-speaking people "who were living in the coastal districts of the Transkei and Ciskei in the sixteenth and seventeenth centuries."[22]

For example, as early as 1552, the Sao Joao foundered just north of the Mzimvubu River in what is now Pondoland. Very close to the site of the disaster, the seamen encountered "Kaffirs," "very black in color with woolly hair." There is every reason to believe that these Kaffirs were Bantu rather than Bushmen or Hottentot, whose click-sounding language was pointedly commented on by later visitors. Survivors of a 1554 wreck saw Africans, some of whom carried assegais with iron points. Surely these were not the primitive Bushmen.

In Wilson's judgment, a 1593 chronicle "proves that the country was occupied by Xhosa-Zulu-speaking people at least to the south of Mtata and possibly further." The people met by this chronicler practiced circumcision, a custom not followed by the Hottentot. Traditions of the Pondomise, Xhosa, and Thembu peoples corroborate the observations of the Portuguese. These traditions place the Bantu on the tributaries of the Mzimvubu for generations before they moved down from the coast. Miss Wilson was convinced that before traveling southward "the ancestors of all the Transkeian groups were in Natal."[23] Another authority on the migrations holds the opinion that, before they crossed the Drakensberg traveling eastward, Bantu people were in the valley of the Vaal River.[24] Hence, it is emphatically untrue that the Africans and Europeans entered the area of present-day South Africa almost simultaneously.

Nevertheless, desirous of preserving political control, fearful of being "mongrelized," and eager to maintain one of the highest living standards in the world, the white South Africans sought historical sanction for their policy of transforming the native reserves into what are euphemistically called "Bantu homelands." Prior occupation, they stubbornly aver, provided that sanction. Those territories "traditionally occupied" by the several Bantu nations were to be developed into "viable," "self-governing" national homelands, or Bantustans. Eight in all were projected. In this spirit of "live and let live—apart," to use Professor Vernon McKay's apt phrase, the whites continued to occupy those areas historically controlled by them. It was maintained that the African should be allowed to enter the urban centers, which are essentially the white man's creation, only when he is willing to minister to the needs of the white man.

Lest the world ask why the various European peoples who comprise South Africa's white population are not each given "independent self-governing" status, the United Nations General Assembly was told in 1963 that "South Africans of European origin have been forged into a single and distinctive nation. It is no longer a European nation, although it is closely linked with Western culture and civilization."[25] Thus, all of European ancestry are conveniently lumped together. This was

109

particularly helpful to those of British stock, whose ancestors admittedly arrived in South Africa much later than the Bantu. But much more importantly, it gave the Europeans the advantages of unity, while disunity was being imposed on the Africans.

Of course, the sizable Asian community centered in Natal was not given the opportunity to determine its future, but then it had no prior claim to land in South Africa.

What of the more than one and a half million Coloureds (of mixed blood), who represented a problem that began about nine months after van Riebeeck's landfall? Though politically silenced, they bore eloquent testimony to the hypocrisy of the South African whites regarding "mongrelization." At least to the extent that the Coloured are partially descended from the Hottentot, they had a claim on South African soil that preceded that of both the Afrikaner and the majority of Bantu. Needless to say, they were not granted self-government.

It is, of course, the Bantu who constituted the real threat to Afrikanerdom, and it was the Bantu who were being divided along tribal lines. They were never asked whether they approved of the Bantustan principle or of the alternative principle of African nationalism, which had been sweeping the continent. Therefore, the claim advanced by Dr. Hilgard Muller, a South African foreign minister, that his country's policies were in line with the African revolution, which had self-determination as its main objective, was preposterous.[26]

For over half a century, South Africa had been one nation. But in the 1960s, to perpetuate white domination in the face of rising international criticism, South Africa was being unilaterally partitioned. The prior settlement by whites of the fertile and mineral-rich areas of the republic that were being retained could not justify that policy. The evidence already presented shows quite clearly that the Bantu and not the Europeans were the first to come to South Africa. If there was an interloper in South Africa, it was the white man. This is not to say that the trek of the Bantu across South Africa from the northwest gave them an exclusive claim to the entire country or even to a portion thereof.

The argument of prior occupation was a weak one. Were it advanced in this country, the Native American, himself incidentally an immigrant from Asia, could claim almost the whole of the United States. Endless migration and unsystematic mating have made prior occupation a most unreliable criterion for determining ethnic ownership of land. This is no less true of South Africa than of scores of other pluralistic nations. Obviously, according each human being regardless of ethnic background, equal personal and property rights is more practical and equitable than fragmentation that is often based on outmoded ethnic lines. To predestine individuals to play particular roles in society on the grounds of heredity was indefensible, even in Calvinist-oriented South Africa. To assign individuals to work at certain jobs or to live in certain areas according to the period in which their ancestors migrated to South Africa made less sense. Sadly, for a time, South Africa had the power to enforce its tyrannical policy. And to buttress that policy, it promoted a distorted historical version of early South African settlement. South Africa's case was an exceedingly feeble one historically. More importantly, it was quite beside the point.

In the 1960s, South Africa's grotesque apartheid had made it the most racially discriminatory place on the planet, and probably the most discriminatory in history. Colin and Margaret Legum described South Africa as a "caste system in which all the Whites are Brahmins and all the rest untouchables."[27]

The country was honeycombed with restrictive laws, ordinances, and practices brutally enforced by the state's police power. Contact between and among the various races of South Africa virtually never took place on a plane of equality. Whites and nonwhites lived separately. They learned in separate schools and were treated in separate hospitals. They ate in separate restaurants and slept in separate hotels. They sat on separate park benches and traveled on segregated trains and buses. Integrated beaches and swimming pools were out of the question. Blacks and whites were punished in separate prison facilities. No surprise, shared toilets were verboten. Whites and nonwhites were interred in different cemeteries. The social system was strikingly similar to that of Mississippi. Prospects for meaningful change were poor. Indeed, not a single black face was seen in parliament. Election Day did not see a single black cast a vote. All South Africans were placed in racial categories that governed every aspect of their lives: where they lived and worshipped, where they could work, whom they could marry, and so on.

One year after Afrikaner nationalists won the 1948 election, mixed marriages were banned. Eight years later came the Immorality Act, which prohibited sexual relations between blacks and whites. It was passed, so Afrikaners said, to protect nonwhites from sexual exploitation. As previously indicated, nocturnal interracial hanky-panky had been going on since the seventeenth century. The very presence of the sizeable mixed-race Coloured population offers eloquent testimony to that. These hypocritical antimiscegenation laws were reminiscent of Hitler's Nuremberg Laws and the antimiscegenation statutes in the United States that were not declared unconstitutional until 1967.[28] In South Africa, they were valid until the 1980s.

Black economic advancement was hindered by an industrial color bar. Provisions for job reservation protected white laborers in the more lucrative positions from black competition.

Adding to the obscenity of apartheid was an educational structure that operated along exclusive racial and tribal lines. Africans were given training that relegated them to subservient positions. When he served in the senate in 1954, Hendrik Verwoerd stated explicitly that no class of Africans should feel that "its spiritual, economic, and political home is among the civilized community of South Africa."[29]

Schools for blacks remained chronically short-staffed. Teachers were often underqualified. Facilities were frequently primitive. And all of this was in one of the richest nations in the world, whose great wealth was made possible by the physically demanding and sometimes dangerous toil of blacks, especially miners who descended into the bowels of the earth to earn a meager living.

Health care was another area in which blacks experienced severe deprivation. As late as 1985, in the waning years of apartheid, the racial disparity in health care was disgraceful. On average, whites lived fifteen years longer than blacks. Tuberculosis was a case in point, disproportionately claiming black lives. There was also a critical shortage of black physicians.[30]

Apartheid was a matter of life and death; let's be clear about that. It was also part and parcel of South African sport. Could it have been otherwise?

South Africa had been an integral feature of the Olympic landscape ever since 1908, when it was still a colonial possession of Great Britain. In May of the previous year, the IOC, without a single dissent, approved of South Africa's official participation in the upcoming London games. In that competition, a South African, Reggie Walker, took the gold medal in the 100-meter dash, and his teammate, Charles Hefferon, finished second in the marathon.[31]

That event was introduced for the first time in the modern Olympics. The Greeks in ancient times believed in the golden mean, doing everything in moderation, and a race covering more than twenty-six miles would not have fit the bill in the ancient Olympics.

South African sportsmen—whites only, of course—won their share of medals. South Africans officiated at many games, and South Africans served as members of the IOC. All that changed to the disappointment of the sports-mad South African white populace. Rome's games in 1960, the XVII Olympiad, was the last in which the all-white South African team was allowed to take part. Storm clouds were gathering. Crises loomed. The beginning of the 1960s ushered in what two South Africans, one being Rudolph W. L. Opperman, who became president of the South African National Olympic Committee (SANOC) in 1971, labeled "the years in the cold."[32]

Race ignited international diplomatic combat in sport between South Africa and the world with increasing frequency and bitterness. Such was the case in 1959, when a scheduled soccer match pitting a multiracial Brazilian side against an all-white team in South Africa did not materialize. Ferreira Santos, a Brazilian delegate to the IOC, told a session in Munich that because some of the Brazilians were dark-skinned they could not play.[33] Brazilians have a broad spectrum of shades, hues, and pigments. Consequently, a Brazilian squad without nonwhite players is inconceivable.

Reginald Honey, who spoke for South Africa at the IOC, rejected Santos's version of what had transpired. He vehemently denied that the South African Olympic Committee or its football federation were responsible for the fiasco. South Africa, according to Honey, set no conditions whatsoever for the South American sportsmen, but Chris De Broglio, an antiapartheid sports activist, later claimed that the visiting colored Brazilians had been required to stay in neighboring Mozambique. The details of the dispute remain murky. In any event, at the eleventh hour, President Juscelino Kubitschek of Brazil canceled the match to the displeasure of South Africans. The affair gave South Africa a black eye. Many more were to come.[34]

Three years later, the racial drama was reprised. Mozambique's government declared that a football team slated to compete in Natal had to include blacks, but the manager of their South African opponent would not agree to that arrangement. He was fearful of incurring the wrath of his own apartheid government. The contest had to be called off.[35]

In 1959–1960, there was a major altercation with New Zealand, a fellow white dominion, over the exclusion of Maoris from the national rugby team, the All-Blacks, so named for the color of their uniforms. Maoris, the indigenous people of New Zealand, brown-skinned Polynesians, were keen and often outstanding rugby competitors. Richard Thompson and John Laurence have both chronicled the controversy.[36] Frightened that Maori players would be embarrassed in South Africa, a coalition of church groups averred no team should be sent unless the South African Rugby Union could give an undertaking that the Maoris would be treated with proper respect. However, the New Zealand Rugby Union buckled and said it would not include Maoris in the planned 1960 tour of South Africa. Popular opposition to discrimination against the Maoris mushroomed in New Zealand. "No Maoris, No Tour" was their slogan, but to no avail. The tour took place. No Maoris or South African blacks were involved in what was an unmitigated defeat for the protestors and the cause of nonracial sport. As Thompson has pointed out, the incident did bring about a reevaluation of white-Maori relations.[37]

As a number of former European colonies in Africa achieved independence, international disapproval of the apartheid regime intensified. Its standing in the Olympic world in the early 1960s was clearly in jeopardy. In 1962, the IOC meeting held in Moscow resolved to warn South Africa that its racial policies had to change before October 1963. Otherwise, the IOC intended to suspend the South African Olympic Committee. Originally scheduled for Nairobi, the venue for the next IOC session had to be switched to Baden-Baden, Germany, because the Kenyan authorities refused to honor South African visas. At Baden-Baden, the South African Olympic Council argued that it had previously sent racially mixed teams abroad, in 1961 and again in 1963. The IOC was having none of it. Their words fell on deaf ears. Absent a change in racial sports policy domestically, South Africa would be barred from the Tokyo Games.

South African delegates at Baden-Baden insisted that apartheid was an internal matter that should not concern the IOC. They said that nonwhite athletes could train among themselves, and competition with whites could take place outside the country.[38] South Africa reiterated its position the following year in Innsbruck, Austria. Frank Braun, president of the South African Olympic Committee, stated that the government would not repudiate its policy of racial separation. He further stated that the South African government categorically refused to see the point of view of the IOC.[39] In other words, it was the apartheid government that called the tune to which the South African Olympic Committee danced.

A fundamental Olympic principle was proving to be a major stumbling block. South Africa's Olympic Committee had to "collectively, clearly, and publicly" disassociate itself from the policy of non-competition in sports and non-integration in the administration of sports in South Africa between Whites and non-Whites. South Africa's response had been found to be inadequate. And so it was that South Africa's eligibility to compete in the Japanese capital in 1964 was canceled. Governmental intransigence on the issue of multiracial sport had doomed its bid to compete in Tokyo. South Africa was suspended.[40]

In April 1966, when the executive board of the IOC met in Rome's posh Hotel Excelsior, South African delegates were in attendance to promote their cause. South Africa subscribed to the IOC regulations, they said. Moreover, they were willing to establish a committee that would be half-white and half-black. Indeed, the government had already approved such a committee. Brundage, for one, saw this as real progress. For apartheid "is a law of the government which cannot be disobeyed without risking severe sanctions."[41] A suspension of the South African Olympic Committee only served to drive that nation out of the Olympic Movement. The athletes would be the losers. Critics of South Africa were not assuaged, and the stalemate continued.

Unfortunately for South Africa, the Olympic debate heated up at a time when two radical Afrikaner nationalists served as prime minister. From 1958 until 1966, the Dutch-born Hendrik Verwoerd led the nation. In August 1966, *Time* magazine called him "one of the ablest white leaders that Africa has ever produced" and quoted him as declaring that "he did not have nagging doubt of ever wondering whether perhaps, I am wrong."[42] Much of the rest of the world had grave doubts.

Verwoerd was the very epitome of racism and has been labeled, quite accurately, the designer of apartheid. Verwoerd attended Stellenbosch University, itself a bastion of Afrikaner nationalism. He was disdainful of blacks, contemptuous of Jews, and antagonistic toward the British.[43] It was Verwoerd who translated into law many of the bedrock tenets of apartheid, and it was Verwoerd who, in 1961, transformed his adopted land into a republic independent of the United Kingdom. Verwoerd was also prime minister when the infamous Sharpeville Massacre occurred in Soweto on March 21, 1960. Peaceful protesters against the restrictive pass laws that required blacks to carry documents bearing the carrier's name, place of birth, and tribal affiliation were attacked by authorities. Sixty-nine were killed, galvanizing world opinion against South Africa.[44] Blacks were expendable. The massacre was a watershed. In 1966, the United Nations proclaimed March 21, the anniversary of Sharpeville, "The International Day for the Elimination of Racial Discrimination."

In 1966 Verwoerd was assassinated. Although Nelson Mandela was convinced that Verwoerd "thought Africans were beneath animals," he said he derived no satisfaction from the assassination" which was perpetrated by a deranged white man.[45]

Verwoerd's successor was Balthazar Johannes Vorster, who occupied the prime minister's office from 1966 to 1968. Vorster had been born in the Cape Province. Like his predecessor, he matriculated at Stellenbosch. Later, he became a leader in the Ossewabrandwag, the Ox-Wagon Sentinel, an organization that embodied fervent, even fanatical, Afrikaner nationalism. It had grown out of the 1938 nationwide centennial celebration of the Great Trek. During World War II, its sympathies were openly with Hitler. Its members sported swastikas and openly gave the Nazi salute.[46]

From a very young age, Vorster shared the unenlightened, condescending opinions of blacks with not only Verwoerd but all Boer South African prime ministers after 1948. Theirs was a view also shared by Adolf Hitler's National Socialist Party. Nelson Mandela, the venerable black leader, saw Vorster as a "man unsentimental in the extreme." "For him," Mandela wrote, "the iron fist was the best and only answer to subversion."[47] For Vorster, all the African nationalist leaders were subversives, which really meant they opposed systemic racism.

Afrikaner leadership was unwilling to bend on the question of sports, which were rigidly segregated along with the rest of South African society. There was some ineffectual internal pressure exerted. After several years of fruitless negotiations with the South African Olympic Committee, in 1962, blacks, Coloureds, and Indians, along with some sympathetic whites, formed the South African Non-Racial Olympic Committee, known by its acronym SAN-ROC.[48] It claimed the backing of more than sixty thousand athletes who opposed racial bigotry in the realm of sports. Their objective was to speak for all South Africans, regardless of race, in the national Olympic committee. Their campaign was in conformity with the Olympic Charter prohibiting racial discrimination.

Foremost among the anti-apartheid sports activists was Dennis Vincent Brutus, the president of SAN-ROC, who long sacrificed and labored tirelessly for integrated sports. Brutus was born in Salisbury, Rhodesia, in 1924 to South African parents, both teachers. His family returned to South Africa when he was a child. Under South Africa's pigmentocratic system, they were classified as Coloured. A graduate of Fort Hare, a public university for nonwhites, he also studied law at the University of Witwatersrand.

Brutus, a poet, journalist, and teacher, bristled at the racism that governed separate athletics. Dennis, a charismatic figure, and his brother, Wilfred, devoted themselves unstintingly to demolishing the segregated sports edifice. In 1960, Dennis was officially banned, which meant that he was prohibited from meeting with more than any two people outside his family. He was forbidden to attend any gatherings, including sport meetings. In fact, Brutus was arrested by the security police in the offices of the South African Olympic Committee![49] Banning was an effective tool for muzzling opponents of apartheid.

Brutus was accused of violating his banning order and was sentenced to prison, but he managed to slip across the border into Mozambique. Because Mozambique was still a Portuguese colony, he was apprehended by the authorities and sent back to South Africa. While attempting to escape, he was shot at point-blank range by a white policeman and nearly bled to death. When he recovered, he was dispatched to Robben Island, the notorious maximum-security prison in windswept Table Bay, off Cape Town, where he spent his days breaking rocks alongside Nelson Mandela. Brutus and Mandela, who had been given a life sentence and spent eighteen of his twenty-seven year confinement on Robben Island, were separated from the general prison population because, as Mandela put it in his autobiography, "we were considered risky from a security perspective, but even more dangerous from a political standpoint. The authorities were concerned we might 'infect' the other prisoners with our political views."[50] Robben Island was a microcosm of South African apartheid. Inmates were allotted varying quantities of certain food staples based on their racial classification, with Indians and Coloureds receiving more generous portions than blacks.[51]

Upon release from prison, Brutus traveled to Great Britain. His anti-apartheid struggle continued uninterrupted. He was indeed the bête noir (no pun intended) of Afrikanerdom.[52]

Another New Zealand rugby tour of South Africa, no longer a dominion but a republic, occurred in 1965. Once again, Maoris were not invited, but no untoward incidents took place, perhaps because there was an understanding that Maoris could take part in the projected 1967 tour. Skepticism in New Zealand was mollified by statements regarding the inclusion of Maoris made by South African rugby officials and by stories in the South African press. Trusting New Zealanders were engaged in wishful thinking. They were deluding themselves.

On September 4, 1965, Dr. Vervoerd made a speech in which he said South Africans visiting abroad, in New Zealand, for instance, abided by the traditions of their host country. Similarly, New Zealand visitors to South Africa would be expected to respect South African laws and mores.[53]

Afrikaner thinking was predicated on the need to preserve the white race. Miscegenation threatened white survival. As *Die Transvaler* explained, social mixing led inexorably to miscegenation, supposedly the goal of Communists. It continued, "In South Africa the races do not mix on the sports field. If they mix first on the sports field then other forms of social mixing are wide open. With an eye to the upholding of the White race and its civilization, not one single compromise can be entered into—not even when it comes to a visiting rugby team."[54]

The minister of the interior and the South African consul general in New Zealand more or less repeated Verwoerd's apartheid mantra. Maoris were not wanted. White workers in New Zealand pushed back. To quote Lawrence, "If an All-White South African sporting team arrived in New Zealand while the present rigid policies of race discrimination applied in South Africa, then New Zealand hotel, transport, dock, and airport workers would stage a mass walk-out."[55] Cancellation of the 1967 tour ensued. Severance of reciprocal rugby relations between New Zealand and South Africa, almost half a century old, was the major casualty. South Africa's sports bigotry had been thrown into sharp relief.

South Africa's Olympic Committee had little latitude to modify its apartheid policy, even if it was inclined to do so. In January 1964, Frank Braun told the IOC at the executive meeting in Innsbruck that he had apprised the South African government of the country's dilemma, but it categorically refused to see the IOC quandary.[56]

Fueled by the expanding membership of black states, African and West Indian, the United Nations passed a plethora of resolutions condemning Pretoria and calling for collective measures.[57] In the 1960s, apartheid was a perennial issue in the UN agenda.

With Brundage in the forefront, many in the IOC tried to resist the anti-apartheid tide, which they sensed would result in expulsion. South Africa fought back, but increasingly the nation was seen as the "skunk of the world," to borrow Nelson Mandela's colorful metaphor.

At an IOC meeting in Teheran in May 1967, the South African Games Association said that in the future, blacks and whites would constitute one team representing all of South Africa. Whereas theretofore nonwhite and white athletes had dressed differently, had separate accommodations, and could not march under the same flag in opening ceremonies, henceforth they would wear the same uniform, lodge together, and march as an integrated ensemble under the South African banner. Previously, South African whites and nonwhites were prevented from competing against each other at Olympiads or other international sports meetings.

This would no longer be standard practice. South Africa's future participation in the Olympic Games would "adequately meet the requirements of opportunity and non-discrimination."[58] Not so. Their response was adjudged to be tepid and cosmetic by much of the Third World, that is, the developing nations wooed by the West and the Soviet Bloc.

The African National Olympic Committees informed the IOC Executive Board convened in Teheran that the South African national team was selected on a racial basis for the sake of presenting one contingent of athletes under the same flag for international sports. Competition outside the country meant that the "highest sports authority in the world" would be recognizing in South Africa "a situation contrary to the Olympic morals and principles."[59]

Racial discrimination was anathema to the African states. They confirmed their adherence to the Olympic Movement and firmly condemned all discrimination in sport. They congratulated the IOC for "its decision to suspend the South African Olympic Committee" and requested the IOC "maintain its decision until racial discrimination has been completely eliminated in South Africa itself and this when all sportsmen in this country could pursue . . . the sport of their choice in the stadiums of their country without any discrimination."[60] They resolved to use any and all means to bring about the "expulsion of the South African Sports Organizations from the Olympic Movement and from the International Federations should the NOC . . . fail to comply fully with the IOC rules."[61] In a thinly veiled threat, the African NOCs reserved their right to drop out of the 1968 Games if South Africa were allowed to participate without complying completely with the Olympic Charter.[62]

Brundage and others understood that this was no bluff. They found themselves on the horns of a dilemma. He had often said that during the Berlin Olympiad of 1936, political interference and racial discrimination had been eliminated, but Nazi policy was not changed. In reality, of course, Nazi concessions had been a charade in Berlin and Garmisch. Accepting two token Jews had been a ruse. Brundage could not bring himself to acknowledge that. Now, in 1967, South Africa was playing the same game. Would they succeed?[63]

In 1967, Brundage, acting on the instructions of the IOC Executive Board, appointed a three-man fact-finding commission to report on the status of sport in the republic. The members were Lord Killanin, president of the Olympic Council in Ireland; R. S. Alexander, chairman of the Kenyan Olympic Association; and Ade Ademola, president of the Nigerian Olympic Committee. The IOC South Africa Commission assembled in Nairobi on September 6 and flew to Johannesburg the next day. In its travels around South Africa, the commission received tremendous attention from the media—newspapers and radio as well as the sporting public. Officials, black and white, of many sports organizations were consulted. Representatives of the SANOC, together with national associations of Olympic sports, individual sportsmen, independent groups, and organizations, met with the commission. All evidence was given in English.

On September 12, 1967, when Prime Minister Vorster met in Pretoria with Lord Killanin as chairman of the commission, he held out the hope that the Bantustan system would provide a means of cutting the Olympic Gordian knot. Millions of Bantu lived in their traditional homelands, mostly under harsh conditions. In essence, they served as reservoirs of cheap labor. They had no political rights within the borders of the republic. Of course, they could not exercise the franchise, but Vorster told Killanin they would become sovereign and independent nations, as sovereign and independent as Ghana.[64] This was a means of circumventing IOC and UN criticism of the South African regime. It was easily recognized as a sham by those who sought the truth.

For the time being, Vorster was fearful that his country would remain in the sports doldrums unless some compromise was made, but he was more fearful that significant concessions would alienate his nationalist adherents. He made it plain that no mixed sport between whites and nonwhites would be practiced locally. By way of explanation, an absurd explanation, Vorster stated that the policy of South Africa, not only that of the Nationalist Party "has never been based on hate or prejudice or fear. . . . [I]t does not mean the denial of a person's humanity. On the contrary, it underlines the diversity of the various population groups which have to find a home in the same geographical area, as in the Republic of South Africa."[65] It was a policy that was aimed at creating opportunities that had previously never existed and avoiding friction and disturbance. If anyone took the attitude that relations with South Africa were only possible if separation in sport were discarded, South Africa would not negotiate or compromise.

Speaking to parliament on April 11, the dogged Vorster stated, almost verbatim, the same policy:

> No mixed sport between whites and non-Whites will be practiced locally, irrespective of the standard of proficiency. . . . If any person, either locally or abroad, adopts the attitude that he will enter into relations with us only if we are prepared to jettison the practicing of

sport prevailing among our own people in South Africa, then I want to make it quite clear that, no matter how important those sports relations are in my view, I am not prepared to pay that price.[66]

According to the *Hansard* account, Vorster continued, noting that even attendance by members of one racial group at recreational events of another racial group could only take place "by way of permit if at all." He admitted that some sports grounds do not allow integration and "that is the affair of those people."[67]

South Africa would not disavow its apartheid policy, the IOC was told in no uncertain terms. Integrated sport was not in the offing, even with the Mexico City Games imminent. Attendance at another group's recreational events would only be permitted where "separate facilities are available and as long as it does not result in situations which are conducive to friction and disturbances, and . . . will not hamper the development of their own facilities." His objective, Vorster said, "is to grant every population group the same sports facilities in their own area and among their own people that I grant the Whites."[68] Because sport in the republic was under the absolute control of the government, the SANOC was hamstrung, and the grip of the sports federations was weakening. Black athletes were barred from national championships by deeply entrenched apartheid. The commission was well aware of this.

Shortly thereafter, F. W. Waring, the South African minister of sport and tourism, indicated that the government spoke with one voice on the subject. According to the *Star*, a Johannesburg newspaper, Waring ruled out trials between whites and nonwhites. South Africa was willing to have the latter take part in the Games, but asserted that "we will pick a white and Black team. However, the IOC allowed a country to send just one team." Waring contended that South Africa provided sporting facilities for nonwhites that were superior to those found anywhere on the globe. That claim was both dubious and irrelevant to the debate.[69]

During the commission's travels, Ade Ademola visited Wilfred Brutus. At the time, Wilfred was banned under the Suppression of Communism Act. Without special permission from a magistrate, he could not have been consulted at all. Wilfred had been the leader of the Western Province Branch of SAN-ROC but was compelled to step down from that position in 1964 because of the banning decree. He was interviewed in his personal capacity.

The South African government had denied Dennis Brutus the right to re-enter the country and speak to the commission. Several months later, Dennis gave testimony to the commission in Lausanne. He testified that

SAN-ROC wanted all South Africans included in the Olympic Games: "[I]t is not exclusion we desire, but we believe that participation must be in accordance with the Olympic Charter. . . . [T]here would be no necessity for SAN-ROC nor would one wish to keep such a body in existence, the moment the SANOC accepts its obligation to treat all South African sportsmen in accordance with the Olympic Charter and does not practice racial discrimination in the organization of sport."[70]

Vorster wanted the IOC to completely dissociate itself from SAN-ROC. In his obviously jaundiced view, Dennis Brutus and "his associates are not interested in sport and have in fact done nothing for the promotion of sport." Vorster saw Brutus not just making waves, but tsunamis.

Unsympathetic to SAN-ROC, the IOC objected to that organization's use of the word "Olympic" in its title. At Teheran, the IOC resolved that "neither the International Olympic Committee nor any of its officials shall have any communication or dealings with it."[71]

SAN-ROC per se was given short shrift by the commission. In the summary of its findings, the commission stated that the evidence showed that SAN-ROC was supported only in spirit by the majority of nonwhites in South Africa. "Its methods," said the commission, "are a cause of embarrassment to the majority in South Africa for whom it claims to speak. The commission must assume that those who gave evidence voluntarily before it, with courage and conviction, were men of truth." The report quoted one anonymous witness, identified as a former leader of SAN-ROC, as follows: "I do feel that those who are outside the country are self-exiled and I feel that wherever they are they should not dictate to us here because we have to face the situation not them."[72] Describing Brutus and many like him as "self-exiled" is analogous to describing Mandela as "self-imprisoned." South Africa was a police state. To incur the displeasure of the government was to court disaster, as Steven Biko and other freedom fighters who were murdered by a regime Brian Bunting called "the South African Reich" discovered.[73]

Due in large measure to Brutus and SAN-ROC, by 1968, many international federations had taken action against the national sports federations of South Africa. Its football federation was suspended in 1964. Both its basketball federation and its fencing federation were also suspended in 1964. Its boxing federation was expelled in 1968. Its judo federation was denied affiliation in 1967–1968. Its volleyball federation was denied affiliation. South Africa's weightlifting body was expelled in 1969, and its Davis Cup team was expelled the next year.[74]

Despite the foregoing, the commission's report did not provide a scathing criticism of South Africa. It appeared to accept South Africa's contention that meaningful strides had been taken toward full compliance with IOC regulations. It appeared to have found credible South Africa's statement that the construction program for sports facilities for nonwhites was rapidly catching up with that for whites.[75]

South African sports authorities were delighted by the commission's report. Opponents of apartheid were dismayed. They were chagrined by Ademola, the Nigerian chief justice, and the only nonwhite member of the commission. There were poor facilities at the Springfield football grounds and golf course, a lack of clubhouses, grandstands, changing rooms, and refreshment stands. Ademola's reaction shocked Natal's Indians, wrote the *Rand Daily Mail*. He asked why they were so dependent on the government and city council for financing: "Why don't you go ahead and do something yourselves? . . . [S]urely there are enough Indians in Natal to provide finance."[76]

The commission's mandate was to collect facts and not make recommendations. Absent any condemnation, the South African delegation to the IOC meeting in Grenoble in February 1968 pounced. They said there was incontrovertible proof that "sportsmen of all races in South Africa are clamoring for admission to the Olympic Games."[77] Great advances had been made by the SANOC since 1963, when South Africa had been suspended. White and, more so, nonwhite athletes were being penalized unfairly. Clearly referring to SAN-ROC, it was stated that "with exception of a few expatriate professional politicians masquerading as sports leaders from London," sportsmen unanimously wished to participate in the Olympics.[78]

In Grenoble, the IOC acknowledged the obvious: racism existed in South Africa. But progress had been made, and it believed South African promises of future compliance with Olympic rules. South Africa's suspension was lifted. The understanding was that SANOC could enter a team that conformed with fundamental IOC principles. South Africa had to vigorously continue its efforts to remove all forms of racial discrimination in amateur sports.

However, the nation of South Africa would suffer a swift reversal of fortune. SAN-ROC lost no time in objecting, saying on March 20, 1968, that the IOC was basically placing its imprimatur on racial discrimination by a member country. It called the decision unconstitutional and said that it threatened not only the Mexican Olympiad but the whole future of the Olympic Movement. To SAN-ROC, it was in reality a minority verdict. Thirty-seven members had voted in favor of South Africa's re-admission, but they represented only twenty-three countries. Twenty-eight votes were recorded against from at least twenty-five countries. SAN-ROC argued that the voting system was loaded in favor of Western nations. Seventy countries were not consulted at all.[79]

The 1968 "D'Oliveira Affair" dimmed South Africa's prospects for Mexico City. Basil D'Oliveira was no firebrand on the issue of desegregation in the land of his birth, although he was one of its victims. He was of Portuguese and East Indian extraction and was classified as Coloured, a classification that guaranteed a life filled with indignities. Among various disabilities, he was prevented from playing cricket at the highest level of competition because his skin was too swarthy for him to be considered white. A star cricketer, he had to journey to England to develop his full athletic potential.[80]

A long-awaited British tour of South Africa precipitated a bitter and protracted dispute in 1968. South African political leaders, including Prime Minister Vorster and Pieter Le Roux, the minister of the interior, made it plain that a racially mixed team that included D'Oliveira would not be gladly received. The governing body for English cricket, the Marylebone Cricket Club (MCC), was conflicted. At first, not choosing D'Oliveira appeared to be the best solution to their problem, and in late August 1968, the MCC announced that they had selected their best cricketers and that D'Oliveira was not among them.

In South Africa, there was much joy, but in Great Britain, the announcement touched off protests. Many Members of Parliament were livid.[81] The MCC blinked and announced that D'Oliveira would go to South Africa as a sports journalist to report on the cricket tour. That seemed to make matters worse. As Richard Lapchick observed, D'Oliveira as a newspaperman "could not obtain a blanket exemption from the Group Areas Act," limiting his movements and denying him access to the white facilities. South African sportswriters also commented that he would not be able to eat or drink with the players for the purpose of interviewing them and "would probably have to sit in the nonwhite stands during the matches."[82]

In mid-September, the MCC, under intense pressure, did a 180-degree turn when it stated that D'Oliveira would be added to the team's roster as a replacement for an injured player. Vorster, speaking in Bloemfontein, said, "[I]t's not the M.C.C. Team, it's the team of the anti-apartheid movement. . . . [I]t's a team of people who don't care about sports relations at all."[83] Crying foul, Vorster blamed SAN-ROC.

Indecision on the part of the MCC had put it in an unfavorable light in international cricket. For South Africa, the episode was a public relations debacle with the Olympics just around the corner. South Africa was isolated from the cricket world, an isolation that would last for more than twenty years because of Basil D'Oliveira. Nelson Mandela called the D'Oliveira incident decisive in defeating apartheid. It certainly diminished its Olympic prospects.[84]

The decision to lift the suspension of South Africa was greeted with rage in many countries. A volcanic reaction from certain quarters was immediate. Several third-world nations, in particular, withdrew from the Mexico City Olympiad because South Africa would be there. Within two days of the IOC action, ten countries announced their withdrawal. India was just one example. Its Olympic association wrote to the IOC in March 1968 that it would not take part if South Africa did. The National Ethiopian Sports Confederation did likewise as well as Libya, Nigeria, Sierra Leone, Sudan, Kenya, Uganda, and Jamaica. Hungary and several Soviet satellites followed suit. Cold War rivalry with the West required the Russians to support black African positions on the South African Olympic issue. Even the Italian and French Olympic committees denounced the new IOC stance. In blistering language, the president of the French Olympic Committee referred to "the most retrograde decision ever adopted by the Olympic Committee."[85] From the United States, there was deafening silence.

By April 1968, when the executive board of the IOC met at its headquarters in Lausanne, Brundage was still struggling to balance competing interests: that of the IOC and the Olympic Movement; that of the Mexican Organizing Committee; that of the South African National Olympic Committee; that of the other national Olympic committees; and that of the international federations. Hovering over deliberations was the threat of boycott, which would torpedo the Games in Mexico.

Brundage, in the sunset of his career, insisted that the sole criterion for excluding South Africa was racial discrimination. He noted that on that basis several nations' policies, including the United States', would warrant exclusion. As he had for decades, Brundage failed to consider the scale of racism, its institutional nature, its legal underpinnings, its pervasiveness, or its longevity. One could make the case that racism was at its zenith at the tip of Africa in 1968. Conversely, South Africa's international sports fortunes were at their lowest ebb. Arthur Ashe, the much admired and popular African American tennis player, had been denied a South African visa. In December 1968, a UN resolution requested that all countries sever sports ties with South Africa.[86]

By the spring, virtually all members of the executive board stood in opposition to South Africa's participation in Mexico City. Even Brundage agreed. He had reluctantly come to the conclusion that the IOC had to withdraw its invitation. He suggested that a telegram be sent at once to all members of the IOC. The entire executive board believed that a team from South Africa ought not put in an appearance. Brundage determined the wording of the cable. Given the available information on global thinking at the time, it was "unanimously of the opinion that it would be most unwise for a South African team to participate in the Games of the XIX Olympiad. Therefore the executive board strongly recommends that you endorse this unanimous proposal to withdraw the invitation to the games."[87] They did. In May 1968, J. W. Westerhoff, the secretary general of the IOC, requested that Ramirez-Vasquez withdraw the official invitation to the SANOC.[88] The potential boycotters reversed their positions. For example, Kenya notified the Mexicans in May 1968 that because the IOC decided to disinvite South Africa, Kenya would be sending its team. Others also did a volte-face.[89]

Unused to defeat, Brundage attempted to put the best possible face on this decision. He emphasized that the IOC was not "bowing to threats or pressures of any kind from those who do not understand the true Olympic philosophy." *Boycott* is not a word customarily employed in sports circles, said he. But Brundage was not telling the whole truth. In his official communiqué on the voting, he averred that the single point on which the executive committee could agree was "that because of the explosive conditions throughout the world and the ugly demonstrations, rioting, and other violent happenings in many different countries during the last sixty days, there was actual danger if a South African team appeared at the Games." The paramount concern was the preservation of the Olympic Movement, which Brundage called "one of the most priceless and powerful instruments of our present civilization."[90] South Africa was out. A crippling boycott by the African states and other developing countries in Asia, plus the Soviet-controlled East European bloc, had been narrowly averted.

Writing to Reginald Honey in South Africa in July 1968, Brundage did not concede that the April executive board decision was a disaster:

> After all, we saved the Games and prevented a complete rupture in international sport. With present conditions in the world, we could not win on a racial issue. It is a sad commentary on our so-called

civilization that games intended to promote international understanding cannot be held without demonstrations, disorder and
violence. The developments since in the United States, France, and
a score of other countries, I am sure you will agree, have justified
our decision.

As late as October 3, practically on the evening of the Games, there
were diehards who still wanted South Africa to compete. Lord Exeter,
who had been the IOC member in Great Britain for three and a half
decades, strongly advocated for the re-admission of South Africa. In
an exclusive interview with the *Sunday Times*, he expressed his opinion that sufficient concessions had been extracted from South Africa's
government. He was convinced that a South African contingent would
be representative of its varied population. No sportsmen would be "left
out on racial grounds."[91] He allied himself with nonwhite athletes in
South Africa who wanted to be in Mexico City. Therefore, they were
at loggerheads with their brethren in Black Africa, Exeter claimed.
Certainly, many nonwhite South African athletes wanted to be able to
compete in Mexico City. It would be their moment to take their places
in sports annals. Others saw a higher purpose and greater benefit for
their people in being forced to stay at home.

Separate trials were unobjectionable in Exeter's view. Moreover, "we
can't interfere with the laws of a country," he said. The IOC had "no
grounds whatever for entering into battle directly with governments
about the internal laws of their country."[92] From Lord Exeter's perspective, it was only the IOC that had successfully cracked the wall of
apartheid.[93] This was fanciful thinking. Surely Exeter understood that
his cause was lost. The clock had run out.

In 1970, South Africa would be removed from the Olympic Movement altogether. Bowing to the Supreme Council in Sport in Africa,
which threatened to give the 1972 Games in Munich a wide berth
unless South Africa was expelled, the IOC caved.[94] South Africa's fate
had been sealed by its dogmatic, messianic racial fanaticism. The nation
would not return to the Olympics until the apartheid regime crumbled.

Isolation from international sports had unquestionably dealt a serious blow to South Africa's national pride and, in so doing, contributed
mightily to the undermining of apartheid. No one understood that
better than the incarcerated Nelson Mandela.

By the late 1980s, international pressure had persuaded the white
power elite that it could no longer sustain white minority rule. It unrav-
eled quickly with almost no warning. In a truly multiracial election,

South Africa's first, Nelson Mandela, recently released from prison, was elected president and sworn in in April 1994. Mandiba, to use Mandela's clan name, the one-time prisoner 466/64, was awarded the Nobel Peace Prize (1993) and became an international idol, even a secular saint. Posterity will doubtlessly share that contemporary assessment of a truly remarkable man.[95]

When he died at the age of ninety-five in December 2013, Mandela was lavishly praised for putting in place a policy of racial reconciliation rather than revenge. The transition to majority rule had been peaceful. Bloodshed had been avoided. It was clear that Mandela deserved to be in the global pantheon of world statesman. He was, to use President Obama's words, the "last great liberator."[96]

Notes

1. Afrikaans incorporated some words from Portuguese and sundry African languages. Afrikaans, Dutch, and Flemish are mutually intelligible.
2. *Facts about South Africa* (Washington DC: Information Counselor of the South African Embassy, 1977).
3. Ibid.
4. The year 2010 marked the 150th anniversary of their initial immigration. There were some free or passenger Indians who paid their own way.
5. The incident is dramatized in the film *Gandhi*. In 1894, he opened an office to practice law in Durban and became the secretary of the Natal Indian Congress. Joseph Lelyveld, *Great Soul: Mahatma Gandhi and His Struggle with India* (New York: Alfred A Knopf, 2011), 4–5, 355.
6. Robert Collins, *African History: Texts and Readings* (New York: Random House, 1971), 465–466.
7. Alfred Leroy Burt, *The British Empire and Commonwealth from the American Revolution* (Boston: D.C. Heath and Company, 1956), 286; T. R. H. Davenport, South Africa—A Modern History, (Toronto: University of Toronto Press, Fourth Edition, 1991) 44–48, 70.
8. Ibid., 287.
9. Burt, *The British Empire and Commonwealth*, 616–621. Also see Monica Wilson and Leonard Thompson, eds., *The Oxford History of South Africa*, vol. 2, *South Africa 1870–1966* (New York: Oxford University Press, 1971), 329.
10. Linda Vergnani, "Scholars Unearth Evidence of the Boer War's Black Victims," *Chronicle of Higher Education*, January 7, 2000. A young Winston Churchill, working at the time of the South African War, as a foreign correspondent, was appalled that "Kaffirs" should be permitted to fire on whites. Churchill made countless racist remarks.
11. *Progress through Separate Development* (New York: Information Service of South Africa, nd), 11.
12. Stanley N. Shaw, *In Defense of South Africa* (Pretoria: Government Printer, nd).
13. *Progress through Separate Development*, 31.
14. Clarence B. Randall, "Why South Africa Needs Time," reprint from *Reader's Digest* (August 1963): 3–4.

15. *Die Burger*, April 1, 1959, 8.
16. Shaw, *In Defense of South Africa*.
17. Randall, "Why South Africa Needs Time," 3–4.
18. Joseph H. Greenberg, "Africa as a Linguistic Area," in *Continuity and Change in African Cultures*, edited by William R. Bascom and Melville J. Herskovits (Chicago: University of Chicago Press, 1951), 20.
19. Ibid., 21.
20. Philip D. Curtin, *African History* (New York: Macmillan, 1964), 31.
21. Monica Wilson, "The Early History of the Transkei and Ciskei," *African Studies* 18 (1959), 167–179.
22. Ibid., 173.
23. Ibid., 174.
24. Alfred T. Bryant, *Olden Times in Zululand and Natal* (London: Longmans, Green and Co., 1929), 6.
25. *Progress through Separate Development*, 47.
26. Ibid., 41.
27. Amelia C. Leiss, ed., *Apartheid and United Nations Collective Measures: An Analysis* (New York: Carnegie Endowment for International Peace, 1965), 31.
28. Occasionally Coloureds, or even whites, were reclassified, which often turned their lives topsy-turvy. The sex laws were not repealed in South Africa until 1985. Also see Alan Cowell, "Change in Sex Law Unsettles Props of Apartheid," *New York Times*, April 30, 1985, and "Sex Laws Repealed," *SA Digest*, April 19, 1985.
29. Monica Wilson and Leonard Thompson, eds., *The Oxford History of South Africa, 1870–1966*, vol. 2 (New York: Oxford University Press, 1971), 78–79.
30. Robert Coles, "Anti-Apartheid Medicine," *New York Times*, January 29, 1985.
31. Rudolf W. J. Opperman and Lappe Laubscher, *Africa's First Olympians: The Story of the Olympic Movement in South Africa, 1907–1987* (Johannesburg: Sanoc-Sanok, 1987), 3.
32. Ibid., 34, 51.
33. Richard E. Lapchick, *The Politics of Race and International Sport: The Case of South Africa* (Westport, CT: Greenwood Press, 1975); minutes of the 55th session of the IOC, Munich, 1959. See Report of the IOC Commission on South Africa (Lausanne: IOC, 1968), 17, and Lapchick's interview with de Broglio on June 6, 1970, in Lapchick, *The Politics of Race*, 30.
34. Ibid.
35. Richard Thompson, *Race and Sport* (London: Oxford University Press, 1964), 32.
36. Ibid.; John Laurence, *The Seeds of Disaster: A Guide to the Realities, Race Policies, and World-wide Propaganda Campaigns of the Republic of South Africa* (New York: Taplinger Publishing Company, 1968). It aroused much passion, especially among Afrikaners. It was interlaced with Afrikaner nationalism, masculinity and their identity. See John Nauricht and Timothy J. L. Chandler, Making Men—Rugby and Masculine Identity, (London: Frank Cass, 1996).
37. Thompson, *Race and Sport*, 54. Rugby in South Africa was overwhelmingly a white sport.
38. Minutes of the 69th session of the IOC Executive Committee, Baden-Baden, October 16–20, 1963. Quoted in the IOC Commission on South Africa Report.

39. Minutes of the IOC Executive Board Meeting, Innsbruck, January 25–26, 1964, ABC, box 88.

40. Opperman, *Africa's First Olympians*, 52–53; minutes of the 61st session of the IOC Executive Board, Innsbruck, January 26–28, 1964.

41. Appendix A of the meeting of the executive board of the IOC, Rome, April 21–24, 1966, ABC, box 88.

42. "South Africa—The Great White Laager," *Time*, August 20, 1966, 25; Alexander Hepple, Verwoerd (Baltimore: Penguin, 1967).

43. In September 1966, possibly for the first time in history, large numbers of Jews paid homage to a man with a notorious anti-Semitic past—Hendrik F. Verwoerd. For this anomaly, see Robert G. Weisbord, "The Dilemma of South African Jewry," *Journal of Modern African Studies*, vol. 5, no. 2 (1967), 233–241.

44. *Time* wrote at the time that Verwoerd had made the pass laws "almost a physical shackle." "The Sharpeville Massacre," *Time*, April 4, 1966, 18. For a comprehensive treatment, see Tom Lodge, *Sharpeville—An Apartheid Massacre and its Consequences* (Oxford: Oxford University Press, 2011).

45. Nelson Mandela, *Long Walk to Freedom: The Autobiography of Nelson Mandela* (Boston: Little Brown and Company, 1994), 431.

46. In general, during the period from 1933 to 1945—one of political and ideological turmoil—Nazism flourished in South Africa. The fraudulent "Protocols of the Elders of Zion" were disseminated, and the Nazi slogans of "Jewish Democracy" and "Jewish Capitalism" were widely adopted. The Nationalist Party press dwelt on "Hoggenheimer," the symbol of Jewish capitalism, who was depicted in political cartoons as an obese Jew smoking a cigar and looking prosperous. New, fanatic Afrikaner groups that accepted the entire Nazi ideology came into existence. One favored wholesale disfranchisement of all elements described as "anti-national, un-national, and un-assimilable"—and the Jews were specifically named. The Nationalists excluded Jews from party membership in the Transvaal, and many Afrikaner leaders were guilty of uttering blatantly anti-Semitic remarks.

Johannes Strijdom, Daniel Malan's successor as prime minister, talked about the "cancer of British-Jewish capitalism." Malan himself made no secret of his hope that Hitler would win, and in 1940, he alleged that South Africa had been transformed into a Jewish imperialistic war machine. Eric Louw, later South Africa's foreign minister, made innumerable anti-Jewish statements during World War II, and Verwoerd, as editor of the newspaper, *Die Transvaler*, in 1936, bitterly attacked Jewish immigration. The anti-Jewish policies of the Nationalist Party subscribed to by these politicians were enunciated in an election manifesto in 1938 and reaffirmed three years later.

47. Mandela, *Long Walk to Freedom*, 338.

48. Obeying the wishes of the IOC, in 1967, the name was changed to South African Non-Racial Open Committee. In 1959, Brutus had founded the Anti-Apartheid South African Sports Association.

49. See Brutus's testimony to the IOC Commission on South Africa, November 25, 1960.

50. Mandela, *Long Walk to Freedom*, 254.

51. *New York Times*, July 6, 2013. Mandela was offered an increased allotment but characteristically refused special treatment.

52. See obituaries in the *Guardian*, February 23, 2010, and the *New York Times*, January 2, 2010.

53. Lawrence, *The Seeds of Disaster*, 254; Lapchick, *The Politics of Race and International Sport*, 69; also, Trevor Richards, *Dancing On Our Bones—New Zealand, South Africa Rugby and Racism* (Wellington, New Zealand: Bridget Williams Books, 1999).

54. Lawrence, *The Seeds of Disaster*, 256–257.

55. Ibid., 264.

56. Minutes of the meeting of the IOC Executive Board, Innsbruck, January 25–26, 1964, ABC, box 88.

57. Leiss, *Apartheid and United Nations*.

58. Meeting of IOC Executive Board with delegates of the National Olympic Committees, Teheran, May 3, 1967, ABC, box 93, IOC archives.

59. Ibid.

60. Ibid., Appendix A, Annex 3.

61. Ibid.

62. Ibid.

63. Report of the IOC Commission on South Africa, 1967.

64. Ibid.

65. *Hansard Report*, April 11, 1967, columns 3959–3964. This may be found in Appendix L of the IOC Commission Report in ABC, box 88, and IOC Commission Report, documents—interviews, telegrams, notes, IOC archives.

66. *Hansard Report*, April 11, 1967.

67. Ibid.

68. Ibid.

69. *The Star*, September 16, 1961.

70. Testimony to IOC Commission on South Africa, Lausanne, November 25, 1967.

71. Letter, Vorster to an unidentified Indian, August 8, 1967, IOC Commission Report—interviews, telegrams, notes, IOC archives.

72. IOC Commission Report.

73. Brian Bunting, *The Rise of the South African Reich* (Middlesex, UK: Penguin Books, 1964).

74. Charges against SANOC addressed to the IOC presented by the National Olympic committees at the general assembly of the Supreme Council for Sport in Africa, Cairo, March 24–26, 1970. See IOC Report, ABC, box 88,. On the grounds of racial discrimination, the South African Amateur Weightlifting Association ought to have been suspended, said SAN-ROC. In 1966, South Africa's Weightlifting Association supported the idea of separate associations for whites and nonwhites, which was contrary to Olympic principles. Moreover, nonwhite weightlifters were barred from South African championships. Nonwhites were never included in South Africa's Olympic team or in the world championships. Precious's Patrick McKenzie, a nonwhite weightlifter, informed the IOC Commission that he had to emigrate to Great Britain to compete on equal terms with white South Africans. See his statement to the commission, November 25, 1967, presented in Lausanne, IOC archives. Dennis Brutus requested the international swimming governing body (FINA) repudiate its recognition of the South African Amateur Swimming Union, which SAN-ROC characterized as a "racist body." *Bulawayo Chronicle*, September 30, 1967.

75. Letter, Brundage to Killanin, August 8, 1967, IOC Report, IOC archives.
76. *Natal Daily Mail*, September 13, 1967.
77. Statement presented by the South African delegation to the IOC meeting in Grenoble, February 3, 1968, IOC archives.
78. Ibid.
79. SAN-ROC news and views (mimeographed). Correspondence of SAN-ROC, 1964–68, IOC archives.
80. Basil D'Oliveira, *The D'Oliveira Affair* (London: Collins, 1968).
81. Lapchick, *The Politics of Race*, 127.
82. Ibid.
83. D'Oliveira, *The D'Oliveira Affair*, 15.
84. Basil D'Oliveira obituary, *New York Times*, November 27, 2011. In 1967, 1968, 1969 the anti-apartheid campaign picked up steam in Australia, Denmark, Norway, Sweden, and Holland. See Peter Hain, *"Don't Play with Apartheid"—The Background to the Stop the Seventy Tour Campaign*, (London: George Allen and Unwin Ltd., 1971), pp. 110–111.
85. SAN-ROC correspondence, March 20, 1968, IOC archives.
86. Lapchick, *The Politics of Race*, 185.
87. Minutes of the executive board of the IOC, Lausanne, April 20–21, 1968, ABC, box 93. The general public and press in the United States and in the United Kingdom were predictably split on the expulsion. One sarcastic letter writer congratulated the secretary general of the IOC for obeying the wishes of the "totalitarian regime in a communist Russia" and asked that the Olympic Games be renamed the "Wishes of the Communists Games." Geoffrey Riddell, April 28, 1968. A Californian said the expulsion of South Africa signified "another stunning victory for the communist conspiracy." Letter, Ralph Russell to IOC, April 25, 1968. Reactions of the general public and press, 1968, IOC archives.
88. Letter, J. W. Westerhoff to Ramirez-Vasquez, May 3, 1968, IOC correspondence with Cojo de Mexico. Ramirez-Vasquez, a very prominent Mexican architect, designed, among other monuments, the National Museum of Anthropology and the Basilica of Guadalupe. In the Olympic records, he is sometimes referred to as Arquitecto Ramirez. Obituary, *New York Times*, April 18, 2013.
89. Letter, Gusaran S. Sehmi of the Kenya Olympic and Commonwealth Games Association to Ramirez-Vasquez, May 9, 1968, IOC archives.
90. Letter, Brundage to Reginald Honey, July 13, 1968, ABC, box 93.
91. *Sunday Times*, October 3, 1968.
92. Ibid.
93. Ibid.
94. Richard E. Lapchick, "The Olympic Movement and Racism: Analysis in Historical Perspective," *Africa Today: Racism in Sport*, vol. 17, no. 6 (November–December 1970), 16; the *Guardian*, May 16, 1970.
95. South African President, F. W. de Klerk was a joint recipient of the prize for the "peaceful termination of the apartheid regime and for laying the foundation for a new democratic South Africa."
96. *Providence Journal*, December 11, 2013; Tom Lodge, *Mandela: A Critical Life*, (Oxford, Oxford University Press, 2006).

6

UDI and the Expulsion of Rhodesia from the Olympic Movement

The crusade against the Nazis, the Italian Fascists, and the Japanese imperialists between 1939 and 1945 left European colonial powers—Britain, France, Holland, and Belgium—economically prostrate. Inevitably, their grip on their possessions in Asia and Africa were loosened. Political freedom came first to the Indian subcontinent and then to places such as Malaysia, Indonesia, and French Indochina. By the 1950s, Africans were increasingly restive under the colonial yoke. The Gold Coast, led by Kwame Nkrumah, became independent of Great Britain as Ghana in 1956. Other British dependencies quickly achieved statehood. Francophone North Africa, Madagascar, and the constituent colonies of French Equatorial Africa and French West Africa followed suit.

In some cases, the transitions to African independence came peacefully. In other cases, Kenya, Algeria, and the Belgian Congo, for example, the path to nationhood was violent. Where mineral wealth, fertile land, or the privileges of a sizable white presence, *uhuru* (freedom), as it was called in Swahili, meant decolonization would likely come about through armed conflict.[1] Such was the case with Rhodesia, formerly Southern Rhodesia, which today is under black rule as Zimbabwe.

As the winds of change blew through the "dark continent" in the post–World War II era, the modern Olympic movement was forced to confront a race-fueled dilemma in Rhodesia, part of the continent's white-dominated redoubt. Named for the imperialist colossus Cecil John Rhodes, Rhodesia's race policies were to lead to a major international donnybrook in global politics and in the Olympic world.

Born in England in 1853, Rhodes, plagued by illness as a young man, emigrated to South Africa at the age of seventeen. Possessed of unbridled ambition and considerable entrepreneurial gifts, he quickly made a fortune in diamonds. Before he was thirty years old, Rhodes was a millionaire. His vehicle for further enrichment was the DeBeers Mining Company, which earned him another fortune in gold mining.

An associate and biographer of Rhodes described him as "morose," "overbearing," and a "good hater." A confirmed bachelor, he was clearly misogynistic. Rhodes, who died in 1902, was also a racist. In the age of the European scramble for Africa, he was the embodiment of imperialism. To achieve his goals, he fomented friction between the Matabele and the Mashona, each of whom desired hegemony in what came to be called "Rhodesia" in his honor. In 1886 and 1887, Rhodesian whites with the armed might of the British Empire behind them overcame the violent resistance of those two peoples.

Beginning in the late 1880s the minions of Rhodes were able to win mineral and metal concessions. They employed trickery to obtain choice land from gullible African chiefs. For twenty-five years, starting in 1889, Rhodes's British South Africa Company ruled Rhodesia in much the same way that another private corporation, the British East Indian Company, had long ruled the subcontinent of India.[2]

Rhodes's power was such that he became the prime minister of the Cape Colony and dreamed of adding Nyasaland (now Malawi) and Northern Rhodesia (now Zambia), areas farther north, as part of the burgeoning British Empire. Rhodes considered the British superior to other peoples, and, in his megalomaniacal fantasies, the empire could and should include all of Africa, some of the Middle East, chunks of South America, and swaths of Asia. Even the recovery of the United States may have been contemplated in his most delusional moments. He is alleged to have said that he would annex the planets if he could.

In 1922, Southern Rhodesia had become a self-governing colony under the British crown. Thirty years later, it was joined with copper-rich Northern Rhodesia and with Nyasaland to form the Central African Federation. White pioneers, many from South Africa, had begun to trek to the area between the Limpopo and Zambezi Rivers, even before the dawn of the twentieth century. They gravitated toward the healthiest regions with the most agreeable climate. Whites appropriated the most arable land. This often necessitated displacing the indigenous African population.

To keep the blacks in their place, literally and figuratively, a rigid color ban was established. In his *Inside Africa*, published in 1953, John

Gunther, the peripatetic and indefatigable American reporter, opined that "segregation is more pronounced in the Rhodesias than anywhere else in Africa. . . . [R]acial discriminations in Rhodesia are among the most barbarous, shameful, and disgusting in the world."[3] That harsh racism would be the crux of Rhodesia's Olympic difficulties.

Self-government, albeit under white minority rule, was the reality brought about by the formation of the Central African Federation. Foreign affairs for Rhodesia remained in the hands of the Parliament at Westminster.

In the 1960s, white Rhodesian politics veered right, a trajectory similar to that followed by the Afrikaners in South Africa, which became a republic in 1961. This trend was pronounced under Roy Welensky, the "Architect of Federation." Half Lithuanian Jew and half Boer, Welensky, a former boxer, witnessed the disintegration of the federation in 1963.[4]

Ian Douglas Smith and his Rhodesian Front, a party that represented white supremacy, came to power determined to resist African demands at all costs. The latter were essentially organized along tribal lines, ZANU for the Shona and ZAPU for the Matabele. Under critical pressure from London, Smith set his sights on a severing of ties with the Mother Country, "Perfidious Albion," as Smith dubbed it.

Smith became prime minister in April 1964. He had been born and raised in Selukwe, Rhodesia, in 1919 and educated at Rhodes University in South Africa. The first white prime minister born in Rhodesia, he was destined to be the last.

Smith had fought valiantly in the British armed forces during World War II. Twice he was shot down, grievously wounded and, as a consequence, disfigured. After the war, he did a stint as a farmer before entering politics, promising to lead his country, Rhodesia, to independence from Britain. "Good Old Smitty" to his admirers, he was the Africans' nemesis. In his dealings with Prime Minister Harold Wilson, Smith was unmovable on the matter of expanding the rights of black populations. Of the African nationalists, Smith was openly contemptuous. Courteous and humble, colorless and introverted, Smith was underrated by many, but his lack of pomposity and pretentiousness made him popular with his constituents. A white adversary once quipped that his modesty was well deserved.[5]

Wilson, a Yorkshireman by birth, a one-time academic, and, after 1963, leader of the Labor Party, moved into number 10 Downing Street as prime minister for the first time in 1964. Smith viewed the portly, pipe-smoking Wilson with disdain. The feeling was mutual.

Smith, like Welensky and many white politicians, saw the hand of the Soviet Union behind African Nationalism, which he equated with Communism and terrorism. Repressive security laws were necessary in his opinion. Smith and his ilk talked of a partnership between the races. What he truly had in mind was the kind of partnership that exists between a horse and a rider. An equitable distribution of land was out of the question as was one man, one vote at the ballot box. Africans had had no say in the creation of the federation. They would have no say in a Rhodesia separate from Britain. Smith prophesied that black rule would not come for a millennium. Perhaps he did not realize that Adolf Hitler, against whom he had courageously waged war and nearly sacrificed his life, had predicted that his Third Reich would last a thousand years. The Führer was off by 988 years. Smith was proven wrong by 1979.

In November 1965, livid over sanctions imposed by the United Nations and chagrined that their "kith and kin" in Britain appeared to share Wilson's hostility to the secessionist regime in Salisbury, Smith and his followers opted for a Unilateral Declaration of Independence (UDI).

At the time of UDI, Rhodesian whites numbered approximately a quarter of a million souls constituting a mere 5 percent of the overall population. Three-fourths of European inhabitants were recent arrivals having entered Rhodesia in the previous two decades, many from South Africa. One out of every four whites had immigrated in the preceding ten years.[6] They were rightfully called "settlers" by the native blacks, who were five million strong and increasing at a rate triple that of the whites. Demographically dwarfed by the Africans, the white community, led by Smith, dug in its heels. With UDI, they had crossed the Rubicon. Much was at stake.

For the most part, whites lived the good life in Rhodesia. Poverty among them was very uncommon. Whites doing menial labor were rare. The percentage of Caucasian home and car ownership was among the highest in the world. Swimming pools could be found in profusion. Even those whites with a somewhat limited income could afford servants because cheap black labor was plentiful. Black maids and gardeners earned a pittance, were considered perks, and not infrequently were abused physically and verbally. Derogatory racial terms such as "coon" were part of the white vocabulary and used freely. This scenario was not unlike that found in ante-bellum and post-bellum southern culture in the United States. Reluctance to give up such a privileged lifestyle made white Rhodesians most adamant about sharing power, political rights, and land.[7]

Viewed through the European racial prism, Africans were primitive, uncivilized, and incapable of self-government. White tutelage was imperative for black progress. Because of their racism and ethnocentrism, many Rhodesians could not bring themselves to see the Great Zimbabwe ruins as the work of indigenous Bantu. The ruins, some of which date back to the eleventh century, consisted of structures with huge walls seventeen feet thick and twenty-four feet high. Located near Fort Victoria, the ruins cover more than sixty acres of ground dominated by a rocky hill with massive walling known as the Acropolis. Stone buildings called Zimbabwes, dwellings of chiefs, had been skillfully erected. Soapstone animal sculptures, especially of birds, added to the wonder and mystery of the site.[8]

Rhodesian whites insisted that the Great Zimbabwe was the workmanship of the Phoenicians or Portuguese, any people other than the indigenous blacks. They were even linked with the fabled King Solomon's mines. In its publications, Rhodesia's National Tourist Board said nary a word about the Bantu provenance of the Great Zimbabwe, Gertrude Caton-Thompson notwithstanding. As early as 1929, Caton-Thompson, a highly respected British archeologist concluded on the basis of her excavations that the Bantu did indeed deserve credit for the Great Zimbabwe, the remarkable ruins in southern Africa. For the Smith government, this interpretation was fraught with danger. It was no surprise that Zimbabwe was selected as the name of the new African nation that replaced Rhodesia named for the white imperialist.[9]

For the large black majority, life under Ian Smith's rule left a great deal to be desired. The economy, the society, and the political systems were patently unfair. The tiny minority of whites ran the government, national and local. Qualifications for exercising the franchise disfranchised most of the Africans. Courts and the military were controlled by whites. Schools were Jim Crowed. The European community received as much of the state education budget as the 95 percent that were black. Twelve times as much money was appropriated for each Caucasian child as for each African child. The rationale for this iniquitous practice was that whites furnished the lion's share of the revenue, but, of course, white wealth was made possible by the miserably paid, arduous, and often backbreaking toil of blacks. Black ownership of the land was proscribed in half of the country. Thousands of Africans were forcibly relocated to preserve white domains.[10]

For much of Rhodesia's history, Africans were acutely aware that they had been conquered by the "Pioneer" whites, and they evinced a sense of inferiority. Their stance vis-à-vis Caucasians was one of subservience. Passing whites on the street, African men doffed their hats as their black counterparts had done in the Southern United States. However, by the critical decade of the 1960s, a generation of African nationalists, dissatisfied, angry, disobedient, bold, and proud, had come to the fore, demanding enfranchisement and a fair share of the country's fertile land. They were determined to bring about change that would create a just society. Smith was no less determined to obstruct change. By maintaining a severe security system, African goals would be thwarted. In Smith's eyes, "self-preservation was the first law of nature."[11]

Unable to bring about meaningful change through peaceable methods, some Africans resorted to violence. Coexistence based on the equality of the races was unthinkable to Smith and his Rhodesian Front. Guerrilla war and bloodshed were made inevitable.

On the very day that Smith and his cabinet severed ties with Britain, he said, "[W]e have struck a blow for justice, civilization, and Christianity and in the spirit of this belief we have this day assumed our Sovereign Independence. God bless you all."[12] Needless to say, "all" did not include the blacks, especially those who were already engaged in armed struggle.

It was November 11, 1965, when the white-dominated government in Rhodesia, led by Smith, unilaterally declared itself independent of Great Britain. Only once before had such a declaration been issued—on July 4, 1776. The 1776 declaration was described by Wilson, the British prime minister, as "one of the historic documents of human freedom."

Few would disagree with the description. Though the similarities of the two cases of UDI are superficial, the Smith government fully exploited the apparent historical parallel to its own advantage. Indeed, the Rhodesian proclamation of independence was shrewdly phrased to be reminiscent of the American Declaration of Independence. The result was somewhat unfortunate for those who believe in the dignity of man, black and white. Not only in Rhodesia itself, but in Great Britain and in the United States, the erroneous and misleading idea was credited that the settlers in Rhodesia were merely following the laudable American precedent of 1776. To accept this idea is to ignore crucial differences between the two rebellions and the two declarations of independence.

Historians have given numerous political, economic, and even religious explanations for the American Revolution. None, however, has suggested that either black-white or Native American–white relations were at issue in 1776. Great Britain was not acting in the interests of blacks or Native Americans in opposing the revolution. The Proclamation of 1763 reserving most land west of the Appalachians for Native Americans had exacerbated feelings between the British and the colonists, especially those in the West. However, the "Indian problem" did not materially contribute to the revolutionary fervor. Although England had abolished slavery by judicial decision in 1772 and abolitionist sentiment was growing in the colonies, in neither place was the African American regarded as fully human.

The deletion from the Declaration of Independence of Thomas Jefferson's indictment of George III for fostering slave trade points up the lack of agreement in America on the "Negro" question.[13] Therefore, while it is true that the American demand for self-determination was not voiced with the black and Native American minorities in mind, it is equally true that the demand was not made, despite those minorities. In fact, black troops played an important role in winning independence for the United States.[14]

The race question, on the other hand, is the heart of the problem in Rhodesia. The Rhodesians dissolved their political bonds with Great Britain to preserve a system firmly based on white supremacy. At the end of the nineteenth century, the "Pioneer Column" had assured white control of Rhodesia through collusion and force. Ever since, the bulk of the blacks had been hewers of wood and drawers of water. They had been segregated in "native" townships, and the least desirable areas in their own motherland had been allocated to them. The ballot had been denied to all but a select few, and successive African nationalist organizations had been forbidden. It is, therefore, preposterous to claim, as the white Rhodesians had in their proclamation of independence, "that the people of Rhodesia fully support the request of their Government for sovereign independence." It is abundantly plain that the Smith-led government represented a tiny minority of the population found between the Zambezi and the Limpopo.

Given the refusal of the Europeans to hold a free election in which the Africans would participate, it is difficult to accurately gauge the popularity of UDI. One can reasonably assume, however, that Smith spoke only for the majority of the 220,000 whites and a handful of tribal chiefs appointed and paid by the government. It should also be noted that there was a small group of moderate whites, silenced by the government, who opposed the rebellion.

In vivid contrast to the unrepresentative character of the Smith regime is the judgment of historians on the American Revolution. Estimates of the "patriot" strength vary, but there is general agreement that the revolution commanded the active support of at least one-third and perhaps as much as one-half of the population. An additional third was neutral.

Thomas Jefferson, as author of the Declaration of Independence, felt that a "decent respect to the opinions of mankind" required a declaration of the causes that impelled the colonies to the separation. As paraphrased by the Rhodesians, the proclamation of November 11 reads as follows: "[A] respect for the opinions of mankind requires them to declare to other nations the causes which impel them to assume full responsibility for their own affairs." The striking similarity in the phraseology of the two statements notwithstanding, the responses of other nations to the American Revolution and the Rhodesian rebellion were markedly different.

As every student of American history knows, France and the United States signed treaties of alliance and commerce, and France entered the war in 1778 without a formal declaration. Spain and Holland also allied themselves with the Americans. The League of Armed Neutrality, formed at the instigation of Russia, was clearly friendly and sympathetic to the American cause.[15] Much of the international support given America during the revolution was unquestionably based on diplomatic and not moral considerations. Nevertheless, the fact is that the mother country and not the United States was the pariah in the international community in our War of Independence.

Just the opposite was the case in the Rhodesian crisis. It was the unrepresentative, rebel regime that outraged the civilized world. On October 12, 1965, 107 nations in the United Nations General Assembly, in a nearly unanimous expression of world opinion, criticized the impending UDI. On November 12, the day after UDI, the isolation of Rhodesia's white minority was underscored. Ten of the eleven members of the Security Council condemned the UDI made by a racist minority in Rhodesia. France abstained on the grounds that the dispute was not an international issue. In the squabble over Rhodesia, only South Africa and Portugal sided with the white settlers. If these settlers had truly had "a respect for the opinions of mankind," there would not have been a declaration of independence.

The difference between the position taken by the mother country in 1776 and that taken by Great Britain on the Rhodesian question is also noteworthy. Whereas in 1776 a concession of independence to the colonies was unthinkable, the necessity of granting independence to Rhodesia had been repeatedly acknowledged by Her Majesty's Government. After 1776, the British Empire in the Americas was partially dismembered. Interest in empire flagged. Yet, a second British Empire was created largely in Africa at the end of the nineteenth century. It, too, disintegrated after World War II, which had weakened the imperial powers.

The principle of self-determination for which the Americans fought in 1776 has been translated into *uhuru* by black Africans fighting to be free of colonial rule. Quite obviously, 1965 and 1776 are worlds apart, and Harold Wilson was not Lord North. The question in the Rhodesian crisis was not "should independence be granted," but rather "independence for whom and under what conditions." Great Britain maintained that independence would be granted if there were sufficient guarantees that political power would, in time, be transferred to the African majority.

Conspicuous by their absence from the Rhodesian proclamation of independence were those ideological assertions, "those self-evident truths," that give the American declaration its historic import. Nowhere in the November 11 decree was it stated that "all men are created equal, that they are endowed by their Creator with certain unalienable Rights, that Among these are Life, Liberty, and the pursuit of Happiness."[16] Such phrases would have had a hollow ring coming from a land where the idea of the inherent inequality of races had been translated into law and the desire to maintain social, economic, and political privileges for the European minority actually prompted the revolution. Nowhere in the Rhodesian proclamation was it stated that governments derive their just powers from the consent of the governed. Such words would sound strange coming from a government that had systematically denied Africans the franchise and had restricted the civil liberties of the entire population.

The truth is that Rhodesia was a police state. The press had been muzzled, and radio listening had been curbed. Opposition to the regime had been met with detention and imprisonment without trial. Ostensibly, even the Rhodesian government, which flouted world opinion and callously ignored the wishes of the majority of its population, was not rash enough to invoke the political philosophy of Locke and Jefferson, which have so changed the course of history.

It can be argued that the "natural" rights claimed in 1776 were not extended to Negroes then. This is unjustifiable from a moral standpoint, if not from an historical one. On both sides of the Atlantic, the African was regarded as primitive, probably uneducable, and certainly inherently inferior to the white man. How much less justifiable and less tenable were such views in the world of the 1960s by which time anthropologists had conclusively rejected the racial myths of earlier centuries? For the whites, some of whom had been in Rhodesia only since the end of World War II, to deny these natural rights to the Rhodesian blacks, many of whose ancestors were in southern Africa by the eleventh century, was indeed the height of cultural arrogance.

Still another difference between the declarations of independence of 1776 and 1965 can be found in the attitudes of the rebels toward the English crown. The American declaration, in its final form, did not contain the word "Parliament." Implicit in the document was the claim that colonists were not then and probably never had been subject to Parliament. It was a voluntary allegiance to the king that connected America with the empire. A contract existed between the colonies and the king. The abrogation of that contract was necessitated by a tyrannical king whose history was the history of "repeated injuries and usurpations." These were duly enumerated in Jefferson's declaration.

The Rhodesians, on the other hand, wanted there to be no doubt that they stood second to none in their loyalty to the queen. Their proclamation of independence ended with the words "God Save the Queen!" It was their intention to continue to fly the Union Jack and to continue to sing the national anthem. They persisted in professing their unswerving loyalty to the queen, even after having ousted her representative, the governor, Sir Humphrey Gibbs. The defiant actions of Ian Smith and his racist colleagues virtually drove one to the conclusion that their professions of loyalty were not directed to the present monarch. What they appeared to ignore is the obvious fact that it was Elizabeth II who reigned and not Victoria. The same lack of historical perspective enabled them to identify their rebellion with that of the Americans two centuries earlier. But the basic issues in the Rhodesian rebellion have no exact historical parallel, not in the Victorian era, not even in the reign of George III.

Perhaps the closest historical parallel to UDI in the Victorian era can be found in events that occurred across the Atlantic in February 1861, when disgruntled Southerners were fearful that the newly elected president, Abraham Lincoln, jeopardized the continuing power of the slaveocracy. In Montgomery, Alabama, they brought into being the Confederate States of America and declared themselves independent of the United States. Their secession ushered in four years of horrific bloodletting, the upshot of which would be the cleansing of the sin of slavery.

Jefferson Davis, a senator from Mississippi, was elected president of the Confederacy. He and his allies saw their efforts as laudably analogous to those of the Founding Fathers.[17] The Confederacy ended in April 1865, after approximately 620,000 lives, maybe more, were forfeited in America's Civil War. Both Ian Smith and Jefferson Davis have been consigned to the scrap heap of history. Whereas the vanquished Confederate states were readmitted into the federal union, within a few years, Rhodesia became independent, but this time under black majority rule.

Not surprisingly, the Soviet bloc, many Western European countries, and the developing states of Africa and Asia were generally unfavorably disposed toward Rhodesia. Mustering support for their cause was deemed essential by the embattled white regime. To that end, some self-styled "patriotic" members of the US Congress, all hardcore conservatives, formed the American-Southern African Council. Their stated purpose was to aid Rhodesia's fight against "Communist aggression." They feared an American military invasion on behalf of the black Marxists at the very time the United States was battling "Communists" in Vietnam. Their stern warning was that the "destruction of anti-communist Southern Africa is a primary objective of the Liberal Red establishment." In this effort, they were aided supposedly, encouraged, and financed by the United Nations and, incredible as it sounds today, by the US State Department.[18]

Strategically, they insisted Rhodesia is the key to Southern Africa: "If this valiant nation falls, every nation will follow swiftly." The Communists had made Rhodesia their number one target, the group declared in a pamphlet dripping with paranoia. White civilization hung in the balance. Chaos and anarchy loomed. They talked of white Rhodesia's rightful heritage. About the Africans' rightful heritage there was a deafening silence. Racism and eagerness to have ready access to mineral resources, especially chrome, clearly provided the underpinnings of the foregoing.[19]

As far as the Olympics were concerned, the Rhodesian quandary manifested itself even before UDI. The National Olympic Committee of Rhodesia had been a constituent part of the National Olympic Committee of the Federation of Rhodesia and Nyasaland. With the breakup of the federation, the national Olympic committees of Malawi and

Zambia, the former Nyasaland and Northern Rhodesia, respectively, were recognized in their own right. Rhodesia's NOC had no need to ask for additional recognition. Because, as Monique Berlioux, the director of information for the IOC, pointed out, since the NOC of the federation had been recognized in 1959 and its status confirmed four years later, Southern Rhodesia was already a bona fide member of the IOC. In other words, it had been grandfathered in.[20]

Many fledgling African states took strong exception to Berlioux's interpretation, and they were troubled by the likelihood that the Salisbury government would send a team to compete in the 1964 Tokyo Games. A crisis threatened, but a compromise was reached. Southern Rhodesia could participate with caveats. They had to compete under the Union Jack, that is, the British flag, and the British anthem, that is, "God Save the Queen." The compromise satisfied no one and did not bode well for future Olympics.

Rhodesians were cautiously optimistic about the Mexico City Games, but the UN sanctions imposed in 1966 were to prove an insurmountable obstacle. Efforts were already underway to marginalize Rhodesia from the sports universe. Demonstrations were organized in Sweden in early May 1968 to prevent a Davis Cup tennis match between the Rhodesians and the Swedes.[21] The demonstrators turned violent, and they succeeded. Then, on May 29, the UN Security Council unanimously passed a strongly worded, comprehensive resolution calling on all members of the world body to refuse admittance to Rhodesian passport holders. Aviation companies were not to operate flights into and out of Rhodesia, which the Security Council called an illegal regime.[22]

A crestfallen Avery Brundage requested the Mexican Organizing Committee issue a statement deploring the fact that the UN resolutions had made it impossible for Rhodesia to compete in Mexico City, although it had been officially invited to do so. Rhodesian citizens could not cross borders. Consequently, they could not make their way to Mexico. Rhodesia had air transportation; however, most countries would not allow them to land.[23] Both Brundage and the Marquess of Exeter saw this as gross political interference in sport. Nevertheless, they were helpless to alter the reality.

Rhodesia's team, an interracial one, had already been selected. A complete list of competitors had been forwarded to the Mexican capital city. However, in accordance with the Security Council resolutions, Mexico had not sent visas or identity cards. In June, Brundage asked the Mexican Organizing Committee to make a public statement that Rhodesia had clearly been invited and that "it deeply deplored the fact that owing to the UN they would not be able to participate in the Games."[24] Vasquez Ramirez hesitated. The committee refused to act precipitously, but it is clear that it was unwilling to defy the United Nations or to alienate the IOC. Consequently, it equivocated. In a letter dated August 9, it stated that it continued to bear in mind the promise of receiving in Mexico all teams recognized by the IOC.[25] At the same time, it stated that Mexico, as a member of the United Nations, would be happy if the Rhodesian team did not take part in the Games as Rhodesia had been excluded from the family of nations, but they were so committed to the organization of the Olympic Games that they did not want to be involved in solving world problems.[26]

Mexico's intentions were unclear. The language of the letter was nebulous and contradictory, and probably deliberately so. It sought to put blame for the dilemma squarely on the shoulders of the United Nations. They ignored Brundage's entreaty to Vasquez Ramirez to see to it that the Rhodesians received the requisite entry forms and identity cards. It was a rare instance in which Brundage had been foiled.[27]

One writer who championed the Rhodesian Olympic cause observed that, "Political interference into the affairs of sport had reached an all-time high. The sacred Olympic truce had been violated." Another battle lay ahead in Munich.[28]

Given their defeat in 1968, what were Rhodesia's prospects in that Bavarian city four years hence? In January 1971, a detailed questionnaire was sent by the International Amateur Athletic Federation to the Rhodesian Amateur Athletic Union (RAAU) to ascertain the precise racial conditions that existed in Rhodesian sports. A reply authored by Eric P. Shore, president of the RAAU, was received in short order. Its major points were that all of the Rhodesian teams in *international competition* were racially mixed. Indeed, "our entire sport is run on multi-racial lines." White clubs did not reject black members, and black clubs welcomed whites, Shore insisted. Athletes competed on a nonracial basis.[29]

The Rhodesian Amateur Athletic Union itself was multiracial. Likewise, coaching and training facilities were open to all, regardless of pigmentation. Africans and whites competed on equal terms at national championships, where there were no racial distinctions. It categorically denied that Rhodesian sports were monochromatic as charged. Among those wearing Rhodesian uniforms, blacks outnumbered whites, it was claimed. In summary, the Rhodesians asserted unequivocally and somewhat disingenuously, "We do not play at multi-racialism or pay lip service to the multi-racial theme in our sport in this country."[30]

Of course, many interpreted this statement as self-serving and deliberately deceptive. It shaded the truth. The Supreme Council for Sport in Africa was most skeptical. Not surprising, in contrast, at the IOC, the statement was received unquestioningly. Writing to Brundage, Lord David Burleigh, the Marquess of Exeter, endorsed the Rhodesian International Amateur Athletic Federation, stating flatly, "[T]here is no discrimination in sport in Rhodesia." But he recommended that a top-level commission of inquiry be sent to Salisbury. In his opinion, this was "monstrous" but necessary. He compared it to saying to "some citizen whom you have no evidence to believe has been guilty of stealing, that in spite of this you are going to send him to Court to be examined in case he has."[31]

Burleigh reiterated that Rhodesian sportsmen had taken part in previous Olympics.[32] On that basis, the IOC had told the Mexicans to extend an invitation to Rhodesia for 1964 in its own right. The notion that Rhodesia was to be treated as a British colony was specifically rejected. The British consulate general in Munich took the diametrically opposite position, stating that "constitutionally Southern Rhodesia is one of Her Majesty's Dominions and a dependent Territory."[33] From the standpoint of the British government, Rhodesia was in a state of rebellion. It was even guilty of treason.

Momentum to exclude Rhodesia from Munich built up in the early 1970s. Newly independent African nations were flexing their muscles on colonial issues. Brundage was apprehensive that Rhodesia would be barred from the All-Africa Games slated for Lagos in 1973. He had been assured that all national Olympic committees recognized by the IOC would be included, but there was the stipulation that only countries deemed to be independent would be invited. Thus, Rhodesia would be disqualified. Brundage believed that such a disqualification could be chalked up to pure politics.[34]

At a meeting of the IOC Executive Board, with seventy-two NOCs in attendance, which took place in Munich in September 1971, Brundage stated that as far as he understood the situation, the Rhodesian National Olympic Committee had complied with relevant Olympic regulations. He recommended that sportsmen from Rhodesia travel with a British passport or with Olympic identification. The African representatives pointed out that no country in the world had recognized the Rhodesian government. Therefore, the Rhodesian Olympic Committee had no

146

standing. Brundage retorted that he was uninterested in what governments did; so long as the Rhodesian NOC conformed to Olympic rules, it should be permitted to participate.[35]

Returning to an old, failed formula, Brundage told the executive board that if Rhodesians carried the British flag with the Southern Rhodesian coat of arms on a royal blue field and used the British anthem, the Africans would not object. Such an arrangement would be acceptable to the Africans on one condition: a commission would investigate Rhodesia following the Munich Games. This was acceptable to the Rhodesians. An article was read to the board arguing that discrimination in sports did not exist in Rhodesia. Rhodesia was invited to take part in the Munich extravaganza, but more problems soon emerged.[36]

The National Olympic Committees of Africa wanted to make sure that "British Subject" would be entered under "Nationality" on identification cards and specified that it had to be clearly understood that Southern Rhodesia participated as a "British colony." They rued the fact that the British passports had not materialized and feared that the Rhodesians were being given temporary nationality by the IOC, a ruse designed to confer on the Rhodesians the recognition the world was eager to deny them. The National Committees quoted the head of the Southern Rhodesian delegation, who, on his arrival in Munich, stated the following: "[W]e are ready to participate under any flag be it the flag of the Boy Scouts or the Moscow flag. But everyone knows very well that we are Rhodesians and will always be Rhodesians."[37]

Furthermore, the National Committees condemned in particular the use of the name "Rhodesia" rather than the designation "Southern Rhodesia" on their equipment and uniform. Without the British passports identifying them as citizens of the United Kingdom and colonies, the Rhodesian team members were to be disentitled to be in the Munich Games. For the time being, the Africans requested the exclusion of the Southern Rhodesian team and the establishment of a commission of inquiry into charges of racial discrimination in sports in Southern Rhodesia. They were clearly determined to prevent Southern Rhodesia entry into the XX Olympiad by the back door, for to do otherwise would be to imply acceptance of UDI.

In assessing the situation in Rhodesia in the aftermath of Munich, the National Olympic Committees insisted that the NOC of Rhodesia was not independent of the Smith government in applying policies of racial bias and segregation.[38] It practiced racial discrimination against African sportsmen. It disallowed multiracial competition and failed to guarantee the equality of training facilities and installations for the practice of sport. Restrictive rules governing the operation of private clubs with respect to membership and the use of athletic facilities excluded blacks. To buttress their charges, the African Olympic committees indicated that several international sporting federations had acted against Rhodesia because of its racism from 1971 to 1975. For example, the Rhodesian Boxing Association had been expelled in 1972 and the Rhodesian Swimming Association in 1973. International bodies suspended the Football Association of Rhodesia and the Rhodesian Amateur Athletic Association.[39]

In May 1971, Brundage had been informed by A. A. Ordia, secretary general of the Nigerian Olympic Committee, that racism was increasingly practiced in Rhodesia, particularly in sport. Recent legislation limited parks and sports facilities therein to Europeans. Ordia underlined the reality that there was "strict racialist exclusion of non-whites from public swimming pools."[40]

A decision by the chief justice of Rhodesia, Sir Hugh Beadle, incidentally a supporter of UDI, had previously held that swimming pools could not remain segregated. It was greeted with ripples of anger on the part of the Europeans, who ignored it. Sharing water with blacks was taboo for them.[41]

Badminton, rugby, and hockey were completely segregated.[42] Many sports were played at the club level, and white clubs routinely barred nonwhites. It was government policy not to interfere in sport in any manner, the Rhodesian foreign minister told the IOC visiting commission at a meeting. If some people wanted exclusive clubs, that was their business.[43]

Clearly Rhodesia was a highly segregated land. Sports and politics were inextricably bound up with one another. There was only a handful of multiracial hotels, and law dictated four separate toilet facilities: for Europeans, racially mixed Coloureds, Asians, and Africans. Public school athletics were not racially integrated. An exception was soccer, where Africans excelled and were able to raise the level of competition.[44]

To deflect criticism, Rhodesia fielded multiracial teams in competitions beyond the country's borders. Illustrative of this was the fact that the majority of Rhodesian competitors in the Mozambique Games had been black.[45] Rhodesia also planned to send a racially mixed team, including several outstanding African runners, to Munich when domestic sports were still racially separate.

On August 19, 1972, with the Munich Games right around the corner, Clifford Buck met with spokespersons for the agitated American track-and-field athletes, some black, some white. A candid discussion took place and ended with an understanding that the entire US men's track-and-field squad would formulate a position. The following day, they drew up a statement that explained their feelings. The team expressed its concern about Rhodesian racism. In its position paper, the American athletes stated, "[T]he IOC principles of free and unrestricted participation of athletes within and among nations is sound. This, however, is not being allowed among athletes competing in S. Rhodesia."[46]

Racial practices had not been mitigated by the decision to allow the Rhodesian contingent to play under the British flag. Reexamination of that decision was warranted, but the American athletes' hope was that the Rhodesians would voluntarily withdraw. If they refused, the IOC ought to reverse its position authorizing their participation. Eliminating the Rhodesian team would "free the Olympic athletes of the moral and political decision presently confronting them" and enable them "to join all other athletes in the free spirit of Olympic competition."[47]

Strong antipathy to Rhodesia was also voiced by Dennis Brutus, the South African activist who spearheaded the campaigns against both South Africa and Rhodesia in Olympic sports. SAN-ROC sent a cable to Lausanne on August 8, 1972, explicitly requesting that the bid to the "racist Rhodesian regime" be nullified.[48]

Also in August, the International Campaign against Racism in Sport, based in Great Britain, called into question the minority Rhodesians' inclusion in the Munich Olympiad. They asked that all "sportsmen who are opposed to racism and especially Black and Asian sportsmen refuse to participate in events in which those drawn from the Rhodesian racist regime are entered." They wanted to "persuade the organizers in Germany, where ironically the great racist festival of sport was held at the time of the Berlin Olympics in 1936, to cancel their invitation to the racists from Rhodesia (Zimbabwe)."[49]

From its headquarters in Cambridge, England, the Zimbabwe Students Union chimed in, lacerating Rhodesia as an international outlaw. At the same time, it took to task the government of West Germany for allowing Rhodesian Olympic athletes, thirty-seven Europeans and seven Africans, to enter their country. Unlike Mexico back in 1968, the Bonn government flouted the Security Council's resolution imposing diplomatic and economic sanctions. West Germany saw fit to accept IOC identity cards, even as Britain continued to withhold British passports. Inasmuch as Rhodesia was a lawless state, an illegal entity, the Zimbabwe students denounced their presence at the XX Olympiad.[50]

West Germany, along with the United States, Japan, France, and Italy, maintained close economic ties with Salisbury. Indeed, West German companies were in the forefront of those undermining the UN sanctions. Harking back to the era of the Nazi games, the Zimbabwe Students Union wrote that they did not want the upcoming Olympiad to become "our Munich agreement that parallels the one signed by Chamberlain in 1938." Prime Minister Neville Chamberlain had famously appeased Hitler by agreeing to the dismemberment of Czechoslovakia. They hoped that "some African leaders will play Churchill and the OAU and friends act like the Allies, Britain, France, USA and USSR, during the Second World War." A failure to unite against Rhodesia in 1972 would embolden Smith, as the 1938 Munich sellout had encouraged the Führer to undertake even more aggressive acts of expansion.[51]

To demonstrate their resolve, the African students wanted the OAU to consider recognition of East Germany. They favored mass rallies against Bonn in Munich, in Africa, in the West Indies, and in the Americas if representatives of Rhodesia somehow managed to compete. As matters turned out, none of these contemplated retaliatory measures were necessary.[52]

For several weeks the Rhodesian athletes in Munich were in limbo. They waited nervously for a final verdict to be reached by the IOC. Back in June, the Rhodesian NOC had furnished the IOC with a list of events in which Rhodesia hoped to compete.[53] They ranged from archery to track and included the javelin, clay pigeon shooting, small bore and pistol shooting, swimming and diving, yachting, and weightlifting. It was not to be.

Seemingly irresistible pressure was exerted on the IOC by African countries individually and as a group through the OAU and its agent, the Supreme Council for Sport in Africa. At the executive board meeting of the IOC (73rd Session) in Munich in September 1972, a cable was read from King Hassan II of Morocco, acting president of the OAU. His Majesty issued an ultimatum. Morocco would withdraw from the games if Rhodesia was included. The organizing committee in Munich had received many threats of withdrawal from African national organizing committees and African ambassadors, as many as twenty-one. A massive boycott was not just possible, but likely.[54]

Chancellor Willy Brandt of West Germany wrote to the IOC pleading the case for saving the Olympics. Brandt's Social Democratic government had been asked by the United Nations whether it would admit

Rhodesia. To do so, would be to violate the UN resolution. Brandt found himself on the horns of a dilemma. West Germany was not yet a member of the United Nations—the war was still a painful memory—but was eager, it said, to promote global solidarity. It was planning to apply for UN membership in the near future. Nevertheless, the government believed that the Olympic Charter ought to take precedence over politics for the duration of the Olympiad. For that reason, Rhodesia had been welcomed. Because the Rhodesian team possessed IOC identity cards, the United Nations could not interfere. These international documents had to be respected, Brundage said in a night letter to Willi Daume, president of the West German Olympic Committee.[55]

As the bruising controversy continued to roil IOC deliberations, Brundage stuck to his guns, arguing that Rhodesia had complied with the terms agreed to at the 72nd meeting in Luxemburg in September 1971, which ratified that "the colonial flag, the British hymn and the same uniform" worn in Tokyo would be employed. At the September 1972 Munich executive committee meeting, a rancorous debate took place about the extent of racial discrimination in Rhodesia and the citizenship, or lack thereof, of Rhodesian athletes. Both pro-Rhodesian and anti-Rhodesian sides wished to score points.[56]

Brundage urged support for Rhodesia. He was confident that if they were welcomed, they would "withdraw voluntarily as a sporting gesture and then everybody would save face." Secret ballots were distributed. When the votes were counted, there were thirty-one in favor of Rhodesian participation, thirty-six against, and three abstentions. Thus, the upshot was that the "invitation to Rhodesia to compete in the Games of the XXth Olympiad was withdrawn."[57]

Africans were jubilant. To put it mildly, Brundage was despondent and irritated by this outcome. His aura of invincibility had been shattered. In a letter to Ian Smith, Brundage assured the prime minister that he had done his best to honor the IOC's bid to the Rhodesians. He repeated his long-held view that the Rhodesians had observed the Olympic regulations and abided by the terms agreed to at the Luxemburg assemblage. For the first time in twenty years, the executive committee had refused approval of his recommendations, he lamented.[58] Then, he hyperbolically declared and prophesied that "if the African politicians think they won a victory, they are much mistaken. This action was denounced unanimously by the whole world of sport and it will take them many years to recover from the hostility which has been aroused."[59] The truth of the matter is that it was Brundage who did not recover. His resignation as president of the IOC was soon forthcoming. He never did abandon his core principle that politics had no place in the Olympic Movement.

The year 1972 was the last hurrah for the blunt-spoken, polarizing Brundage. He wielded more power than any IOC president before his time or after. Perhaps it was not too much to say that he was the pope of the modern Olympic Movement, believing as he did in his own infallibility. After he left the presidency, he was a lost soul. He visited his old Lausanne office uninvited, to the embarrassment of his successor, Lord Killanin. Madame Berlioux has been quoted as saying, "He would call me from Geneva and ask me to keep him company. I would just wander through the streets with him aimlessly for hours on end. He would not speak much. He was totally lost. He was desperately lonely." The Olympics had been his whole life. On one occasion, he had predicted egomaniacally, "[W]hen I'm gone, there's nobody rich enough, thick-skinned enough, and smart enough to take my place, and the Games will be in tremendous trouble."[60]

As of 1972, on the bitter Rhodesian matter, the Gordian knot had been cut at long last. Response to the snub of Rhodesia by the IOC had been fast and furious. Innumerable examples of letters, telegrams, and newspaper editorials have been preserved in the Brundage Papers at the University of Illinois and in the archives of the IOC in Switzerland.

The papers reveal the depth of animosity toward people of color, which was so much a part of the Rhodesian conundrum. Over the top was an anonymous letter written in French in September 1972 and addressed to the president of the IOC. It said that the Olympic Games should be "reserved for the civilized and not for singes [monkeys]." The author's admonition to the IOC was, "Do not give in to savages." For Arabs there was to be no pity, nor for the "Arab invasion," nor for the "Black invasion." Long live American whites, continued the letter. Long live Rhodesia. Exclude Collett and Mathews, who were described inaccurately as "Black Panthers."[61]

Equally intemperate and racist was the communication sent by someone who identified himself as the former chief medical officer at the University of Nigeria. "So you niggers have won! You picked on little Rhodesia. That is so typical for niggers. Especially the ones who got their education from the whites (UK or USA). Congratulations you bastards. May your bones bleach among the black vultures." It was directed at Ordia at the "International Olympic Body."[62]

Another pro-Rhodesian correspondent, a Canadian, added a bizarre criterion. All black athletes deserved to be expelled because their body builds were different from those of Caucasians. *No blacks* competed in the Greek games in antiquity. Perhaps, the writer wondered, there should be two Olympics—one for whites or others with similar physiques and one for blacks and those whose bodies were built more like African ones.[63]

Britons also weighed in on the Rhodesian expulsion. While the matter was still unresolved, a letter writer asked that Lee Evans's demand for barring Rhodesia be rejected. Ninety-five percent of the British people agreed, he told Brundage, "[I]f the blacks want to walk out of the Olympics let them."[64]

Support for Rhodesia and Brundage emanated from some surprising quarters, among them the little known National Front of Liberation of Romania. Rhodesia's expulsion was patently unfair. To be fair, the IOC should have expelled the Soviet Union because of their occupation of countries behind the Iron Curtain, "for the killing of millions of innocent people . . . for the persecution of the scientists, of the Hebrew [sic] and all the human thinking people in Soviet Russia." Rhodesia, they asserted, defends human rights on their soil, whereas Russia oppresses half the world. Therefore, it is Russia, "a country of criminals that ought to be expelled."[65]

Editorializing against the dismissal of the Rhodesian team was the *Toronto Star*, which found the move ignoble. The *Star* saw the decision as a wrongheaded response to political blackmail. Threatened by a black African boycott, the IOC buckled. The editorial made a distinction between South Africa's odious racial policies and its hard-line refusal to integrate its Olympians on the one hand, and a Rhodesian team that consisted of both black and white athletes. Nails had been driven into the coffin of the Olympic ideal, said the *Star*.[66]

Where would the "blackmail" stop? asked the *Star*. Could the Soviet Union be barred from the Olympics because it discriminated against Jewish athletes, a highly debatable charge? Could Francophone nations expel Canada if the French speakers were not treated properly? Of course, there was not a scintilla of proof that French Canadians were the victims of discrimination. Just the opposite.[67]

Some of the same points were made in an editorial titled "Olympic Disgrace" published in the *Los Angeles Herald Examiner*. Olympic idealism collapsed "when the very men pledged to keeping the Games free and above political trickery and aggrandizement surrendered to the demands that Rhodesia be dumped." The *Herald Examiner* went on to argue against booting out a country's athletes because that nation's government was at odds with the spirit of the Olympics.[68]

Where would such thinking lead? Counted among the nations in the Munich Games would be the East African state of Uganda. Both the *Star*, the *Herald Examiner*, and others took aim at Uganda, a former British colony, for its deportation of tens of thousands of its Asian inhabitants. The *Herald Examiner* wrote that you had "to go back to Hitler to find a more sweeping and crueler case of mass social outrage." Ending the editorial were these words: "the kicking out of Rhodesia was enough to blow out the Olympic torch."[69]

A closer examination of the Ugandan situation is in order inasmuch as it was so frequently alluded to by those who pilloried the IOC for supposedly utilizing a double standard to the detriment of Rhodesia. In August 1972, as the Rhodesian altercation swirled around the Olympic world, Uganda's despotic, mercurial, and brutal dictator, General Idi Amin, purged the country of its Asian community. They were given ninety days to depart Uganda. Perhaps fifty thousand, most of whom held British passports, were forced out. Their businesses and homes were summarily expropriated. The Asians—persons of Indian and Pakistani background—had been ubiquitous in the Ugandan retail economy. Indeed, they were sometimes described as the very backbone of the nation's economy. Overwhelmingly indigent with meager prospects, the Africans often viewed the Asians with resentment. The latter were labeled "bloodsuckers" and stereotyped as dishonest.

Amin had seized power in a 1971 coup d'état. Although physically gigantic—he had once been the boxing champion of Uganda—he was clearly mentally unstable. He said that the idea to banish the Asians had come to him in a dream. Thus, expulsion was not the result of any legislative process, but it was a godsend to the Rhodesian's public relations cause.[70]

At the Olympic memorial service for the slain Israeli athletes in Munich, Brundage, who was the last to speak, observed that the XX Olympics had been subjected to two savage attacks, pairing the killings that Serge Groussard described as "one of the most atrocious massacres since World War II" with the Olympic exclusion of Rhodesia. The latter, Brundage said, had been fought against "naked political blackmail." Not only blacks in Africa and in the United States, but people around the globe were affronted by the outgoing president's insensitive utterance. Within twenty-four hours, Brundage backtracked, stating that he did not have the "slightest intention of linking the Rhodesian question, purely a matter of sport, with an act of terrorism universally condemned."[71]

Still, Brundage came under fire for coupling the slaughter of the Israelis with the Rhodesian ejection. How could the IOC leader even mention the two phenomena in the same sentence? asked a bitter writer. "It shows a horrifying want of proportion Mr. Brundage, to consider the non-violent tactic of boycott as remotely related to the terrorism of the Black September group."[72]

The New York *Amsterdam News* deplored the use of the word "savage," which it surely thought had racial overtones. The parallel of the boycott with the Israeli tragedy was unwarranted.[73]

One black Londoner expressed an opinion that people of Brundage's type should quit the Olympic committee for the good of the Olympic Movement. In reference to the Mathews and Collett tiff, Miss Titi Paul, a self-described black Londoner, inquired why two African American athletes should have been taken to task for standing casually for the "Star Spangled Banner" when Brundage "could say that the games of the twentieth Olympiad have been subjected to two savage attacks." Miss Paul added, "[Y]ou and your committee should know that the Rhodesian question at such time was offensive to everyone and particularly to we Blacks sitting in front of you mourning. For your speech to us I had to leave the Olympic stadium and return home."[74]

Of course, Jews were pained and appalled when Brundage put the murder of eleven Israeli Olympians on a par with the Rhodesian problem. For one, the Olympics had proven to the world at large, as it had back in 1936, just how cheap Jewish blood was. To Brundage, Allan R Freedman of Teaneck, New Jersey, wrote, "[Y]our upholding of the vaunted Olympic ideal over more human suffering or grief is completely in character."[75]

A telegram from Dr. Lawrence Reddick, an esteemed African American academic, lambasted the Olympic president along similar lines. He wrote that Brundage had disgraced his position when he connected with terrorism the legitimate protest of African nations and athletes from Africa and Afro-America against "racist Rhodesia." Reddick wanted Brundage to retract the charge of blackmail against the African states and their supporters.[76] There was never to be a retraction. Brundage remained refractory and combative to the end. His long tenure as president of the IOC began with the disputatious Berlin Games and ended with the controversial Munich Games.

For white Rhodesians, the defeat at Munich was emblematic of their deteriorating predicament. Smith's government had very few friends in the family of nations. Its government had been delegitimized. Mainly because of UN sanctions, the economy became increasingly precarious. Race relations were worsening.[77] In many rural areas, whites slept with weapons under their pillows, fearful of those they called terrorists. For seven years, a bloody civil war raged, a war punctuated by horrendous atrocities.[78]

Finally, in December 1979, insurgent forces agreed to a British-brokered cease-fire. Transition to majority rule came the following year when Smith capitulated. Independence was formally granted by the United Kingdom. Salisbury, which had been named for a British foreign secretary in the colonial era, was renamed Harare. Rhodesia was rechristened Zimbabwe. The new nation entered the Olympic fold and participated for the first time in the Moscow Games in 1980. Self-determination certainly did not produce a utopia, but rather an increasingly autocratic and repressive regime headed by Robert Mugabe.

Notes

1. John Hatch, *A History of Postwar Africa* (New York: Frederick A. Praeger, 1965).
2. Sir Lewis Michell, *The Life of the Right Honourable Cecil John Rhodes*, vol. 1, 180–181, and vol. 2, 311–312; Bruce Fetter, *Colonial Rule in Africa* (Madison: University of Wisconsin Press, 1979), 64–67.
3. John Gunther, *Inside Africa* (New York: Harper and Brothers, 1955), 632.
4. See Garry Allighan, *The Welensky Story* (London: MacDonald, 1962).
5. Edwin S. Munger, *Prime Minister Ian Smith of Rhodesia*, American Universities Field Staff Reports, Central & Southern Africa Series, vol. 13, no. 3, *Rhodesia*, October 1969, 2.
6. *Rhodesia or Zimbabwe: No Middle Ground in Africa* (African Fund—American Committee on Africa, September 1969), 1. In addition, there were about 25,000 East Asians and persons of mixed racial background.
7. Henry Kamm, "White Rhodesians Intent on Preserving 'Easy Life,'" *New York Times*, March 17, 1976; Richard West, "Rhodesia: Echoing England," *New York Times*, February 28, 1979.
8. On the Zimbabwe ruins, see Brian Fagan, "Zimbabwe: A Century of Discovery," *African Arts*, vol. 2 (3) (Spring 1969): 20–24, 85; Tony Clifton and Ronald Legge, "The Glory That Was Rhodesia," *Atlas* (November 1971), 40–41.
9. Fagan, "Zimbabwe," 24.
10. Kevin Lowther, "Rhodesia Alphabet," *Africa Today*, vol. 13, no. 6 (June 1966): 9–10.
11. Nathan M. Shamuyarira, *Crisis in Rhodesia* (London: Andre Deutsch, 1965), 234. For a month-to-month account of the Rhodesian government's moves toward UDI, see *Mr. Smith's Illegal Declaration* (Exeter, UK: Africa Research Limited, nd).
12. *New York Times*, November 12, 1965.
13. King George III had "waged cruel war against human nature itself, violating the most sacred right of life and liberty in the persons of a distant people who never offended him, captivating and carrying them into slavery in another hemisphere, or to incur miserable death in their transportation

thither," Jefferson wrote hypocritically. Jefferson owned 150 fifty slaves when he penned the Declaration.

14. For the black role in the revolution, see Benjamin Quarles, *The Negro in the American Revolution* (Chapel Hill: University of North Carolina Press, 1961). The British governor of Virginia, Lord Dunmore, declared Negro slaves free and invited them to enlist and fight for the British. The colonists responded by recruiting blacks, so Negroes fought on both sides.

15. European countries, both large and small, joined the League of Armed Neutrality mainly to protect their commercial interests and to limit British influence. Spain coveted Gibraltar and declared war on Britain in June 1779.

16. American patriot leaders incessantly demanded liberty from Britain. The hypocrisy of doing so while denying liberty to American slaves was not lost on thinkers on both sides of the Atlantic. Perhaps Samuel Johnson stated the contradiction most pungently when he asked, "How is it that we hear the loudest yelps for liberty among the drivers of Negroes?" Thomas Paine made the same point. Darlene Clark Hine, William C. Hine, and Stanley Harrold, *The African-American Odyssey*, combined volume, 4th edition (New Jersey: Pearson-Prentice Hall, 2008), 87.

17. Arnold Whitridge, "Jefferson Davis and the Collapse of the Confederacy," *History Today* (February 1961): 79–89.

18. American-Southern African Council, *Aid Rhodesia's Fight against Communist Aggression* (nd), 1.

19. Ibid.

20. Letter from Monique Berlioux to A. A. Ordia, Nigerian Olympic Committee, September 19, 1970, participation of Rhodesia files, International Olympic archives.

21. Richard E. Lapchick, *The Politics of Race and International Sport: The Case of South Africa* (London: Greenwood Press, 1975), 123–124.

22. UN Security Council Resolution 253 (1968) of May 29, 1968. S/Res/253 (1968). The resolution urged member states to render moral and material assistance to the people of Southern Rhodesia in their struggle to achieve their freedom and independence.

23. Letter, Avery Brundage to J. W. Westerhoff, June 10, 1968, ABC, box 179. Three days earlier, Westerhoff had informed Brundage that the president of the Mexican Olympic Organizing Committee had said at a press conference that he would not allow any Rhodesian competitors to participate in the Mexico City Games. That report was unconfirmed. The Mexican policy was much more nuanced. Letter, J. W. Westerhoff to Brundage, June 7, 1968, ABC, box 179.

24. Letter, Brundage to Westerhoff, June 10, 1968, ABC, box 179.

25. Letter, Monte R. Gomez to Brundage, August 9, 1968, ABC, box 179.

26. Ibid.

27. Letter, Brundage to Vasquez-Ramirez, August 27, 1968, ABC, box 179.

28. John Cheffers, *A Wilderness of Spite: Rhodesia Denied* (New York: Vantage Press, 1972), 135. Cheffers, an Australian, was a track-and-field coach for the Rhodesians. Speaking of Mathias Kanda, a black marathoner, he wrote bitterly, "What right had vindictive and smelly politicians to deprive this lad of his life's ambition." He denied categorically that there was any discrimination in Rhodesian sports. See 16–17.

29. Statement by Frederick W. Holder, hon. secretary treasurer of the International Amateur Athletic Federation, April 5, 1971, ABC, box 183.
30. Ibid.
31. Letter, David Burleigh to Brundage, September 3, 1971, ABC, box 88. David Burleigh was a member of the IOC Executive Board for almost half a century.
32. Ibid.
33. Undated document, ABC, box 183.
34. Letter, Brundage to Berlioux, August 22, 1970, thematic correspondence, IOC Archives.
35. IOC Executive Board meeting of National Olympic Committees, Munich, September 1971, IOC archives.
36. Ibid.
37. Resolution of the National Olympic Committees of Africa concerning the new problems raised by the participation of Southern Rhodesia in the Games of the XX Olympiad in Munich, 1972, IOC archives.
38. Ibid.
39. Correspondence (1971–1975) concerning charges submitted to the IOC against the NOC of Rhodesia for its exclusion from the IOC, IOC archives.
40. Letter, Ordia to Brundage, May 22, 1971, IOC archives.
41. Shamuyarira, *Crisis in Rhodesia*, 214.
42. Weightlifting appears to have been an exception. Letter, general secretary of the International Weightlifting Federation to I. E. Vino, IOC member from Denmark, December 28, 1973, in commission of inquiry—Rhodesia correspondence, IOC archives.
43. IOC commission of inquiry—Rhodesia correspondence, 1974, IOC archives. In 1969, the Rhodesian Front stated the following among its principles:

> The Party opposes compulsory integration and believes that the peaceful co-existence of people can only be achieved when communities have the right and opportunity to preserve their own identities, traditions, and customs, and therefore recognizes the obligation of government and respective communities where necessary to ensure the provision of such separate facilities as will make this possible.

    See Reginald Austin, ed., *Racism and Apartheid in Southern Africa: Rhodesia* (UNESCO Press, 1975).
44. IOC meeting with the Rhodesian Olympic Committee, May 3, 1974, commission of inquiry—Rhodesia, 1974, IOC archives. The commission met personally with Prime Minister Ian Smith, who said he was eager to see Rhodesia in the Olympic Games.
45. Minutes of IOC Executive Board meeting, 69th session, Amsterdam, May 1970, IOC archives.
46. General position of the USA Olympic track-and-field team concerning Southern Rhodesia's participation in the XX Summer Olympic Games, nd, ABC, box 183.
47. Ibid.
48. Cable, Brutus to IOC, August 8, 1972, ABC, box 183.
49. Statement of the International Campaign against Racism in Sport, August 22, 1972, ABC, box 183.

50. Statement on the Southern Rhodesian controversy and the 1972 Munich Olympic Games, undated, ABC, box 183.
51. Ibid.
52. Ibid.
53. Letter, NOC of Rhodesia to Herbert Kunze, secretary general, Organizing Committee for the XX Olympiad, June 12, 1972. Participation of Rhodesia correspondence, 1971–1972, IOC archives.
54. Minutes of Executive Board meeting, 73rd session, Munich, September 1972, IOC archives.
55. Letter, Brundage to Willi Daume, August 8, 1972, ABC, box 183.
56. IOC Executive Board meeting, 73rd session, Munich, September 1972, IOC archives.
57. Ibid.
58. Letter, Brundage to Prime Minister Ian Smith, November 19, 1972, ABC, box 184.
59. Ibid.
60. Allen Guttmann, *The Games Must Go On*, 253; William Oscar Johnson, "Avery Brundage: The Man behind the Mask," *Sports Illustrated* 53 (6) (September 4, 1980): 58, 63.
61. Letter, Anonymous to Brundage, September 10, 1972, participation of Rhodesia correspondence, IOC archives.
62. Letter, Rolf von Scorebrand to Ordia, received at the IOC on September 4, 1972, ABC, box 183.
63. Letter, A. Keksis to IOC, August 28, 1972, participation of Rhodesia correspondence, IOC archives.
64. Letter, V. Roberts to Brundage, August 8, 1972, participation of Rhodesia correspondence, IOC Archives.
65. Letter, National Front of Liberation of Romania to IOC, September 10, 1972, participation of Rhodesia correspondence, IOC archives.
66. "Political Blackmail at the Olympics," *Toronto Star*, August 24, 1972. Correspondents supporting Rhodesia frequently used the word "blackmail." One wondered "what financial gain prompted the betrayal of a country which had been invited to take part and who had met every requirement." Letter, Mary Cargill to IOC, August 8, 1972, participation of Rhodesia correspondence, community and public, IOC archives.
67. Ibid.
68. "Olympic Disgrace," *Los Angeles Herald Examiner*, August 25, 1972.
69. Ibid.
70. An expansionist war with neighboring Tanzania led to the end of Amin's power. He died in exile in Saudi Arabia in 2003.
71. Groussard, *The Blood of Israel*, 442. In a press statement dated September 7, 1972, Brundage said that, "as President of the IOC we regret any misinterpretation of the remarks made during the solemn memorial services in the stadium yesterday."
72. Letter, Dorothy A. Brewster to Brundage, September 6, 1972, participation of Rhodesia correspondence, IOC archives.
73. *New York Amsterdam News*, September 9, 1972.
74. Letter, Titi Paul to Brundage, September 10, 1972, ABC, box 183.

75. Letter, Freedman to Brundage, September 6, 1972, ABC, box 183. One Chicagoan blamed the Israeli massacre on Brundage and his supporters. What happened at the Olympics "was the outcome of the decision 'you men' made against the Rhodesians." Brundage supposedly had given the "'radicals' an inch and now they were taking a mile." Letter, Christ to Brundage, August 4, 1972, participation of Rhodesia correspondence, IOC archives.

76. Telegram, Lawrence Riddick to Brundage, nd, ABC, box 183.

77. In the 1970s, whites were completely in charge. In 1976, in excess of 70 percent of the most fertile land was still in white hands. Government spending for the education of white children was roughly eleven times its spending for blacks. Pejorative language about blacks was still rife. They were sometimes called baboons by white managers. "Stone age dwellers" was a description of blacks used by one white supervisor. Quoted in the *New York Times*, March 19, 1976.

78. Editorial, "The Killings in Rhodesia," *New York Times*, June 27, 1978.

7

Aftermath: Outlaw Nations as Olympic Hosts—Gays and Others as Targets of Discrimination

Even with the outcast South Africa debarred from the Olympic Movement, the Pretoria regime was central to the instability of the Games in 1976 in Montreal. For the first time in history, an Olympiad was held in Canada, perhaps because the IOC believed that choosing a moderate nation instead of one of the two superpowers would reduce the chances of strife and even boycott. Events in 1980 in Moscow and four years hence in Los Angeles gave some substance to this theory. Ongoing racial turmoil in the United States, where the gathering strength of the Black Power movement was much in evidence, continuing UN pressure to embargo South African sports, and decolonization unfolding on the African continent all contributed to the woes of the IOC and the Canadian Olympic organizers.

A racial altercation involving the New Zealand–South Africa rugby rivalry played havoc with the Montreal Games. The conflict took place against the backdrop of the Soweto student uprising that began on June 16, 1976, a month prior to the opening of the Olympiad. Soweto, an acronym for Southwest Township, was inhabited by blacks who were legally prohibited from lodging in white Johannesburg. Many of the Soweto Africans had been forcibly relocated from Johannesburg. The "Children's Revolt" was triggered by an educational decree that mandated the use of Afrikaans, which Bishop Desmond Tutu, the African Nationalist campaigner, called the "Language of the Oppressor" for the teaching of certain subjects. Several thousand black youngsters rallied against not just the required introduction of Afrikaans but against the entire ethos it symbolized. Carrying placards, one of which read, "If we must do Afrikaans, Vorster must do Zulu," they peacefully challenged Afrikaner domination.

As happened so often in South Africa, violence ensued. The authorities sicced snarling dogs on the demonstrating youth. They also shot and killed many. Casualty figures are still in dispute, but it is highly probable that hundreds were killed and perhaps a thousand injured. It was Sharpeville redux.[1] Around the globe, South Africa received abundant negative publicity. On the horizon was the Olympics in Montreal, which was severely impacted.

The Games commenced with much ceremony, fanfare, and pageantry.[2] Ninety-four countries were represented, and nine thousand of the world's best athletes entered the Olympic stadium, a structure recently and frantically completed. As is the Olympic custom, Greece led the march past the viewing stand, with the other countries following in alphabetical order. As host, Canada, with 478 athletes, came into the stadium last. The United States had four fewer. Soviet athletes numbered 526. Wearing black memorial patches on their uniforms, Israel's contingent received an especially warm welcome from the sympathetic crowd mindful of the 1972 Munich massacre. Accompanied by Prince Philip, Queen Elizabeth, in pink, officially opened the Games. She spoke in both French and her native English.

There had been heated quarreling over the status of Taiwan. Canada was at loggerheads with the IOC. The host country recognized the Communist regime on the mainland. In contrast, the United States recognized Taiwan, Chiang-Kai Shek's anti-Communist nationalists, as the Republic of China. The IOC insisted that the name Taiwan, not the Republic of China, be used for that nation and its team. Taipei, Nationalist China's capital, insisted on using its own colors and national anthem. When no satisfactory compromise could be reached, Taiwan withdrew.[3]

A second debate centered on New Zealand's ongoing sports ties to South Africa. New Zealand had no major domestic racial problem, but numerous African nations, seething over the apartheid situation in South Africa, castigated New Zealand for conducting a rugby tour in South Africa at the very time the Olympics were getting underway. Nigeria, the most populous sub-Saharan African state, withdrew from Montreal, citing New Zealand's "continuing collaboration with South Africa."[4] Others threatened to leave. On July 17, the *New York Times* wrote that nineteen African nations had refrained from attending the opening ceremonies. Four Arab countries were also absent. Kenyan athletes and officials were particularly vociferous. Mike Boit, a standout twenty-seven-year-old half-miler, lamented the pullout of his country. "Why didn't New Zealand wait until after the Olympics for that tour?" he asked plaintively. Isaac Luzongo, chairman of Kenya's National Sports Council, chimed in, "We will not align ourselves with a country that has sports ties with South Africa," ignoring the fact that several countries had sports, industrial, and diplomatic links with South Africa.[5]

A public relations–conscious newspaper in Montreal ignored the burgeoning tumult. Its headline on July 18 summarized the Olympic happenings to that point: "Opening: Tears, Awe, No Politics." The Pollyannish Madame Berlioux wishfully minimized the danger to the Games: "The talk we have heard so far is all rumor." But the ripple effect of the African defections was already being felt. Coordinating a secondary boycott were Jean Claude Ganga, a Congolese who was vice-president of the Supreme Council of Sport for Africa; Abraham Ordia; and, no surprise, the ubiquitous Dennis Brutus. It was conceded that New Zealand had violated no Olympic regulations, and there was little support for kicking New Zealand out of the Games. The spokesman for Zambia explained, "[W]e're in the front-line of the whole apartheid thing. Any nation that condones that, we just can't take part with them."[6]

Among sub-Saharan countries, only the Ivory Coast and Senegal, both francophone former colonies, resisted the emotional appeal of fellow African states. On the other hand, there were unanticipated defections. One was Guyana, formerly British Guiana. Located on the northern coast of South America, sandwiched between Venezuela and Surinam, its population was of African and East Indian heritage. Its spokesman asserted that principle was more important than gold.[7]

What exactly were the consequences of the walkout? Many athletes, including potential medal winners, were denied the opportunity to compete and to fulfill their dreams; however, the Olympiad continued uninterrupted. World antagonism to apartheid was highlighted once again. On July 22, in the midst of the Olympic brouhaha, the International Amateur Athletic Federation that governed track and field, made permanent the expulsion of South Africa's Amateur Athletic Union. With this action, individual South African athletes were precluded from competing in any meet operated under the aegis of the federation. South African teams were already banned. FIFA, the governing body of soccer, also expelled South Africa.[8]

In the 1970s and 1980s, although the republic was outside the Olympic family, the IOC policy on apartheid was sometimes evaded. In a July

1984 letter to Juan Antonio Samaranch, then president of the IOC, Sam Ramsamy of SAN-ROC, lamented the fact that South African athletes were "sneaking into Olympic participation by acquiring passports of convenience."[9] Some were able to acquire Portuguese, West German, or Israeli citizenship. Sydnee Maree, an elite nonwhite middle distance runner born in South Africa, became an American citizen in 1984. He was a member of the United States Olympic squad in 1984 and 1988.[10]

Probably the best known of the holders of passports of convenience was the discalced, pert South African track star Zola Budd, who had been born in the Orange Free State. She was described as "South Africa's Barefooted Wonder Runner" in South African government publications. Portraying Budd as a victim of the anti-apartheid campaign, the *South African Digest* informed American readers that her considerable track records could not be officially acknowledged because of her nationality.[11]

Budd, in her autobiography, described herself as "shy, impressionable, and easily influenced."[12] She became a British subject in April 1984 at the age of seventeen. In Zola's own telling, to a large degree, she was manipulated by London's *Daily Mail* working in concert with Zola's father and her coach, all of whose motives were crassly pecuniary. Zola's paternal grandfather was English, thereby providing Great Britain with the pretext for granting her citizenship. The *Mail* wrote that Zola's heart lay in England. But she claimed that that was news to her. From the instant she was granted British citizenship, she felt like a "commodity" and accused the *Mail* of transforming her into "some kind of circus animal."[13] Budd later relocated to South Africa, where her heart lay all the time. What we have in her case is a subterfuge used by a London tabloid to sell more newspapers and a technicality employed by British Olympic officials hoping to be more competitive in Los Angeles.

Zola Budd is best remembered because of an unfortunate incident that occurred in the women's 3,000-meter final at the Los Angeles Olympiad. Budd's legs became entangled with those of her arch-competitor, the American runner Mary Decker. The latter was left sprawled on the ground, her dreams of Olympic gold in tatters. A very disheartened and badly shaken Budd, who was injured in the collision, finished seventh to loud choruses of boos.

Boycotts beset both the XXII Olympiad held in Moscow in 1980 and the XXIII Olympiad held in Los Angeles in 1984, but they had nothing to do with race. Instead, they were casualties of Cold War rivalry.

The Soviet capital had been selected to host the Games of 1980 back in 1974. They were the first ever hosted by a Communist country, but the December 1979 Soviet attack on neighboring Afghanistan led to a boycott movement spearheaded by the United States, which also sent arms to Afghanistan, many of which would later be used against their country of origin. The United States Olympic Committee had always been seen as a nongovernmental, nonpolitical, privately funded independent entity, but the Cold War and specifically the Soviet invasion prompted a political response, again demonstrating that divorcing sports from politics was not always possible or desirable. Some would call it a moral response. President Jimmy Carter whispered in the ears of the USOC that the United States should not participate in Moscow, and he pressed other nations to do likewise, even dispatching an emissary to plead his case.[14] Of course, US government involvement had been eschewed at the time of Hitler's 1936 Games. Clearly, it was a matter of whose ox was being gored.

In Great Britain, Prime Minister Margaret Thatcher and the House of Commons wanted British athletes to stay home, but the British Olympic Committee strongly disagreed and sent a team. All in all, the boycott failed. Some eighty-five nations went to the Moscow festivities, even though the Soviet Union was then at war, a war which it initiated. Of course, the absence of many outstanding athletes from some stay-at-home countries inevitably detracted from the luster of the competition.[15]

Negotiations in 1983 between the US and Soviet representatives were aimed at heading off a retaliatory Soviet and Soviet-satellite boycott of the Los Angeles Olympics. Chances of success in doing so were minimal, given the tense, mutually mistrustful political atmosphere. President Ronald Reagan had dubbed the Soviet Union the "Evil Empire" in 1983, and much shrill criticism of the Kremlin had been heard as arrangements for the Games were being completed. There were those who wanted to exclude Russian competitors even if they wanted to partake. For its part, the USSR was concerned about threats of violence directed at its athletes. In May 1984, the Soviets made it official. The hammer and sickle would not be unfurled in the City of Angels. They would not be present.[16]

The Los Angeles Organizing Committee worked tirelessly to prevent other countries from withdrawing.[17] To put it mildly, they were euphoric when "Red China," as it was still called in the "free world," Russia's main rival in the Communist sphere, decided it would indeed send a team to Los Angeles.[18] Four days after the announce-ment, Peter Ueberoth, chairman of the LA Organizing Committee, was informed that China would challenge Soviet hegemony on the Olympics, thereby guaranteeing that the Games would be a success. That announcement was followed by strongman Nicolae Ceauşescu of Romania declaring that it would not go along with the Soviet boycott. In the final analysis, 14 states boycotted, while 140 went to California. Moscow had been sanguine and predicted that no fewer than 100 nations would stay away from Los Angeles.[19] The Games did succeed, even financially. They finished in the black, a rare phenomenon for an Olympiad.

Year after year, sports crazy South Africa's frustration deepened because of the train of rejections directed at it. The republic was cold shouldered by most of the world, and it had no reason to be optimistic. In October 1979, to retain a toehold in the sports world and perhaps even win an international boxing crown, apartheid was briefly relaxed so that a promising Afrikaner heavyweight pugilist, Gerrie Coetzee, could challenge an African American, John Tate, for the World Boxing Association title.

The match occurred in Pretoria in an arena where black fans had previously been excluded, and Tate was accommodated in Johannes-burg in an area reserved by law for whites. For one night and one night only, seating was integrated, and the audience, a miscellany of celebri-ties, included Prime Minister P. W. Botha. Their presence indicated the importance attached to the biracial sports event being hosted in South Africa, and not in comparatively liberal Cape Town but in Pretoria, a bastion of Afrikanerdom. There was a touch of irony in that Coetzee, who lost, had been vocal more than once in criticizing apartheid, whereas Tate's willingness to fight in South Africa flouted the sports boycotts of South Africa.[20]

In the sport of tennis, both on the individual and the team levels, South Africa had long enjoyed a high profile in international competi-tion. After the Olympic expulsion, the country was repeatedly called to account because of apartheid. Leading the campaign to totally exclude South Africa was Richard E. Lapchick, an academic and activist. In 1979, he wanted South Africa to be ousted from Davis Cup tourna-ments. To that end, he traveled to Nashville, Tennessee. To parry the anti-apartheid thrust, South Africa fielded a racially integrated team consisting of one mixed race (Coloured) player, eighteen-year-old Peter Lamb. They hoped to score a public relations coup.[21]

Where racial justice was concerned, Richard was following in the illustrious footsteps of his father, a member of the Original Celtics and a legendary basketball coach at St. John's University in New York City and later the New York Knicks. The senior Lapchick is generally credited with integrating professional basketball. Despite opposition, he signed Nat "Sweetwater" Clifton of the Harlem Globetrotters to a Knicks contract. Professional basketball was never the same again.

Richard paid a heavy price for his unstinting humanitarian efforts. On the evening of Valentine's Day 1978, he was viciously assaulted in his office at Virginia Wesleyan. During the brutal attack, the assailants carved the word "niger" (a misspelling of "nigger") on his stomach. He was bludgeoned, called a "nigger lover," and told he had no business involving himself in South African matters. Richard had heard the "nigger" expletive before. When he was a five-year-old child growing up in Yonkers, a suburb of New York City, telephone callers trying to intimidate his father used it.[22]

As an activist, the younger Lapchick helped to organize protests against visiting South Africans, but the United States Tennis Association was unwilling to sever relations with South Africa. Many countries had done so.[23]

Lapchick also tried to block the South African Springboks rugby team from touring the United States in 1981.[24] Some cities where matches were scheduled canceled, but some did not. South Africa was boycotted, snubbed, and reviled until the end of the white minority rule. The disappointment and anger of South African sports enthusiasts surely contributed to the end of apartheid.

Israel had participated in the Olympic Games for the first time in Helsinki in 1952. For the Jewish state, the Games are important not because of the opportunity to demonstrate Jewish athletic prowess but because participation in international sports competitions is additional confirmation of Israel's nationhood and its standing in the global community. Especially since the Six-day War of 1967, there have been countless attempts by Arabs and their allies to transform Israel into an international pariah. This is no less true in the field of international sports than elsewhere.

In September 1974, Israel was all but officially expelled from the Asian Football Confederation. The decision was taken at a meeting held in Teheran on the occasion of the Seventh Asian Games. Delegates of the Asian Football Confederation Congress in Teheran voted seventeen to twelve to support a Kuwaiti resolution that stated that in the future

Israeli teams should not be invited to tournaments organized by Asian Football Confederation members nor should Israel be permitted to host any Asian Football Confederation competitions. Passage of the resolution was facilitated by the admission to the Confederation of Qatar, the United Arab Emirates, Bangladesh, North Korea, and the People's Republic of China as new members. Many of the countries voting to banish Israel had never even competed in international soccer.

In his response to the Teheran decision, Israeli education minister Aharon Yadlin linked the rebuff to the Munich massacre two years earlier. Attempts to isolate Israel in the world was one Arab tactic, he said. Barbaric physical attacks were a second tactic. Yadlin further asserted that "Israel will not forfeit its right and duty to appear at international and Olympic meets." He added that continuing participation in sports events would be proof of Israeli determination and of Israeli faithfulness to the legacy of the Munich martyrs. Yadlin, whose ministry was in charge of sports in Israel, insisted on his country's right to affiliate with Asian sports federations.

In 1977, Israel's expulsion from the Asian Football Confederation was made official. Early in 1978, Dr. Joao Havelange of Brazil, president of the International Football Federation (FIFA), the governing authority of international soccer, visited Israel to attend celebrations of the fiftieth anniversary of the founding of the Israeli Soccer Federation and assured the Israelis that he would help them overcome their difficulties in international soccer. He also told Haskell Cohen, an American with close ties to Israeli sports, that "Although Israel has been forced out of the Asian Soccer Federation, I will do everything to have them admitted to the European confederation." Nevertheless, in April 1978, Israel's bid to join the European Football Union (UEFA) failed to win approval. A three-quarters majority of the congress of the union was necessary for admission, and the Israelis were able to garner only sixteen of thirty-four votes. Opposition from the Soviet Union and other Communist nations had left Israeli soccer in international limbo.

Israel's position in Asian sports deteriorated further in June 1978, when the council of the Asian Games Federation voted to bar Israel from the Eighth Asian Games scheduled for Bangkok in December, despite the fact that Israel had taken part in the Asian games since 1954 and was a member in good standing of the federation. As early as December 1976, the council had decided to keep the Jewish state out of the games, ostensibly because of security problems. Both Israeli officials and the International Olympic Committee rejected the security argument. Lord Killanin pointed out that the same reasoning could be used against any other country. Consequently, the games would not be recognized by the IOC. Five oil-rich Arab countries—Kuwait, Saudi Arabia, Iraq, Qatar, and the United Arab Emirates—all adamantly opposed to competing with Israel, pledged $2 million to finance the games in Thailand. Israeli sports officials responded to that pledge with the assertion that their own nation is "part of the Asian continent, a fact which no force in the world and no amount of money can change."[25]

Discrimination against Israeli sportsmen continued in 1979. Camp David notwithstanding, Egypt's Ani Nazar refused to play his Israeli opponent in the World Cup junior tennis championships in Mexico City. Cricketers from Sri Lanka refused to play a match against Israel in the second Prudential World Cricket Cup in England. Host nation Japan, which was almost completely dependent on Arab oil, balked at inviting Israel to the third Asian track-and-field meet. In April, Israel was excluded from the thirty-fifth table tennis championship in North Korea, and the exclusion was endorsed by the International Table Tennis Federation. In July, a Kuwaiti fencer was expelled from the Stoke Mandeville games for paralyzed athletes because he was unwilling to compete against an Israeli.

The Arabs found in the Soviet Union an ally willing, even eager, to join the movement to ostracize Israel from the international sports world. Events that had occurred at the 1973 World University Games in Moscow, in which a forty-member Israeli contingent participated, raised doubts about the Soviet willingness to separate politics and international athletics. To politically neutralize the Israeli presence, the Soviets invited Yasir Arafat, head of the Palestine Liberation Organization.

More distressing to the Israelis than the invitation to Arafat was the fact that disorderly crowds repeatedly harassed and vilified Israeli athletes. They were hooted and verbally abused on several occasions during competition. Special security measures were imposed upon the Israeli sportsmen, and, following fraternization between them and their Russian coreligionists, the Soviet authorities attempted to minimize contact between the two groups. During the games, unruly mobs physically assaulted Russian Jews who had the courage to cheer Israeli teams. At one point, a cluster of Soviet Jews waving an Israeli flag during a basketball game between Puerto Rico and Israel was set upon by "fans" abetted by uniformed Russian soldiers.

When the Israeli athletes returned home, Yigal Allon, then the deputy prime minister, charged that his nation's athletes had experienced "racism and anti-Semitism" at the World University Games. Allon expressed his belief that Moscow ought not to be selected as the site of the 1980 Olympics.

In light of the foregoing, rumors to the effect that the Soviet Union as host of the 1980 Olympics would exclude Israel from the Games aroused considerable concern in some quarters. The certainty of Israel's exclusion from the 1980 Olympics was the central theme of a number of nationally syndicated columns published in a three-month span during 1977. All were written by well-known conservative columnists.[26]

The Soviets sought to scotch recurring rumors of troubles concerning Israel at the Games. They repeatedly stated that they abide by International Olympic Committee rules and regulations. When Moscow made a bid for the Games, its mayor made a solemn pledge to that effect. When Moscow won the right to host the Games, the government of the USSR promised to admit the athletes of all national Olympic committees recognized by the International Olympic Committee. Soviet President Nikolai Podgorny guaranteed that his country would live up to its obligations. All athletes and journalists accredited to the Games would be granted the right to enter the Soviet Union. In March 1977, a letter was submitted to the IOC from Leonid Brezhnev reaffirming that the Games would be conducted under IOC regulations and principles. Premier Alexei Kosygin gave similar assurances.

What would happen should the Soviets break their word? Shortly after the 1976 Montreal Olympiad ended, Lord Killanin told the press that if even one athlete were denied entry by a host country, he would cancel the 1980 Olympic Games. The United States Olympic Committee (USOC) had not been quite so unequivocal. Robert Kane, president of the USOC, said that the USOC never would stand idly by when the rights and privileges guaranteed a country under the regulations of the IOC were infringed or abrogated.

Trials of Soviet dissidents, notably Anatoly Sharansky and Alexander Ginzburg, provided the impetus for a movement to boycott the Moscow Olympics. Congressman Jack Kemp introduced a resolution in the House asking the USOC to take such measures as may be necessary to have the IOC select a site for the 1980 Summer Olympics outside the Soviet Union. Ronald Reagan called on the International Olympic Committee to transfer the Games to another locale.[27] In this fashion, the world could express its outrage over the "Kremlin's intolerance for dissent and human freedom." Liberal congressman Father Robert F. Drinan of Massachusetts, who disagreed with Reagan about almost every other issue, also believed that the United States should think about finding an alternative site. Father Drinan optimistically voiced the opinion that removing the Olympics from Moscow would force a change in the Soviet treatment of dissidents.[28]

While American sports and governmental authorities had been unresponsive to the boycott idea, it is noteworthy that, in August 1978, Dr. David Owen, then the British foreign secretary, was quoted as saying that the Russians should not take it for granted that the Olympic Games would be held in Moscow. Owen stated, "If the British people and people around the world grew to feel that the Soviet Union was just totally riding roughshod over the ethics and principles that still underlie the Olympics, then I believe the Olympics would come under increasing pressure."[29]

There were those, Anthony Lewis of the *New York Times* for one, who believed that withdrawal from the Moscow Olympics was an appealing notion advanced by good people. On the other hand, Lewis contended that thousands of visitors from abroad could be a modest force for opening up Soviet society. To those who rightly observed that holding the Olympics in Nazi Germany hardly liberalized Hitler's Reich, John Rodda, an advocate of infiltration not boycott, pointed out that nightly television coverage was not a fact of life in 1936 at the Berlin Olympics.[30]

Israeli sensitivity about possible exclusion from the Moscow Olympiad was underscored in January 1979, when Yitzhak Ofek, chairman of the Israeli Olympic Committee, announced that his country was cutting all of its sports ties with the Republic of South Africa because of the latter's apartheid racial policy. Ofek explained that he was unwilling to give the Soviets any pretext for keeping Israel out of the 1980 Games. Ofek's statement, which was made unilaterally without consulting the other members of the Israeli Olympic Committee, angered the foreign ministry and raised hackles at the ministry of culture and education. In short order, after a meeting of the Israeli Olympic Committee, the Ofek statement was withdrawn. As had previously been the case, Israel would adhere to the rules enunciated by international sports federations regarding South Africa. This meant there would be some South Africa–Israeli sports competition. Presumably, South Africa would continue to participate in the quadrennial Maccabiah Games for Jewish athletes. It's possible that the Israeli Olympic Committee and Israeli government officials realized that to sever sports links with

South Africa for "political" reasons would be to set a precedent that could boomerang against another international pariah, namely Israel, at some time in the future.

As far as the 1980 Moscow Olympiad was concerned, the Israelis were absent, not because they were excluded by the host, but because they took part in the boycott organized by their staunch friend and ally, the United States.

Racism in the context of the Olympics receded in the 1970s and 1980s with the absence of Rhodesia and South Africa. It did not vanish altogether, of course. So long as racism exists, there will be racism and perceptions of racism in sports, and that includes the Olympics. Racial dissatisfaction came to the fore prior to the 1996 centennial games in Atlanta. That caused some apprehension among Olympic boosters, such as Atlanta mayor Andrew Young, a former aide to Martin Luther King Jr. and UN ambassador in Jimmy Carter's presidency. Many local black Atlantans maintained that the Olympic organizers were insufficiently responsive to the educational, employment, and housing ills of the black community. Martin Luther King III was especially outspoken, and some reforms were made. No boycott took place. In the end, 197 countries, an Olympic record, took part in the Games, which were not marred by racial strife but by the apolitical Olympic Park explosion.

Periodically, racial incidents occurred in the Olympics. For example, at the 2012 London Games, a female Greek Olympian, a triple jumper, was banned by Greek officials for ridiculing immigrants from Africa. A Swiss soccer player who insulted South Koreans as a "bunch of Mongoloids" was ejected from the Games for his offensive behavior.

Playing for Italy in the 2008 London Olympiad, Mario Balotelli, a black, was subjected to racist invective. In the face of this vilification, an emotionally exhausted Balotelli collapsed.

Blatant racism is a constant in international soccer competition. Bananas are frequently hurled onto the pitch to taunt black players. Grunts by fans, which are meant to imitate ape vocalization, are also common. Inevitably, crude anti-black sentiment has crept into the Olympic Movement.

Choosing a host nation for the Games is often a major headache for the IOC. Because of astronomical costs incurred, the roster of potential bidders is diminished. One can ask, is the experience of being bathed in the Olympic spotlight likely to bring democratic change to an undemocratic host nation? In the case of Nazi Germany, it did not even happen in the short term. Viewed historically, the 1936 Games were an unmitigated disaster. On the other hand, hosting the 1988 Games in Seoul had, to some degree, pushed South Korea, a military dictatorship, sharply toward reform. What about the 2008 Beijing Olympiad?[31]

In the new century, China understood that its human rights record could be an impediment to getting the Games. Consequently, as Minky Worden of Human Rights Watch has pointed out, "Top officials made human rights improvements a cornerstone of their case to be an Olympic host."[32] Liu Qi, the mayor of Beijing and also president of the bidding committee for 2008, asserted that the Olympics would prove to be a fillip to their human rights progress.[33] Alas, it was not to be. Skeptics were legion. Dissenting voices inside and outside China were vindicated by events after 2008. Post-Olympic China remained an authoritarian state.

China's persecution of the Tibetans has continued unabated since 2008. Self-immolation among the Tibetans has been well reported in the West. The self-immolators, people of all ages, have come from many walks of life. Nuns, monks, and especially disciples of the Dalai Lama are well represented among those who publically set themselves aflame. The Dalai Lama, a pacifist and Nobel Peace Prize recipient, personifies the nationalist aspirations of the Tibetans. The government goes to great lengths to see to it that Tibetans have no access to his message or likeness.[34] He is blamed by the Chinese authorities for fomenting sedition among his people. Others who incinerate themselves are students, farmers, and nomads. Precise numbers cannot be ascertained because the government keeps the media on a tight leash. To the Tibetans, the Chinese are imperialists who deny them religious and linguistic freedom. The resistance to Chinese rule is coordinated by the Tibetan government in exile in India. Protesters, Tibetan and other, are not handled with kid gloves. Some vanish into the night and fog of Chinese gulags.

China's catalog of civil liberties violations remains long and appalling. Freedom of expression is hard to find, press freedom a chimera. P.E.N. has taken the government to task for suppression and censorship. Complaints of child labor abuse abound, and corruption is commonplace. Pollution is a scourge, and environmental rights given short shrift.[35]

Tibetan activists and other dissenters were under no illusions about their chances of dissuading the IOC from going to Beijing. A syndicated cartoon published in April 2008 showed a Chinese figure wearing a hat sporting the five Olympic rings and saying, "Those horrible protestors are going to ruin my coming out party." He is talking to Hitler, who retorts, "Nonsense! Everyone came to my party. They'll come to yours." Hitler's sentiment was borne out by the Olympiad.[36]

Uighurs, another ethnic minority, fared no better than the Tibetans in the wake of the Beijing Olympiad. For these Turkik-speaking Muslims living predominantly in the Xinjiang region, autonomous in name if not in fact, the situation remained unchanged. If anything, it deteriorated. Almost thirteen hundred had been taken into custody before the Games because they endangered state security. An official Chinese report admitted as much in 2009. The Uighurs have been alienated by many governmental policies. One is discrimination in employment that favors ethnic Han people. Uighurs allege that this bias is on the upswing. Preference for the Mandarin language is also seen as an attempt to solve the Uighur problem by assimilation. Religious oppression is another grievance of the Uighurs. Worship in public is limited, and the wearing of head scarves by Uighur women is frowned upon. Uighurs claim they are targets of nothing less than cultural genocide, and their protestations have led to many deaths.[37]

China's part in the ethnic cleansing that took place in Darfur, the western area of the Sudan, was widely condemned by the international community. Sudan is the largest nation of the African continent, as large as France. The Arab central government in Khartoum has long been at odds with darker-skinned non-Arab people in the south and west. Starting in 2003, violence perpetrated by the Janjaweed Arab militias at the behest of the Khartoum authorities, created a humanitarian crisis of frightening proportions that included torture, rape, mass killing, and expulsion. The United Nations estimated that as many as 300,000 had been killed in Darfur. Hundreds of thousands fled to neighboring Chad. The US Congress called it "genocide" and imposed sanctions. Also, an arrest warrant was issued for the Sudanese strongman Omar Hassan Ahmad Al-Bashir by the International Criminal Court.

Despite the foregoing, China served as the principal supplier of arms to this murderous regime. Ruth Messenger, once the borough president of Manhattan, was quoted as saying, "China is the reason that Darfur is happening."[38] Sudanese oil was the quid pro quo for Chinese weapons, and China acted as the guardian of Sudan in the Security Council.

Celebrities and dignitaries reproached the Chinese for their misconduct. Mia Farrow was especially prominent in the pro-Darfur campaigning. After initial hesitation producer/director Steven Spielberg gave up his role of artistic adviser to the Beijing Olympics. Many Nobel laureates objected to China's policies. Some corporate sponsors spoke critically to the IOC, but it was adamant about not rebuking China. The IOC president, Belgian-born O. John Rogge, made a statement worthy of Avery Brundage to the effect that his organization was not a political entity. It was a sports body and would not become involved in politics. In a press conference he said, "[I]t is not the task of the International Olympic Committee to get involved in monitoring and/or lobbying and/or influencing."[39]

In the end, of course, the human rights crusades failed. It was 1936 Berlin once again. The "Genocide Olympics" went forward and dazzled billions, but the eyes of the world were focused on the Birds Nest, the national stadium in Beijing. Darfur was eclipsed. What really counted for many American sports fans was that the US team won the most medals, 110. Somewhat disappointing was the fact that China was first in the number of gold medals garnered.

Numerous proposals to find an unobjectionable host for the Games have been propounded. Some say, in the event that the practice of rotating hosts picked from national bids were to be jettisoned, Greece, as the birthplace and continuing site of the Olympics in antiquity, could and should be designated as the permanent site of the modern Olympics. This is not novel. In 1896, the king of Greece said that his nation had been the "mother and nursery of athletic contests in Pan Hellenic Antiquity."[40] He voiced his hope that the world would choose it as a "peaceful meeting place of the nations, as a continuous and permanent field for the Olympic Games."[41]

A miffed de Coubertin disagreed sharply. As the founder of the reborn Games, he felt that he had been snubbed by the Greek hosts in 1896. Furthermore, Greek chauvinism was growing at the time and went hand in hand with the king's notion of Greece as a fixed locale for future Games. Olympic authorities Findling and Pelle have written that in Coubertin's judgment, changing Olympic sites would publicize the Olympic ideal and broaden its international flavor. Coubertin wrote that France would be the host in 1900, and in the future, the Games might take place in New York, Stockholm, or in Berlin.[42]

Over the decades, the permanent site solution has periodically surfaced, especially after acrimonious Olympiads. Bill Bradley, who represented New Jersey in the US Senate from 1979 to 1997, introduced a resolution in May 1984. It favored Greece as the permanent Olympic site. Bradley, a Princeton-educated Rhodes Scholar, had earned a gold medal as a member of the US Olympic basketball team in Tokyo in 1964. He went on to play for the New York Knicks in the professional ranks and was subsequently elected a member of the Basketball Hall of Fame. In his resolution, Bradley opined that with increasing frequency, the Olympics had become "an arena not for sport but for nations to further their political goals."[43] Athletes had been the losers. Bradley wanted the Olympics to be insulated from politics.

While his nonbinding resolution was adopted, nothing happened. There was no follow-up. Is there any reason to believe that if Greece were designated the permanent Olympic site, it would have the effect of divorcing the Olympics from politics? Certainly not. Would it even reduce the likelihood of a crippling boycott? Hardly.

Back in April 1967, army officers in Greece seized power in a coup d'état and held the nation in their iron grip for seven years. Under their dictatorship, civil liberties vanished, the fundamental right of assembly was abrogated, and press freedom disappeared. Dissidents were incarcerated and often tortured. While the government insisted that it had saved the nation from Communism, there was much international criticism, and Amnesty International condemned the regime in very strong terms. Had Athens been the venue for the 1968 Olympiad instead of Mexico City or served as the site of the 1972 Olympiad instead of Munich, boycott would have been inevitable.

Switzerland has also been a nominee for the permanent Olympic venue. In a 2010 op-ed piece for the *New York Times*, Charles Banks-Altekruse, a one-time American rower who lost his opportunity to win Olympic gold because of the US boycott of the Moscow Olympiad, wrote in support of permanently basing "all Olympic activities in the traditionally neutral Switzerland which has the geography, weather, expertise, and transportation necessary to host winter and summer games."[44] It can boast of its political stability and is democratic. It already has the international Olympic headquarters in Lausanne, but some would surely see the choice of Switzerland as Eurocentric and therefore objectionable.

Switzerland is best known for its banks, its ski resorts, its watches, and its chocolate. Additionally, it is rarely involved in geopolitical battles. However, it does have a growing demographic dilemma. Its Muslim population is still small compared to several other European countries. Muslims number roughly 310,000, approximately 4.5 percent of the overall Swiss population. They dwell mostly in the German-speaking cantons. In 2007, controversy swirled around a decision of the city council in Bern, the Swiss capital, to reject a proposal to construct a huge Muslim cultural center. Two years later, there was a protracted legal squabble over the building of a minaret to call the faithful to prayer. A national plebiscite to prohibit any new minarets won with a majority of 57.5 percent. In 2013, residents in Switzerland's Italian-speaking region, following the precedent of France, voted to bar the wearing of full-face burqas or veils. These actions infuriated the Muslim population and were deemed xenophobic and Islamophobic. Will this problem worsen? If so, would it not be a prelude to a boycott by Muslim and other nations if future Olympiads were slated for Switzerland?[45]

To avert a future boycott, some have suggested designating multiple *permanent* Olympic locations in various countries. Holding events in two or three nations for Olympiads is another possibility. Such arrangements and holding opening and closing ceremonies in more than one nation in a single Olympiad would not necessarily eliminate chances of a disrupting boycott. An objectionable country would still remain objectionable. Ostensibly, there is no panacea, no cure-all to guarantee a smooth transition from one quadrennial Olympiad to the next.

Many concur that a higher standard should be employed in determining the venue for Summer and Winter Olympics. Violations of the Olympic Charter should be exclusionary. Those that discriminate in the realm of sport should not be considered either as hosts or participants. Egregious international outlaws—for example, Nazi Germany in 1936, China in 2008, and Russia under Putin in 2014—should not have qualified as hosts. Their choice made a mockery of international fraternalism.

In general, the bar for participation should be set much lower than the mark for hosting. How low must be calculated on an ad hoc basis. Prating about removing political motives will not lead to consensus because what some consider politics others regard as morality. Boycotts that blacklist secondary targets should not be countenanced.

In 2013, the word "boycott" was much bandied about in connection with the Sochi Winter Olympics. Antigay propaganda was on the upswing in Russia, as was evidenced by a newly enacted law that prohibited the dissemination to minors of what was euphemistically called propaganda about "non-traditional sexual relations," meaning, of course, homosexuality.[46]

Whereas in the West considerable progress has been made in societal acceptance of gays, Russia still lags behind. Furthermore, under Vladimir Putin there has been an intensification of repression and a growing intolerance of dissent in recent years.

A furor over the new anti-gay law occurred outside Russia. One of the most eloquent condemnations of the homosexual-baiting statute came from Stephen Fry, the British writer and actor, who coupled Putin and Sochi with Hitler and Berlin. Both, he saw as stains on the "Five Rings." Fry faulted the Olympic leadership for the blind eye it turned to the Führer's wrongdoing in 1936 that had such tragic consequences. He accused Putin of "eerily repeating this insane crime, only this time against LGBT Russians." In an open letter to his prime minister, David Cameron, and to IOC president Jacques Rogge, Fry, who is Jewish and gay, argued that an "absolute ban on the Russian Winter Olympics of 2014 in Sochi is simply essential." Stage them somewhere else, Fry pleaded.[47]

Human Rights Watch called the IOC to account, chiding it because it "refused to sound its voice against bigotry and systematic homophobia in Russia." In its newsletter, the watchdog group published a photograph of Russian police confiscating a signature rainbow banner from gay rights activists in Moscow in May 2013.[48]

French President Francois Hollande announced that he would not attend the Sochi Games and so did President Obama. Lest the reason for the snub be unclear, Obama included two open lesbians in the American delegation: Billie Jean King, the retired tennis superstar, and hockey player Caitlin Cahow.[49] Shortly thereafter, figure skating Olympic medal–winner Brian Boitano was added to the Sochi-bound US delegation. He acknowledged that he was homosexual at that time. An Italian member of the IOC scolded the United States for "absurdly" politicizing the Games by appointing gays to its delegation.

Some athletes, one a New Zealand speed skater said he would wear gay pride paraphernalia in Russia, an act which could be construed as a transgression of Russian law and of Article 50 of the Olympic Charter outlawing "political" demonstrations. Fans were likely to do the same. There were calls in the United States for boycotts of Russian vodka, much of which, it turned out, was actually made in Latvia. In September 2013, pickets appeared at the Metropolitan Opera's opening night gala, which featured a Russian theme. The chances of disruptions at the Black Sea Olympic venue seemed substantial.

Dick Pound, a veteran delegate to the IOC from Canada, found the Russian legislation revolting. Nevertheless, he opined that the athletes in Sochi should regard themselves as guests.[50]

Thomas Bach, a German attorney and the newly chosen IOC president, took the position that inside an Olympic facility athletes forfeited the right to express their "political" views.[51] This prompted some to ask, would even subtle expressions of opinion such as donning a rainbow patch or wearing nail polish symbolic of gay rights lead to sportsmen being removed from the games, à la Smith and Carlos? Altogether overlooked, as it had been in Mexico City, was whether the demonstrators' point of view interfered with the orderly conduct of the Games.

In October 2013, Putin feared derailment of the Sochi Games and retreated somewhat. Addressing Russian sports leaders in the presence of Thomas Bach, Putin pledged that gays would be welcomed.[52] His precise meaning was unclear.

However, when Putin gave his annual state of the nation speech to Parliament in December, he forcefully defended his anti-gay law, which, he said, protected the traditional values of most Russians. It opposed "genderless" Western tolerance; for Putin, it was a matter of good versus evil.[53] In reality, faced with an international outcry, he was trying to save what was being called "Putin's Games" by placating conservatives such as the Russian Orthodox Church without further alienating critics outside the country.

In January 2014, Putin equated homosexuals with pedophiles and connected his anti-homosexual law with what he saw as Russia's demographic dilemma. A gay population, out of the closet and free to propagandize, would lead to a lower birthrate.[54]

One day before the official Olympic opening, LGBT (lesbian, gay, bisexual, transgendered) demonstrators targeted leading Olympic sponsors such as McDonald's and Coca-Cola in St. Petersburg, Jerusalem, London, and elsewhere. On the very day Putin formally declared the Games open, gay activists were arrested in Moscow and St. Petersburg.[55]

Several homosexual athletes recognized as such won medals in Sochi. The first was a Dutch female speed skater, Irene Wust, who won a gold. To the astonishment of many, Putin congratulated her and hugged her. The Russian leader was on his best behavior at what some referred to as the "Homophobia Olympics," and the Wust incident was part of his charm offensive.[56]

Sochi's seventeen-day Olympiad turned out to be an unexpectedly placid one. It was free of terrorism, and, at least at the athletic venues, gay activism was absent. There were no podium pronouncements. Gay spectators and sportsmen were not harassed as promised by the Russian authorities. Among civil rights advocates, there was much trepidation that gays would be subject to mistreatment in the future after the crowds had departed Sochi.

The 2014 Olympiad is the first but possibly not the last to be threatened by an ideological struggle over sexual preference. Gender, that is, opportunities for women in sport, or lack thereof, is another potentially divisive issue, most likely involving a conservative puritanical Middle Eastern nation such as Saudi Arabia.

As Human Rights Watch has observed, "Saudi Arabia has one of the worst records of respecting and protecting women's rights." The government's views on women's rights is ante-diluvian. Under much duress, in 2012, two Saudi women were allowed to represent their nation in track and field and judo at the London Olympiad. But on Saudi soil, "millions of women and girls are still banned from taking part in sport in state schools," Human Rights Watch claimed. This policy clearly violated the Olympic Charter, which declared the practice of sport to be a human right. The Saudi sports minister saw it differently. He called the inclusion of women in sports, "steps of the devil."[57]

Then there is the specter that the anti-Israeli "boycott, divestment and sanctions" campaign will be extended to the Olympics. Although there is no charge of sports discrimination against Arabs in Israel, there is a concerted and relentless movement to delegitimize, defame, and demonize the Jewish state. Back in February 2009, a female Israeli tennis player, Shahar Peer, was refused a visa to play in an international tournament in Dubai.[58]

Gaining momentum is an academic boycott of Israeli universities. Two-thirds of the members of the American Studies Association voted to support a resolution that prohibits collaboration with Israeli institutions of higher learning. This was done because of the Palestinian issue. Earlier in 2013, the Association for Asian American Studies had taken similar action.[59]

As we have seen, for the better part of the last century, it was the racial question that plagued the Games. Olympiads obviously have never taken place in a vacuum, nor can they. Racially troubled societies have racially troubled athletics.

In 1900, four years after the first Olympics, W. E. B. du Bois, speaking at the first Pan African Conference in London, prophetically told the assemblage that the problem of the twentieth century is the problem of the color line.[60] Du Bois understood that sports cannot be disentangled from the community at large. Wherever there are Caucasians, they harbor condescending hostile attitudes toward persons of African heritage. Thus, race was a major stumbling block in 1936, 1940, 1968, and 1976 at the Olympics. In the decades of the 1960s and 1970s, the status of blacks in Rhodesia and South Africa was the major bone of contention. How could it have been otherwise?

For at least the first three-quarters of the 1900s, the Olympic Movement was guided by the predilections and prejudices of Avery Brundage. In fact, sports journalist Dave Zirin has written that Brundage, not supernovas Jesse Owens, Carl Lewis, or Mark Spitz, was the "dominant Olympic figure of the twentieth century," and he was benighted on racial issues.[61] He reflected the illiberal, sometimes retrograde mentality of all too many wealthy industrialists and European aristocrats among Olympic moguls.

A new era if not a utopian world followed Brundage's departure, and even though there is no good reason to think that he had the Olympics in mind, Du Bois predicted in 1920 that the "dark world is going to submit to its present treatment just as long as it must and not one moment longer."[62] It has taken a long while, and the struggle for racial equality continues. But Du Bois has been proven right.

Notes

1. "Soweto Uprising," *Wikipedia*, en.wikipedia.org/wiki/Soweto_uprising; Davenport, *South Africa: A Modern History*. On commission found that by February 1977, the number of fatalities had reached 575.
2. Red Smith, "Opening of Olympics is Hailed in Montreal," *New York Times*, July 18, 1976, 1.
3. Ibid., July 16, 1976, 1.
4. Steve Cady, "Taiwan, Nigeria Quit Olympics," *New York Times*, July 17, 1976, 1.
5. Steve Cady, "Opening Ceremony of Olympic Games," *New York Times*, July 18, 1976, 1.
6. Ibid.
7. Steve Cady, "Olympic Games Started: Guyana Joins in Boycott," *New York Times*, July 19, 1976, 1.
8. Bruce Kidd, "Montreal 1976," in John E. Findling and Kimberly D. Pelle, eds., *Encyclopedia of the Modern Olympic Movement* (Westport, CT: Greenwood Press, 2004): 191–198.
9. Letter, Sam Ramsamy to Juan Antonio Samaranch, July 4, 1984, SAN-ROC file, 1976–1988, IOC correspondence.
10. Maree later returned to South Africa where he ran afoul of the law and served prison time.
11. *South African Digest*, March 2, 1984. It was published for American consumption. *Track and Field News* had named her the world's best 5,000-meter runner in 1983.
12. Zola Budd and Hugh Eley, *Zola: The Autobiography of Zola Budd* (London: Partridge Press, 1989), 1.
13. Ibid., 3.
14. Findling, *Historical Dictionary*, 163.

15. Ibid., 163–164.
16. John E. Findling and Kimberly D. Pelle, *Encyclopedia of the Modern Olympic Movement* (Westport, CT: Greenwood Press, 2004), 211–212.
17. Ibid., 173.
18. Ibid., 174.
19. *New York Times*, July 14, 2008.
20. Trevor Sachs, "A Hollow Sporting Footnote in Apartheid-era South Africa," *New York Times*, October 21, 2012.
21. Richard E. Lapchick, *Smashing Barriers: Race and Sport in the New Millennium* (Oxford: Madison Books, 1991), 3–4.
22. Ibid., 5–9
23. Ibid., 18.
24. Ibid., 91.
25. *New York Times*, June 7, 1978.
26. Jeffrey Hart of Dartmouth College told his readers that sources close to the Olympic scene had informed him that the "chances of Israeli athletes competing in the 1980 Moscow Games are exactly zero." *Manchester Union Leader*, July 2, 1977.
27. *New York Times*, July 29, 1978.
28. *U.S. News and World Report*, August 28, 1978.
29. *Jewish Chronicle* (London), September 1, 1978.
30. *New York Times*, September 1, 1978; the *Guardian*, August 25, 1978.
31. Richard Pound, "Olympian Changes: Seoul and Beijing," in Minky Worden, *China's Great Leap: The Beijing Games and Olympian Human Rights Challenge* (New York: Seven Stories Press, 2008), 85–97.
32. Worden, *China's Great Leap*, 26.
33. Ibid.
34. *New York Times*, November 3, 2013.
35. Jane Cohen, "China's Air Stinks of Larger Problem," *Providence Journal*, October 31, 2013.
36. *Providence Journal*, April 21, 1968.
37. *New York Times*, October 8, 2013, and October 30, 2013. On March 1, 2014, a deadly knife attack by Uighur militants on a Chinese railroad station in Kunming (Yunnan) claimed at least twenty-nine lives. See *USA Today*, March 3, 2014 and *New York Times*, March 3, 2014. That spasm of violence was reminiscent of killings carried out by mobs of Uighurs back in 2009. See Andrew Jacobs, "Train Station Rampage Further Strains Ethnic Relations in China," *New York Times*, March 4, 2014.
38. Ilan Greenberg, "Changing the Rules of the Games," *The New York Times Magazine*, March 30, 2008: 54.
39. Sharon K. Hom, "The Promise of a Peoples Olympics," in Minky Worden, *China's Great Leap*, 70–71.
40. Quoted in Findling, *Historical Dictionary*, 8–9; Pierre de Coubertin, "The Olympic Games of 1896," *Century Magazine* 53 (1896): 39.
41. Findling, *Historical Dictionary*, 9.
42. Ibid., 9–10.
43. *Congressional Record*, Senate, May 16, 1984, 12459. In 2000, Bradley was offered the chairmanship of the United States Olympic Committee but declined.

44. Charles Banks-Altekruse, "Give the Olympics a Home," *New York Times*, March 1, 2010.

45. See *Wall Street Journal*, Europe, November 6, 2009; *Swissinfo*, May 3, 2007.

46. Even a favorable allusion to Tchaikovsky's gayness could result in imprisonment, some feared. A state-financed biopic of Tchaikovsky will give the composer's nontraditional sex life short shrift. In addition to the national law signed by Putin, there were at least twelve regional legislatures that had enacted similar laws. See Michael Newcity, "Russia 'Gay Propaganda' and the Games," *Providence Journal*, December 21, 2013. Sochi's mayor stated that no gays were to be found in his city; they would be unwelcome there. *Good Morning America*, February 10, 2014, ABC.

47. "Olympic Games Fry Letter to Cameron," *Pink News*, August 7, 2013. Other personalities who spoke out in favor of a boycott of Sochi were Lady Gaga and Harvey Fierstein, the gay activist, playwright, and actor, whose best-known credit is for *La Cage Aux Folles*.

48. *Human Rights Watch Newsletter*, December 2013.

49. King could not attend the opening ceremonies because of her mother's illness but did join the US delegation for the closing ceremonies.

50. Jeré Longman, "IOC Names New President amid Concerns over Athlete Protests in Sochi." *New York Times*, September 11, 2013, B12.

51. Ibid.

52. *New York Times*, October 29, 2013.

53. *Boston Herald*, December 12, 2013; *Providence Journal*, December 13, 2013; the *Guardian.com*, December 12, 2013. A gay activist was arrested for having held aloft a sign that read, "Being gay and loving gays is normal, beating gays and killing gays is criminal." *New York Times*, December 20, 2013.

54. The ban on demonstrations at Sochi would be allowed by permit only and would be restricted to a special zone miles away from the Olympic venues. The idea was to prevent victory podium protests, thus effectively quashing antigovernment expressions. *New York Times*, January 11 and 20, 2014.

55. *Providence Journal*, January 8, 2014.

56. ABC via *Good Morning America*, February 10, 2014.

57. Human Rights Watch, "Saudi Arabia: Let Women and Girls Play Sports," http://www.hrw.org/let-them-play.

58. *New York Times*, February 16, 2014.

59. Ibid., December 17, 2013.

60. David Levering Lewis, *W. E. B. Du Bois: Biography of a Race, 1868–1919* (New York: Henry Holt and Company, 1993), 251.

61. Dave Zirin, "The Ghosts of Olympics Past," in Worden, *China's Great Leap*, 74.

62. John Bartlett, *Familiar Quotations* (Boston: Little, Brown and Company, 1980), 725. This statement was taken from du Bois's *Darkwater: The Souls of White Folk*.

Bibliography

Books and Chapters in Books

Allighan, Garry. 1962. *The Welensky Story*. London: MacDonald.

American Olympic Committee, ed. 1935. *Fair Play for American Athletes*. Chicago.

American–Southern-African African Council. nd. *Aid Rhodesia's Fight against Communist Aggression*.

Archer, Robert, and Antoine Bouillon. 1982. *The South African Game: Sport and Racism*. London: Zed Press.

Ashe, Arthur, R. 1988. *A Hard Road to Glory: A History of the African-American Athlete*. Vol. 2. New York: Warner Books.

———. 1993. *A Hard Road to Glory: A History of the African-American Athlete since 1946*. Vol. 3. New York: Amistad Press.

Austin, Reginald. 1975. *Racism and Apartheid in Southern Africa: Rhodesia*. Unesco Press.

Bachrach, Susan D. 2000. *The Nazi Olympics: Berlin 1936*. Boston: Little, Brown and Co.

Baker, William J. 1988. *Jesse Owens: An American Life*. New York: Free Press.

Barry, James P. 1975. *The Berlin Olympics, 1936: Black American Athletes Counter Nazi Propaganda*. New York: Franklin Watts, Inc.

Bass, Amy. 2002. *Not the Triumph but the Struggle: The 1968 Olympics and the Making of the Black Athlete*. Minneapolis: University of Minnesota Press.

Bass, Charlotte A. 1960. *Forty Years: Memoirs from the Pages of a Newspaper*. Los Angeles: Charlotte Bass.

Becker, Carl L. 1958. *The Declaration of Independence: A Study in the History of Political Ideas*. New York: Vintage Books.

Beinart, William. 2001. *Twentieth-century South Africa*. New York: Oxford University Press.

Blackmon, Douglas. 2008. *Slavery by Another Name: The Re-enslavement of Black Americans from the Civil War to World War II*. New York: Doubleday.

Boatner, Mark Mayo III. 1966. *Encyclopedia of the American Revolution*. New York: David McKay Company, Inc.

Bogle, Donald. 1974. *Toms, Coons, Mulattoes, Mammies, and Bucks*. New York: Bantam Books.

Borut, Jacob. 2006. "Jews in German Sports during the Weimar Republic." In *Emancipated Through Muscles: Jews and Sports in Europe*. Edited by Michael Brenner and Gideon Reuveni. Lincoln: University Press.

Brinton, Crane. 1965. *The Anatomy of Revolution*. New York: Vintage Books.

Brown, Daniel James. 2013. *The Boys in the Boat: Nine Americans and Their Epic Quest for Gold at the 1936 Berlin Olympics*. New York: Viking.

Bryant, Alfred T. 1929. *Olden Times in Zululand and Natal*. London: Longmans, Green and Co.

Budd, Zola, and Hugh Eley. 1989. *Zola: The Autobiography of Zola Budd*. London: Partridge Press.

Bunting, Brian. 1964. *The Rise of the South African Reich*. Harmondsworth, Middlesex, UK: Penguin Books.

Burt, Alfred Leroy. 1956. *The British Empire and Commonwealth from the American Revolution*. Boston: D.C. Heath and Company.

Bytwerk, Randall L. 1983. *Julius Streicher*. New York: Dorset Press.

Carlos, John, and Dave Zirin. 2011. *The John Carlos Story: The Sports Moment That Changed the World*. Chicago: Haymarket Books.

Carlos, John, and C. D. Jackson Jr. 2000. *Why?: The Biography of John Carlos*. Los Angeles: Milligan Books.

Carpentier, Florence. 2004. *Le Comité International Olympique en Crises: La Presidence de Henri de Baillet-Latour 1925–1940*. Paris: L'Harmittan.

Carter, Dan. 1971. *Scottsboro: A Tragedy of the American South*. Oxford: Oxford University Press.

Cayleff, Susan E. 1996. *Babe: The Life and Legend of Babe Didrickson Zaharias*. Urbana, IL: University of Chicago Press.

Cheffers, John. 1972. *A Wilderness of Spite: Rhodesia Denied*. New York: Vantage Press.

Chodes, John. 1975. *Corbitt: The Story of Ted Corbitt, Long Distance Runner*. Los Altos, CA: TAF News.

Clark, Kristine Setting. 2002. *Undefeated, Untied, and Uninvited: A Documentary of the 1951 University of San Francisco Dons Football Team*. Irvine, CA: Griffin Publishing Group.

Cohen, Joshua. 2012. "Fencing for Hitler, Helene Mayer (1910–1953)." In *Jewish Jocks: An Unorthodox Hall of Fame*. Edited by Franklin Foer and Marc Tracy. New York: Twelve.

Collins, Robert. 1971. *African History: Texts and Readings*. New York: Random House.

Constable, George. 1996. *The Olympic Century: The XI, XII, and XIII Olympiads*. Los Angeles: World Sport Research and Publication.

Cosell, Howard. 1973. *Cosell*. Chicago: A Playboy Press Book.

Coubertin, Pierre de. 1997. *Olympic Memoirs*. Lausanne: International Olympic Committee.

———. 1909. *Une Campagne de Vingt-et-Un Ans 1887–1908*. Paris: Librairie de L'education Physique.

Creighton, T. R. M. 1960. *The Anatomy of Partnership: Southern Rhodesia and the Central African Federation*. London: Faber and Faber.

Cripps, Thomas. 1974. *Slow Fade to Black: The Negro in American Film, 1900–1942*. London: Oxford University Press.

Curtin, Philip. 1964. *African History*. New York: Macmillan.

Davenport, T. R. H. 1991. *South Africa: A Modern History*. Toronto: University of Toronto Press.

Davis, Michael B. 1992. *Black American Women in Olympic Track and Field*. Jefferson, NC: McFarland and Co.

Dawidowicz, Lucy S. 1979. *The War against the Jews, 1933–1945*. New York: Bantam.

Dodd, Martha. 1939. *Through Embassy Eyes*. New York: Harcourt, Brace and Co.

D'Oliveira, Basil. 1969. *The D'Oliveira Affair*. London: Collins.

Edwards, Harry. 1969. *The Revolt of the Black Athlete*. New York: The Free Press.

———. 1980. *The Struggle That Must Be: An Autobiography*. New York: Macmillan.

Espy, Richard. 1979. *The Politics of the Olympic Games*. Berkeley: University of California Press.

Facts about South Africa. 1977. Washington DC: Information Counselor of South Africa.

Fetter, Bruce. 1979. *Colonial Rule in Africa*. Madison: University of Wisconsin Press.

Findling, John E., and Kimberly D. Pelle, eds. 1996. *Historical Dictionary of the Modern Olympic Movement*. Westport, CT: Greenwood Press.

———. 2004. *Encyclopedia of the Modern Olympic Movement*. Westport, CT: Greenwood Press.

Fisher, Marshall Jon. 2009. *A Terrible Splendor—Three Extraordinary Men, A World Poised for War, and the Greatest Tennis Match Ever Played*. New York: Crown Publishers.

Fromm, Bella. 1992. *Blood and Banquets: A Berlin Diary 1930–1938*. New York: Simon and Schuster.

Gilmore, Al-Tony. 1975. *Bad Nigger!: The National Impact of Jack Johnson*. Port Washington, NY: Kennikat Press.

Glickman, Marty, and Stan Isaacs. 1996. *The Fastest Kid on the Block: The Marty Glickman Story*. Syracuse: Syracuse University Press.

Gluck, Gemma La Guardia. 2007. *Fiorello's Sister: Gemma La Guardia Gluck's Story*. Edited by Rochelle G. Saidel. Syracuse: Syracuse University Press.

Good, Robert C. 1973. *U.D.I.: The International Politics of the Rhodesian Rebellion*. Princeton, NJ: Princeton University Press.

Green, Constance McLaughlin. 1967. *The Secret City: A History of Race Relations in the Nation's Capital*. Princeton, NJ: Princeton University Press.

Groussard, Serge. 1975. *The Blood of Israel: The Massacre of Israeli Athletes—The Olympics 1972*. Translated from the French by Harold J. Salemson. New York: William Monroe & Co., Inc.

Grundlingh, Albert, André Odendaal, and Burridge Spies. 1995. *Beyond the Tryline: Rugby and South African Society*. Johannesburg: Ravan Press.

Guiney, David. 1982. *The Friendly Olympics*. Dublin: P R Books.

Gunther, John. 1955. *Inside Africa*. New York: Harper and Brothers.

Guttmann, Allen. 1984. *The Games Must Go On: Avery Brundage and the Olympic Movement*. New York: Columbia University Press.

———. 1992. *Olympics: A History of the Modern Games*. Champaign, IL: University of Illinois Press.

Guttmann, Allen, Heather Kestner, and George Eisen. 2000. "Jewish Athletes and the 'Nazi Olympics.'" In chapter 3 of *The Olympics at the Millennium: Power Politics and the Games*. Edited by Kay Schaffer and Sidonie Smith. New Brunswick, NJ: Rutgers University Press.

Hain, Peter. 1971. *Don't Play with Apartheid: The Background to the Stop the Seventy Tour Campaign*. London: Allen and Unwin.

Hamilton, Cynthia. nd. *Apartheid in an American City: The Case of the Black Community in Los Angeles*. Los Angeles: Labor/Community Strategy Center.

Hart-Davis, Duff. 1986. *Hitler's Games: The 1936 Olympics*. New York: Harper and Row Publishers.

Hartmann, Douglas. 2003. *Race, Culture and the Revolt of the Black Athlete: The 1968 Olympic Protests and Their Aftermath.* Chicago: The University of Chicago Press.

Hatch, John. 1965. *A History of Postwar Africa.* New York: Frederick A. Praeger, Publishers.

Hepple, Alexander. 1967. *Verwoerd.* Baltimore: Penguin Books.

Hine, Darlene, William C. Hine, and Stanley Harrold. 2008. *The African American Odyssey.* Combined volume. NJ: Pearson-Prentice Hall.

Hitler, Adolf. 1971. *Mein Kampf.* Translated by Ralph Manheim. Boston: Houghton Mifflin Company.

Hoffer, Richard. 2009. *Something in the Air: American Passion and Defiance in the Mexico City Olympics.* New York: Free Press.

Ince, Basil A. 2005. *Trinidad and Tobago at the Olympic Games: From Rodney Wilkes to George Bovill III.* Trinidad.

International Olympic Committee. 1994. *One Hundred Years–The Idea–The Presidents–The Achievements.* Volume 1. Lausanne: International Olympic Committee.

Jaspin, Elliot. 2007. *Buried in the Bitter Waters: The Hidden History of Racial Cleansing in America.* New York: Basic Books.

Johnson, Jack. 1969. *Jack Johnson Is a Dandy: An Autobiography.* New York: Chelsea House Publishers.

Kandel, Eric R. 2006. *In Search of Memory.* New York: W. W. Norton and Company.

Killanin, Lord and John Rodda, eds. 1979. *The Olympic Games.* London: MacDonald and Janes.

Korr, Chuck, and Marvin Close. 2008. *More Than Just a Game: Soccer vs. Apartheid—The Most Important Soccer Story Ever Told.* New York: St. Martin's Press.

Kruger, Arnd, and William Murray, eds. 2003. *The Nazi Olympics: Sports, Politics and Appeasement in the 1930's.* Urbana, IL: University of Illinois Press.

Lambert, Margaret Bergmann. 2005. *By Leaps and Bounds.* Washington DC: The United States Holocaust Memorial Museum and the Holocaust Survivors Memoirs Project.

Lapchick, Richard E. 1991. *Smashing Barriers: Race and Sport in the New Millennium.* Oxford: Madison Books.

———. 1975. *The Politics of Race and International Sport: The Case of South Africa.* Westport, CT: Greenwood Press.

Large, David Clay. 2007. *Nazi Games: The Olympics of 1936.* New York: W. W. Norton and Company.

Larson, Erik. 2011. *In the Garden of the Beasts: Love, Terror and an American Family in Hitler's Berlin.* New York: Crown.

Laurence, John. 1968. *The Seeds of Disaster: A Guide to the Realities, Race Policies and World-wide Propaganda Campaigns of the Republic of South Africa.* New York: Taplinger Publishing Company.

Leiss, Amelia C., ed. 1965. *Apartheid and United Nations Collective Measures: An Analysis.* New York: Carnegie Endowment for International Peace.

Lelyveld, Joseph. 2011. *Great Soul: Mahatma Gandhi and His Struggle with India.* New York: Alfred A. Knopf.

Lodge, Tom. 1986. *Black Politics in South Africa since 1945.* London: Longman.

———. 2006. *Mandela: A Critical Life.* Oxford: Oxford University Press.

———. 2003. *Politics in South Africa: From Mandela to Mbeki.* Bloomington, IN: Indiana University Press.

———. 2011. *Sharpville: An Apartheid Massacre and Its Consequences.* New York: Oxford University Press.

Loney, Martin. 1975. *Rhodesia: White Racism and Imperial Response.* Baltimore: Penguin Books.

Lusane, Clarence. 2003. *Hitler's Black Victims: The Historical Experiences of Afro-Germans, European Blacks, Africans, and African-Americans in the Nazi Era.* New York: Routledge.

Madigan, Tim. 2001. *The Burning: Massacre, Destruction and the Tulsa Race Riot of 1921.* New York: St. Martin's Griffin.

Mallon, Bill. 1999. *The 1904 Olympic Games: Results for All Competitors in All Events, with Commentary.* London: McFarland and Co.

Mandela, Nelson. 1994. *Long Walk to Freedom: The Autobiography of Nelson Mandela.* Boston: Little, Brown and Company.

Mandell, Richard. 1971. *The Nazi Olympics: Sport, Politics, and Appeasement in the 1930's.* Urbana, IL: University of Illinois Press.

Margolick, David. 2002. *Strange Fruit: The Biography of a Song.* New York: The Ecco Press.

Matthews, George R. 2005. *America's First Olympics: The St. Louis Games of 1904.* Columbia: University of Missouri Press.

Matthews, Vincent, and Neil Amdur. 1974. *My Race Be Run.* New York: Charter House.

McRae, Donald. 2002. *Heroes without a Country: America's Betrayal of Joe Louis and Jesse Owens.* New York: Harper Collins Publisher.

Michell, Lewis. 1910. *The Life of the Right Honorable Cecil John Rhodes.* 2 volumes. London.

Mr. Smith's Illegal Declaration: Month by Month Account from January, 1964 to October, 1965 of the Rhodesian Government's Moves towards a Unilateral Declaration of Independence. nd. Exeter, UK: Africa Research Limited.

Munger, Edwin S. 1969. *Prime Minister Ian Smith of Rhodesia.* American University Field Staff Reports—Central and Southern Africa Series. Vol. 13. No. 3.

Murphy, Frank. 2006. *The Last Protest: Lee Evans in Mexico City.* Kansas City: Windsprint Press.

NAACP. 1919. *Thirty Years of Lynching in the United States 1889–1918.* New York: NAACP.

Nauright, John, and Timothy J. L. Chandler, eds. 1996. *Making Men and Masculine Identity.* London: Frank Cass.

Nazis against the World. 1934. New York: Non-Sectarian Anti-Nazi League to Champion Human Rights.

Nell, William C., 1968. *The Colored Patriots of the American Revolution.* New York: Arno Press and *New York Times.*

Olympic. 1930. Official Publication of the Organizing Committee—Games of X Olympiad. No. 1. Los Angeles.

Opperman, Rudolf W. J., and Lappe Laubscher. 1987. *Africa's First Olympians: The Story of the Olympic Movement in South Africa 1907–1987.* Johannesburg: SANOC-SANOK.

Oriard, Michael. 2001. *King Football: Sport and Spectacle in the Golden Age of Radio and Newsreels, Movies, and Magazines, the Weekly and the Daily Press.* Chapel Hill: The University of North Carolina Press.

Otty, Harry. 2006. *Charley Burley and the Black Murderers Row.* UK: Tora.

Owens, Jesse, and Paul G. Neimark. 1970. *Blackthink: My Life as Black Man and White Man.* New York: William Morrow and Company, Inc.

Page, James A. 1991. *Black Olympian Medalists.* Englewood, CO: Libraries Unlimited, Inc.

Palley, Claire. 1966. *The Constitutional History and Law of Southern Rhodesia 1885–1965 with Special Reference to Imperial Control.* Oxford: Clarendon Press.

Peterson, Robert. 1970. *Only the Ball Was White: A History of Legendary Black Players and All Black Professional Teams.* New York: Oxford University Press.

Piascik, Andy. 2009. *Gridiron Gauntlet: The Story of the Men Who Integrated Pro Football.* Toronto: Taylor Trade Publishing.

Pieroth, Doris H. 1996. *Their Day in the Sun: Women of the 1932 Olympics.* Seattle: University of Washington Press.

Poniatowska, Elena. 1975. *Massacre in Mexico.* New York: The Viking Press.

Progress through Separate Development. nd. New York: Information Service of South Africa.

Quarles, Benjamin. 1961. *The Negro in the American Revolution.* Chapel Hill: University of North Carolina Press.

Rampersad, Arnold. 1997. *Jackie Robinson: A Biography.* New York: Alfred A Knopf.

Rhodesia or Zimbabwe: No Middle Ground in Africa. 1969. New York: The Africa Fund.

Richards, Trevor. 1999. *Dancing on Our Bones: New Zealand, South Africa, Rugby and Racism.* Wellington: Bridget Williams Books.

Ross, Charles K. 1999. *Outside the Lines: African Americans and the Integration of the National Football League.* New York: New York University Press.

Schaap, Jeremy. 2007. *Triumph: The Untold Story of Jesse Owens and Hitler's Olympics.* Boston: Houghton Mifflin Company.

Schirach, Baldur von. 1967. *Ich Glaubte an Hitler.* Hamburg: Mosaic Verlag.

Schmeling, Max. 1998. *Max Schmeling: An Autobiography.* Edited and translated by George B. Von Der Lippe. Chicago: Bonus Books.

Schwab, Gerald. 1990. *The Day the Holocaust Began: The Odyssey of Herschel Grynszpan.* New York: Praeger.

Senn, Alfred E. 1999. *Power, Politics and the Olympic Games: A History of the Power Brokers, Events, and Controversies that Shaped the Games.* Champaign, IL: Human Kinetics.

Shamuyarira, Nathan M. 1965. *Crisis in Rhodesia.* London: Andre Deutsch.

Shaw, Stanley N. nd. *In Defense of South Africa.* Pretoria: Government Printer.

Shirer, William L. 1984. *20th Century Journey: A Memoir of the Life and the Times.* Volume 2. *The Nightmare Years, 1930–1940.* Boston: Little, Brown and Company.

Sitcoff, Harvard. 1981. *The Struggle for Black Equality, 1954–1980.* New York: Hill and Wang.

Smith, Tommie, and David Steele. 2007. *Silent Gesture: The Autobiography of Tommie Smith.* Philadelphia: Temple University Press.

Sparks, Allister H. 1990. *The Mind of South Africa.* New York: Alfred A. Knopf.

Thompson, Richard. 1964. *Race and Sport.* London: Oxford University Press.

Tygiel, Jules. 1984. *Baseball's Great Experiment: Jackie Robinson and His Legacy.* New York: Vintage Books.

Walters, Guy. 2006. *Berlin Games: How the Nazis Stole the Olympic Dream.* New York: William Morrow.

Ward, Geoffrey C. 2004. *Unforgivable Blackness: The Rise and Fall of Jack Johnson.* New York: Alfred A. Knopf.

Washington, Harriet A. 2007. *Medical Apartheid: The Dark History of Medical Experimentation on Black Americans from Colonial Times to the Present.* New York: Doubleday.

Wells, Robert E. 2010. *Sport and the Talented Tenth: African American Athletes in Colleges and Universities of the Northeast, 1879–1920.* New York: iUniverse, Inc.

Wilson, Monica, and Leonard Thompson, eds. 1971. *The Oxford History of South Africa, 1870–1966.* Volume 2. New York: Oxford University Press.

Wiltse, Jeff. 2007. *Contested Waters: A Social History of Swimming Pools in America.* Chapel Hill: The University of North Carolina Press.

Witherspoon, Kevin. 2008. *Before the Eyes of the World: Mexico and the 1968 Olympic Games.* DeKalb, IL: Northern Illinois University Press.

Worden, Minky. 2008. *China's Great Leap: The Beijing Games and Olympian Human Rights Challenges.* New York: Seven Stories Press.

Zaharias, Babe Didrickson [as told to Harry Paxton]. 1955. *The Life I've Led: My Autobiography.* New York: A.S. Barnes and Co.

Articles

Banks-Altekruse, Charles. 2010. "Give the Olympics a Home." *New York Times.* March 1.

Barney, Robert K. 1996. "Resistance, Persistence, Providence: The 1932 Olympic Games in Perspective." *Research Quarterly for Exercise and Sport* 67 (June): 148–160.

Bartholet, Jeffrey. 2013. "Aflame: A Wave of Self-immolations Sweeps Tibet." *The New Yorker* July 8 and 15: 44–49.

Berkow, Ira. 1990. "The Man Who Told Hitler 'No.'" *New York Times.* August 28.

Bernett, Hajo. 1980. "Das Scheitern der Olympischen Spielen von 1940." *Stadion* 6: 251–290.

Calan, Susan. 2004. "'Cinderellas' of Sport: Black Women in Track and Field." In *Sport and the Color Line: Black Athletes and Race Relations in Twentieth Century America.* New York: Routledge: 211–232.

Clifton, Tony, and Ronald Legge. 1971. "The Glory That Was Rhodesia." *Atlas* (November).

Coles, Robert. 1985. "Anti-apartheid Medicine." *New York Times.* January 29.

Corbitt, Ted. 2007. Obituary. *New York Times.* December 13.

Coubertin, Pierre de. 1896. "The Olympic Games of 1896." *Century Magazine* 53: 39–53.

Crouse, Karen. 2012. "From Striking Symbol of Segregation to Victim of Golf's Success." *New York Times.* April 3.

Dickey, A. Glenn, 1984. "Hitler's Games: A High Time for Gold Medalist." *San Francisco Chronicle.* June 12.

Diem, Carl. 1938. "The Meeting on the Nile." *Olympische Rundschau* (July).

Dyreson, Mark. 1995. "Marketing National Identity: The Olympic Games of 1932 and American Culture." *Olympika: The International Journal of Olympic Studies* 4: 23–48.

"Eddie Tolan: A Victim of Race Prejudice." Eddie Tolan Vertical File. Bentley Historical Library, University of Michigan.

Eisen, George. 1984. "The Voices of Sanity: American Diplomatic Reports from the 1936 Berlin Olympiad." *Journal of Sport History* 2 (3) (Winter).

"Facilities for Games of Tenth Olympiad." 1932. In *Olympic News* 6 (January–February): 7, 8, 10, 11.

Fagan, Brian. 1969. "Zimbabwe: A Century of Discovery." *African Arts* 2 (3) (Spring): 21.

Fenster, Julie. 2001. "A Deadly Inheritance." *American Legacy* (Winter).

"Forget Hitler: It Was America That Snubbed Black Olympian Jesse Owens." 2013. *Daily Mail* (UK). Online. August 12.

Forrest, Brett. 2014. "Putin's Party." *National Geographic* 225 (1) (January): 110–129.

Freedman, Samuel G. 2009. "Southern White Teams Just Didn't Play Black Ones, but One Game Ended That." *New York Times*. October 26.

Gerstenfeld, Manfred, 1999. "Wartime and Postwar Dutch Attitudes toward the Jews: Myth and Truth." *Jerusalem Letter/Viewpoints*. August 15.

"The Glory That Was Rhodesia: Yes, It Was the Blacks Who Built It." 1971. *Atlas* (November): 40–41.

Greenberg, Ilan. 2008. "Changing the Rules of the Games." *The New York Times Magazine*. March 30: 52 ff.

Greenberg, Stanley. 1951. "Africa as a Linguistic Area." In *Continuity and Change in African Cultures*. Edited by William R. Bascom and Melville Herskovits. Chicago: University of Chicago Press: 15–27.

Grundlingh, Albert. 1996. "Playing for Power?: Rugby, Afrikaner Nationalism and Masculinity in South Africa, c. 1900-c. 1970." In *Making Men: Rugby and Masculine Identity*. Edited by John Nauright and Timothy J. L. Chandler. London: Frank Cass: 181–204.

Human Rights Watch Newsletter. 2013. December.

Jacobs, Andrew. 2014. "Train Station Rampage Further Strains Ethnic Relations in China." *New York Times*. March 4.

Johnson, William, Oscar. 1980. "Avery Brundage: The Man behind the Mask." *Sports Illustrated* 53 (6) (September 4): 50 ff.

Kamm, Henry. 1976. "White Rhodesians Intent on Preserving 'Easy Life.'" *New York Times*. March 17.

Kandel, Eric R. 2012. "A Conversation with Eric R. Kandel." *New York Times-Science Times*. March 6.

Kidd, Bruce. 2004. "Montreal 1976." In *Encyclopedia of the Modern Olympic Movement*. Edited by John E. Findling and Kimberly D. Pelle. Westport, CT: Greenwood Press: 191–198.

Kruger, Arnd. 1978. "Fair Play for American Athletes: A Study in Anti-Semitism." *Canadian Journal of History of Sport and Physical Education* (May): 43–57.

Lambert, Margaret. 1980. "A Jewish Athlete and the Nazi Olympics of '36." *New York Times*. February 3.

Lapchick, Richard E. 1970. "The Olympic Movement and Racism: An Analysis in Historical Perspective." In *Africa Today: Racism in Sport* 17 (6) (November–December): 14–16.

Laskau, Henry. 2000. Obituary. *New York Times*. May 9.

Lebowitz, Arieh. 1996. "Labor's 1936 Counter-Olympics." *Unionist*. December 8.

Lipsyte, Robert. 1999. "Evidence Ties Olympic Taint to 1936 Games." *New York Times*. February 21.

Longman, Jeré. 2009. "Reaching Back 73 Years for Inspiration." *New York Times*. November 15.

———. 2013. "I.O.C. Names New President Amid Concerns Amid Athlete Protests in Sochi." *New York Times*. September 11, p B12.

Lowther, Kevin. 1966. "Rhodesian Alphabet." *Africa Today* 13 (6) (June): 9–11.

Maloney, Larry. 1996. "Atlanta 1996: The Games of the XXVIth Olympiad." In *Historical Dictionary of the Olympic Movement*. Edited by John E. Findling and Kimberly D. Pelle. Westport, CT: Greenwood Press: 194–200.

Meyer, Gaston. 1979. "St. Louis 1904." In *The Olympic Games*. Edited by Lord Killanin and John Rodda. London: MacDonald and Janes.

Meyers, Steven Lee. 2014. "Putin's Olympic Fever Dream." *New York Times Magazine*. January 26: 18 ff.

Moor, Robert. 2012. "Pygmy Caged in Monkey House." *New York*. April 9: 8.

Musburger, Brent. 1968. "Bizarre Protest by Smith, Carlos Tarnishes Medals." *Chicago American*. October 19.

Nauright, John, and David Black. 1996. "'Hitting Them Where it Hurts': Sprinbok—All Black Rugby, Masculine National Identity and Counter-hegemonic Struggle, 1959–1922." In *Making Men: Rugby and Masculine Identity*. Edited by John Nauright and Timothy J. L. Chandler. London: Frank Cass: 205–226.

"Nazis, Negroes, Jews, and Catholics." 1935. *The Crisis* 42 (9) (September): 273.

Northern Illinois University Alumni News. 1984. (Summer).

"Olympic Disgrace." 1972. *Los Angeles Herald Examiner*. August 25.

"Political Blackmail at the Olympics." 1972. *Toronto Star*. August 24.

Racism in Sport: Africa Today 17 (6) (November–December 1970).

Randall, Clarence B. 1963. "Why South Africa Needs Time." Reprint from *Reader's Digest* (August).

Reeves, Jay. 2010. "F.B.I. Had Monitored Lawsuit by Blacks versus Tide's Bryant." *Providence Journal Sports*. August 22.

Rhoden, William C. 2008. "Enduring Image Coupled with an Enduring Dispute." *New York Times*. February 22.

———. "Vilified to Glorified: Olympic Redux." 2005. *New York Times*. October 17.

Rivers, Eunice, and Stanley H. Shuman, Lloyd Simpson, and Sidney Olansky. 1953. "Twenty Years of Follow-up Experience in a Long-range Medical Study." *Public Health Reports* 68 (4) (April): 391–392.

Ruck, Robert. 2004. "Sports and Black Pittsburgh 1900–1930." In *Sport and the Color Line: Black Athletes and Race Relations in Twentieth Century America*. Edited by Patrick B. Miller and David K. Wiggins. New York: Routledge: 3–24.

Sachs, Trevor. 2012. "A Hollow Sporting Footnote in Apartheid-era South Africa." *New York Times*. October 21: 8.

Scheck, Rafael. 2005. "The Killing of Black Soldiers from the French Army by the Wermacht in 1940: The Question of Authorization." *German Studies Review* 28 (3): 595–605.

Sell, Christine M. 2007. "The 1940 Tokyo Games: The Games That Never Were—The Art Contests and the XIIth Olympiad." *Journal of Olympic History* 15 (2) (July): 40–49.

Shapiro, Edward S. "The World Athletic Carnival of 1936: An American Anti-Nazi Protest." *American Jewish History* 74: 265–266.

Southgate, Martha. 2012. "Water Damage." *New York Times*. August 11.

Spivey, Donald. 2004. "End Jim Crow in Sports: The Leonard Bates Controversy and Protest at New York University, 1940–1941." In *Sport and the Color Line: Black Athletes and Race Relations in Twentieth Century America*. Edited by Patrick B. Miller and David K. Wiggins. New York: Routledge: 147–166.

"Stay Out of Nazi Olympics." 1935. *The Crisis* 42 (9) (September): 273.

Stein, Joshua. 2004. "Olympic Games Comparison Doesn't Measure Up." *Jewish Voice and Herald*. September 10.

"Stories from the Berlin Olympics: Herman Neugass." 1997. *United States Holocaust Memorial Museum Update* (Spring).

Stump, A. J. 1982. "The Olympics That Almost Wasn't." *American Heritage* 33.

Tahara, Junko. 1993. "A Study of the Responses of Foreign Countries to the Cancellation of the Games of the XIIth Olympiad, Tokyo: Through the Analysis of the Documents in the Possession of the Diplomatic Record Office, the Ministry of Foreign Affairs of Japan." *Japanese Journal of Physical Education* 38 (July): 87–98 [in Japanese].

———. 1992. "Count Michimasa Toyeshima and the Cancellation of the XIIth Olympiad in Tokyo: A Footnote to Olympic History." *The International Journal of the History of Sport* 9 (3) (December): 468–471.

Thamel, Pete. 2006. "Taking on the Governor and Winning." *New York Times*. January 1.

Vergnani, Linda. 2000. "Scholars Unearth Evidence of the Boer War's Black Victims." *Chronicle of Higher Education* 46 (18) (January 7): AM.

———. 2007. *Journal of Olympic History* 2 (July 15): 40–49.

Vertinsky, Patricia, and Gwendolyn Captain. 1998. "More Myth Than History: American Culture and Representation of the Black Female's Athletic Agility." *Journal of Sport History* 25 (3) (Fall): 532–561.

Wallenstein, Peter. 2002. "Interracial Marriage on Trial: Loving vs. Virginia." In *Race on Trial: Law and Justice in American History*. Edited by Annette Gordon-Reed. New York: Oxford University Press: 177–196.

Ward, Geoffrey C. 1992. "The Man in the Zoo." *American Heritage* (October): 12, 14.

Weintraub, Robert. 2012. "Two Lives after Losing to Jesse Owens." *New York Times*. July 21.

Weisbord, Robert G. 1967. "The Dilemma of South African Jewry." *The Journal of Modern African Studies* 5 (2).

Weisbord, Robert G., and Thomas D. Morin. 1977. "The Caribbean Refuge." *Congress Monthly* (February): 13–16.

Weisbrot, Robert. 1991. *Freedom Bound: A History of America's Civil Rights Movements*. New York: Plume.

Welky, David. 1997. "Viking Girls, Mermaids, and Little Brown Men: U.S. Journalism and the 1932 Olympics." *Journal of Sport History* 24 (1) (Spring): 24–49.

West, Richard. 1979. "Rhodesia: Echoing England." *New York Times*. February 28.

Whitridge, Arnold. 1961. "Jefferson Davis and the Collapse of the Confederacy." *History Today* (February): 79–89.

Wilkins, Roy. 1932. "Negro Athletes at the Olympic Games." *The Crisis* 39 (8) (August): 252–253.

Wilson, Monica. 1959. "The Early History of Transkei and Ciskei." *African Studies* 18: 167–179.

Winn, Stephen R. 1989. "A Tale of Two Diplomats: George S. Messer Smith and Charles H. Sherrill on Proposed American Participation in the 1936 Olympics." *Journal of Sport History* 16 (1) (Spring): 27–43.

Wolken, Dan. 2014. "Activists Worry Post-games." *USA Today.* February 24.

Zirin, Dave. 2008. "The Ghosts of Olympics Past." In *China's Great Leap: The Beijing Games and Olympian Human Rights Challenges.* Edited by Minky Worden. New York: Seven Stories Press: 73–84.

Newspapers, Journals, Magazines

Afro-American. 1932. August 13 and August 20.

Boston Herald. 2013. December 12.

Bulawayo Chronicle. 1967. September 30.

Chicago Daily News. 1968. October 3.

Chicago Sun-Times. 1968. September 25 and September 26.

Chicago Tribune. 1968. August 29 and September 26.

The Crisis. 1932. 9 (8) (August); 42 (September); 39 (October); and 39 (November).

———. 1935. 42 (September).

Daily Worker. 1932. July 27; and August 1, 2, and 15.

———. 1936. August 15.

Die Burger. 1959. April 1.

Guardian. 2010. February 23.

Jewish Chronicle [London]. 1978. September 1.

Jewish Post [Chicago]. 1967. December 29.

Los Angeles Times. 1968. October 18.

Manchester Union Leader. 1977. July 2.

Natal Daily Mail. 1967. September 13.

Newsweek. 1968. October 28.

New York Amsterdam News. 1935. June 22 and August 24.

———. 1972. September 9.

New York Times. 1938. June 20.

———. 1965. November 12.

———. 1968. October 26, 27, and 28.

———. 1970. June 7.

———. 1972. September 8 and 9.

———. 1976. March 19.

———. 1978. June 27.

———. 2010. January 2.

———. 2013. July 6.

Olympic Review, July 1940; January 1941.

Pink News. 2013. August 7.

Pittsburgh Courier. 1935. December 14.

Providence Journal. 2013. December 11.

South African Digest. 1984. March 2.

Star [Johannesburg]. 1961. September 16.

Sunday Worker. 1936. August 1.

U.S. News and World Report. 1978 August 28.

Wall Street Journal [Europe]. 2009 November 6.

Manuscript Collections, Reports, Documents

Avery Brundage Collection (hereinafter ABC). University of Illinois. Boxes 10, 25, 29, 41, 42, 57, 88, 93, 156, 179, 183, 184, and 330.

Baillet-Latour correspondence. International Olympic Committee archives. Lausanne.

Brundage, Avery. "Olympic Story." Chapter manuscript, chapter 15, ABC, box 350.

Congressional Record. Senate. May 16, 1984.

"Criminal Activities at the 1968 Olympic Games in Mexico City, Foreign Police Corporation, George Washington University." National Security archive. FBI Report—Document 94. September 6, 1968.

Executive Committee meeting transcript. March 23, 1968. USOC archives, Colorado Springs, Colorado.

Gustavus T. Kirby Papers. Box 6. USOC archives. Colorado Springs, Colorado.

Hansard Report [South Africa]. April 11, 1967.

1968 Post-Olympic File, Letters on Smith Carlos Incident. USOC archives.

Official Bulletin of the International Olympic Committee. October 1937.

Participation of Rhodesia Correspondence. IOC archives.

Proces-Verbal De La Reunion De La Commission Executive, Londres. June 6, 1938, IOC archives.

"Quadrennial Review of Activities 1965–1969." Presented at the Quadrennial Meeting of the USOC. Denver Hilton Hotel, Denver, Colorado. April 18–20, 1969. USOC archives.

Report of the Organizing Committee on Its Work for the XIIth Olympic Games of 1940 in Tokyo until Relinquishment. 1940. Tokyo: Organizing Committee of the XIIth Olympiad. IOC archives.

Robert Kane Papers. Box 12. Board minutes and reports, folder 12–1979. USOC archives. Colorado Springs, Colorado.

———. Box 4A, 4–38. USOC archives.

Rubien, Frederick W., ed. 1936. *Report of the American Olympic Committee, Games of the XIth Olympiad, Berlin, Germany August 1 to 16, 1936. IXth Olympic Winter Games, February 6 to 16, 1936.* American Olympic Committee.

Sulger, Jack. 1968 Report. Robert Kane Papers, box 12, 12–182. USOC archives.

Tolan, Eddie. Vertical file, Bentley Historical Library, University of Michigan.

United States Department of State/Foreign Relations of the United States, Diplomatic Papers, 1935. 1954. Volume 4. Europe/Washington DC.

United States Olympic Committee 4 (6). December 1968.

United States Olympic Committee archives. Colorado Springs, Colorado.

Vorbereitungen Zu Dem V Olympischen Winterspielen 1940. Amtlicher Bericht. 1940.

Winter Olympics, Garmisch-Partenkirchen Official Press Service. June 25, 1939. IOC archives.

Films

Banished. 2007. Directed by Marco Williams. Two Tone Productions and the Center for Investigative Reporting. Film.

Congressman Ralph H. Metcalfe: The Man, the Legacy. USOC archives, Colorado Springs, Colorado. DVD.

Glory Road. 2006. Directed by James Gartner. Film.

Hitler's Pawn. 2004. Directed by George Roy. HBO Sports. Film.
1968 Olympics: The Black Power Salute. 2012. YouTube video.
Stride to Glory. 1996. Warner Vision Australia, International Olympic Committee, and Trans World. Film.
Watermarks. 2004. Directed by Yaron Zilberman. DVD.

Interviews

Glickman, Marty. Personal interview. Kingston, RI. June 29, 1989.
Kohanik, Laurie. Telephone interviews with the author. December 18, 2008, and January 5, 2009.
Metcalfe, Ralph Jr. Personal interview. Chicago. August 14, 2009.
Wottle, Dave. Telephone interview. May 26, 2010.

Public Lecture

Brophy, Alfred. Public lecture on the Tulsa Race Riot. Brown University. November 30, 2004.

World Wide Web

"Howard P. Drew: The Original 'World's Fastest Human.'" www.howarddrew.com.
"Soweto uprising." *Wikipedia*. http://en.wikipedia.org/wiki/soweto_uprising.
"Tinus Osendarp." *Wikipedia*. http://en.wikipedia/org/wiki/tinus_osendarp.
Wen. Wikipedia.org.

Index

Page numbers followed by n indicate notes.